INDIAN MYSTICISM

INDIAN MYSTICISM

Editor-in-Chief

Swami Chidatman Jee Maharaj

ANMOL PUBLICATIONS PVT. LTD.

NEW DELHI - 110 002 (INDIA)

ANMOL PUBLICATIONS PVT. LTD.
H.O.: 4374/4B, Ansari Road, Daryaganj,
New Delhi-110 002 (India)
Ph.: 23278000, 23261597
B.O.: No. 1015, Ist Main Road, BSK IIIrd Stage
IIIrd Phase, IIIrd Block,
Bangalore - 560 085 (India)
Visit us at: www.anmolpublications.com

Indian Mysticism

First Published, 2009
ISBN 978-81-261-3626-1

PRINTED IN INDIA

Printed at Mehra Offset Press, Delhi.

Contents

Preface

India colourful and vibrant, a land as diverse as its people. A mosaic of faiths, cultures, customs and languages that blend harmoniously to form a composite whole. One of the world's oldest living civilizations—which gave to the world—the concept of zero, the primordial sound Aum..., Yoga and Buddhism.

She is old. She is young. The two diametrically opposite, different yet unique and dynamic faces of India coexist even at this turn of the millennium. With a history of heritage, learning and civilisation dating back to almost 5000 years or perhaps even more, the modern India presents itself as an ideal country. From snow clad mountains to breezy sparkling blue sea side. From arid deserts with shifting sand dunes to lush green country sides. From ancient relics and architectural ruins dating back into antiquity to modern cities, India has it all.

To the north it is bordered by the world's highest mountain chain, where foothill valleys cover the northernmost of the country's maximum states. Further south, plateaus, tropical rain forests and sandy deserts are bordered by palm fringed beaches. Its southernmost tip is the meeting point of three Oceans.

India is a land of staggering contrast with a mingling of the tradition and modernity that is an unique experience to be in India. One will forever remember the stay in this wonderful Homeland-a land truly of mystery and enchantment. Only India can offer such an astonishing variety of contrasts.

She has given birth to numerous spiritual leaders and founders of some of the popular religions of the present day world. India probably has the most religious diversity in any country. It's the birthplace of Hinduism, Buddhism, Sikhism and Jainism and is among the few places to have a resident

Zoroastrian population. India with her veritable treasure trove of culture, mysticism, philosophy, art, music and architecture to name a few. Much of India's classical music is devotional and the North Indian Hindustani and South Indian Carnatic streams are distinct and both have a complex 'raga' framework. The legacy of dance in India is tremendous. The classical dances of India are numerous such as Kathakali of Kerala, Bharatnatyam of Tamil Nadu, Kuchipudi of Andhra Pradesh, Manipuri and Odissi from Orissa are the prominent dance forms in this country that sways to an altogether novel beat. The Yakshagana, nautanki and puppetry are ancient folk forms that live on till date. The earliest specimens of Indian painting are the ones on the walls of the Ajanta Caves dating back to 2nd century BC. The Mughals had a huge impact on Indian art. The influence of Persian art brought placid garden scenes, illustrations from myths, legends and history into Indian art. Word craft, handicrafts, architecture and sculpture all contribute to this rich and varied domain. Indian literature, both in English and in the vernacular, is ever more popular around the world.

The book aims at presenting perspectives of different aspects of Indian culture. It has topics on Indian classical music and dance, painting, ayurveda and yoga which are traditional and indigenous system of physical and mental wellbeing, language, philosophy and excellence achievements by Indian in the different branches of science and social sciences. It also includes our ancient religious and classic literature.

It is hoped that this book will be welcomed by the general readers as also scholars who are interested in the Indian heritage.

—Editors

1

Reincarnation—Its Meaning and Consequences

The concept of reincarnation seems to offer one of the most attractive explanations of humanity's origin and destiny. It is accepted not only by adherents of Eastern religions or New Age spirituality, but also by many who don't share such esoteric interests and convictions. To know that you lived many lives before this one and that there are many more to come is a very attractive perspective from which to judge the meaning of life. On the one hand, reincarnation is a source of great comfort, especially for those who seek liberation on the exclusive basis of their inner resources.

It gives assurance for continuing one's existence in further lives and thus having a renewed chance to attain liberation. On the other hand, reincarnation is a way of rejecting the monotheistic teaching of the final judgment by a holy God, with the possible result of being eternally condemned to suffer in hell. Another major reason for accepting reincarnation by so many people today is that it seems to explain the differences that exist among people. Some are healthy, others are tormented their whole life by physical handicaps. Some are rich, others at the brink of starvation.

Some have success without being religious; others are constant losers, despite their religious dedication. Eastern religions explain these differences as a result of previous lives, good or bad, which bear their fruits in the present one through the action of karma. Therefore reincarnation seems to be a perfect way of punishing or rewarding one's deeds, without the need of accepting a personal God as Ultimate Reality.

Given the huge interest in this topic today, let us examine it more closely under the following headings:

(A) Reincarnation in world religions;

(B) Past-life recall as proof for reincarnation;

(C) Reincarnation and Christianity.

Reincarnation in Eastern Religions

The reincarnation of an entity which is the core of human existence (*atman* or *purusha*) in a long cycle that implies many lives and bodies, is not so old a concept as it is claimed today. Neither is it a common element for most of the oldest known religions, nor does its origin belong to an immemorial past. The classic form of the reincarnation doctrine was formulated in India, but certainly not earlier than the 9th century BC, when the Brahmana writings were composed. After the Upanishads clearly defined the concept between the 7th and the 5th century BC, it was adopted by the other important Eastern religions which originated in India, Buddhism and Jainism. Due to the spread of Buddhism in Asia, reincarnation was later adopted by Chinese Taoism, but not earlier than the 3rd century BC.

The ancient religions of the Mediterranean world developed quite different kinds of reincarnationist beliefs. For instance, Greek Platonism asserted the preexistence of the soul in a celestial world and its fall into a human body due to sin. In order to be liberated from its bondage and return to a state of pure being, the soul needs to be purified through reincarnation. In stating such beliefs Plato was strongly influenced by the earlier philosophical schools of Orphism and Pythagoreanism. The first important Greek philosophical system that adopted a view on reincarnation similar to that of Hinduism was Neo-Platonism, in the 3rd century AD, under certain Eastern influences.

In the case of ancient Egypt, *The Egyptian Book of the Dead* describes the travel of the soul into the next world without making any allusions to its return to earth. As it is well known, the ancient Egyptians embalmed the dead in order that the body might be preserved and accompany the soul into that world. This suggests their belief in resurrection rather than in reincarnation. Likewise, in many cases of ancient tribal religions that are credited today with holding to reincarnation, they rather teach the preexistence of the soul before birth or its independent survival after death. This has no connection with the classic idea of transmigration from one physical body to another according to the demands of an impersonal law such as karma.

Reincarnation in Hinduism

The origin of *samsara* must be credited to Hinduism and its classic writings. It cannot have appeared earlier than the 9th century BC because the Vedic hymns, the most ancient writings of Hinduism, do not mention it, thus proving that reincarnation wasn't stated yet at the time of their composition (13th to 10th century BC). Let us therefore analyse the development of the concept of immortality in the major Hindu writings, beginning with the Vedas and the Brahmanas.

Immortality in the Vedic Hymns and the Brahmanas

At the time the Vedic hymns were written, the view on afterlife was that a human being continues to exist after death as a whole person. Between humans and gods there was an absolute distinction, as in all other polytheistic religions of the world. The concept of an impersonal fusion with the source of all existence, as later put forth by the Upanishads, was unconceivable. Here are some arguments for this thesis that result from the exegesis of the funeral ritual:

1. As was the case in other ancient religions (for instance those of Egypt and Mesopotamia), the deceased were buried with the food and clothing that were seen as neçessary in the afterlife. More than that, the belief of ancient Aryans in the preservation of personal identity after death led them to incinerate the dead husband together with his (living) wife and bow so that they could accompany him in the afterlife. In some parts of

India this ritual was performed until the British colonisation.

2. Similar to the tradition of the ancient Chinese religion, the departed relatives formed a holy hierarchy in the realm of the dead. The last man deceased was commemorated individually for a year after his departure and then included in the mortuary offerings of the monthly *shraddha* ritual (*Rig Veda* 10,15,1-11). This ritual was necessary because the dead could influence negatively or positively the life of the living (*Rig Veda* 10,15,6).
3. According to Vedic anthropology, the components of human nature are the physical body, *ashu* and *manas*. *Ashu* represents the vital principle (different from personal attributes), and *manas* the sum of psycho-mental faculties (mind, feeling and will). The belief in the preservation of the three components after death is proved by the fact that the family addressed the departed relative in the burial ritual as a unitary person: "May nothing of your *manas*, nothing of the *ashu*, nothing of the limbs, nothing of your vital fluid, nothing of your body here by any means be lost" (*Atharva Veda* 18,2,24).
4. Yama, the god of death (mentioned also in old Buddhist and Taoist scriptures) is sovereign over the souls of the dead and also the one who receives the offerings of the family for the benefit of the departed. In the *Rig Veda* it is said about him: "Yama was the first to find us our abode, a place that can never be taken away, where our ancient fathers have departed; all who are born go there by that path, treading their own" (*Rig Veda* 10,14,2). Divine justice was provided by the gods Yama, Soma and Indra, not by an impersonal law such as karma. One of their attributes was to cast the wicked into an eternal dark prison out of which they could never escape (*Rig Veda* 7,104,3-17).

The premise of reaping the reward of one's life in a new earthly existence (instead of a heavenly afterlife) appeared in the Brahmana writings (9th century BC). They spoke of a limited heavenly immortality, depending on the deeds and the quality of the sacrifices performed during one's life. After reaping the reward for them, humans have to face a second death in the heavenly realm (*punarmrityu*) and thereafter return to an earthly existence. The proper antidote to this fate came to be considered esoteric knowledge, attainable only during one's earthly existence.

Reincarnation in the Upanishads

The Upanishads were the first writings to move the place of one's "second death" from the heavenly realm to this earthly world and to consider its proper solution to be the knowledge of the *atman*-Brahman identity. Ignorance of one's true self (*atman* or *purusha*) launches karma into action, the law of cause and effect in Eastern spirituality. Its first clear formulation can be found in the *Brihadaranyaka Upanishad* (4,4,5): "According as one acts, according as one behaves, so does he become. The doer of good becomes good.

The doer of evil becomes evil. One becomes virtuous by virtuous action, bad by bad action." Reincarnation (*samsara*) is the practical way in which one reaps the fruits of one's deeds. The self is forced to enter a new material existence until all karmic debt is paid: "By means of thought, touch, sight and passions and by the abundance of food and drink there are birth and development of the (embodied) self. According to his deeds, the embodied self assumes successively various forms in various conditions" (*Shvetashvatara Upanishad* 5,11).

We can therefore witness a fundamental shift in the meaning of afterlife from the Vedic perspective. The Upanishads abandoned the goal of having communion with the gods (Agni, Indra, etc.), attained as a result of bringing good sacrifices, and came to consider man's final destiny to be the impersonal fusion *atman*-Brahman, attained exclusively by esoteric knowledge. In this new context, karma and reincarnation are key elements that will define all particular developments in Hinduism.

Reincarnation in the Epics and Puranas

In the *Bhagavad Gita*, which is a part of the *Mahabharata*, reincarnation is clearly stated as a natural process of life that has to be followed by any mortal. Krishna says:

> *Just as the self advances through childhood, youth and old age in its physical body, so it advances to another body after death. The wise person is not confused by this change called death (2,13). Just as the body casts off worn out clothes and puts on new ones, so the infinite, immortal self casts off worn out bodies and enters into new ones (2,22).*

In the Puranas the speculation on this subject is more substantial and therefore specific destinies are figured out for each kind of "sin" one performs:

> *The murderer of a brahmin becomes consumptive, the killer of a cow becomes hump-backed and imbecile, the murderer of a virgin becomes leprous-all three born as outcastes. The slayer of a woman and the destroyer of embryos becomes a savage full of diseases; who commits illicit intercourse, a eunuch; who goes with his teacher's wife, disease-skinned. The eater of flesh becomes very red; the drinker of intoxicants, one with discolored teeth.... Who steals food becomes a rat; who steals grain becomes a locust... perfumes, a muskrat; honey, a gadfly; flesh, a vulture; and salt, an ant.... Who commits unnatural vice becomes a village pig; who consorts with a Sudra woman becomes a bull; who is passionate becomes a lustful horse.... These and other signs and births are seen to be the karma of the embodied, made by themselves in this world. Thus the makers of bad karma, having experienced the tortures of hell, are reborn with the residues of their sins, in these stated forms (Garuda Purana 5).*

Similar specific punishments are stated by *The Laws of Manu* (12, 54-69). As the karmic debt one recorded in the past is considerably large, a single life is not enough to consume it. Therefore, in order to attain liberation, many lives become a necessity. The external intervention of a god or a human guru is useless since it would compromise the role of karma.

Who or What Reincarnates in Hinduism?: According to the Upanishads and Vedanta philosophy, the entity that reincarnates is the impersonal self (*atman*). *Atman* does not have a personal nature, and so the use of the reflexive pronoun "self" is not suitable. *Atman* can be defined only through negating any personal attributes. Although it constitutes the existential substrata of human existence, *atman* cannot be the carrier of one's "spiritual progress," because it cannot record any data produced in the illusory domain of psycho-mental existence. The spiritual progress one accumulates toward realising the *atman-Brahman* identity is recorded by karma, or rather by a minimal amount of karmic debt. The whole physical and mental complex a human being consists of is reconstructed at (re)birth according to one's karma. At this level, the newly shaped person experiences the fruits of "his" or "her" actions from previous lives and has to do his best to stop the vicious cycle *avidya-karma-samsara*.

As a necessary aid in explaining the reincarnation mechanism, Vedanta adopted the concept of a subtle body (*sukshma-sharira*) which is attached to *atman* as long as its bondage lasts. This is the actual carrier of karmic debts. However, this "subtle body" cannot be a form of preserving one's personal attributes, *i.e.*, of any element of one's present conscious psycho-mental life. The facts recorded by the subtle body are a sum of hidden tendencies or impressions (*samskara*) imprinted by karma as seeds that will generate future behaviour and personal character. They will materialize unconsciously in the life of the individual, without giving one any hint at understanding his or her actual condition. There can be no form of transmitting conscious memory from one life to another, since it belongs to the world of illusion and dissolves at death.

In the Samkhya and Yoga *darshanas*, the entity that reincarnates is *purusha*, an equivalent of *atman*. Given the absolute duality between *purusha* and *prakriti* (substance), nothing that belongs to the psycho-mental life can pass from one life to another because it belongs to *prakriti*, which has a mere illusory relation with *purusha*. However, the *Yoga Sutra* (2,12) defines a similar mechanism of transmitting the effects of karma from one life to another, as was the case in Vedanta.

The reservoir of karmas is called *karmashaya*. It accompanies *purusha* from one life to another, representing the sum of impressions (*samskara*) that could not manifest themselves during the limits of a certain life. In no way can it be a kind of conscious memory, a sum of information that the person could consciously use or a nucleus of personhood, because *karmashaya* has nothing in common with psycho-mental abilities. This deposit of karma merely serves as a mechanism for adjusting the effects of karma in one's life. It dictates in an impersonal and mechanical manner the new birth (*jati*), the length of life (*ayu*) and the experiences that must accompany it (*bhoga*).

Reincarnation in Buddhism

Buddhism denies the existence of a permanent self that reincarnates from one life to the next. The illusion of an existing self is generated by a mere heap of five aggregates (*skandha*), which suffer from constant becoming and have a functional cause-effect relation: (1) the body, also called the material form (*rupa*), (2) feeling (*vedana*)-the sensations that arise from the body's sense organs, (3) cognition (*sanna*)-the process of classifying and labelling experiences, (4) mental constructions (*sankhara*)-the states which initiate action, and (5) consciousness (*vijnana*)-the sense of awareness of a sensory or mental object. The five elements are impermanent (*anitya*), undergo constant transformation and have no abiding principle or self.

Humans usually think that they have a self because of consciousness. But being itself in a constant process of becoming and change, consciousness cannot be identified with a self that is supposed to be permanent. Beyond the five aggregates nothing else can be found in the human nature.

However, something has to reincarnate, following the dictates of karma. When asked about the differences between people in the matters of life span, illnesses, wealth, etc., the Buddha taught:

Men have, O young man, deeds as their very own, they are inheritors of deeds, deeds are their matrix, deeds are their kith and kin, and deeds are their support. It is deeds that classify men into high or low status (Majjhima Nikaya 135,4).

If there is no real self, who inherits the deeds and reincarnates? The Buddha answered that only karma is passing from one life to another, using the illustration of the light of a candle, which is derived from another candle without having a substance of its own. In the same manner there is rebirth without the transfer of a self from one body to another. The only link from one life to the next is of a causal nature. In the *Garland Sutra* we read:

According to what deeds are done
Do their resulting consequences come to be;
Yet the doer has no existence:
This is the Buddha's teaching.

The Tibetan Book of the Dead describes in detail the alleged experiences one has in the intermediary state between two incarnations, suggesting that the deceased keeps some personal attributes. Although it is not clear what actually survives after death in this case, it mentions a mental body that cannot be injured by the visions experienced by the deceased:

When it happens that such a vision arises, do not be afraid! Do not feel terror! You have a mental body made of instincts; even if it is killed or dismembered, it cannot die! Since in fact you are a natural form of voidness, anger at being injured is unnecessary! The Yama Lords of Death are but arisen from the natural energy of your own awareness and really lack all substantiality. Voidness cannot injure voidness! (Tibetan Book of the Dead, 12)

Whatever the condition of the deceased after death might be, any hypothetical personal nucleus vanishes just before birth, so there can be no psycho-mental element transmitted from one life to another. The newborn person doesn't remember anything from previous lives or trips into the realm of the intermediary state (*bardo*).

Another important element is the extreme rarity of being reincarnated as a human person. The Buddha taught in the *Chiggala Sutta* (*Samyutta Nikaya* 35.63):

> *Monks, suppose that this great earth were totally covered with water, and a man were to toss a yoke with a single hole there. A wind from the east would push it west, a wind from the west would push it east. A wind from the north would push it south, a wind from the south would push it north. And suppose a blind sea-turtle were there. It would come to the surface once every one hundred years. Now what do you think: would that blind sea-turtle, coming to the surface once every one hundred years, stick his neck into the yoke with a single hole?*
>
> *It would be a sheer coincidence, lord, that the blind sea-turtle, coming to the surface once every one hundred years, would stick his neck into the yoke with a single hole.*
>
> *It's likewise a sheer coincidence that one obtains the human state. It's likewise a sheer coincidence that a Tathagata, worthy and rightly self-awakened, arises in the world.*

If one tried to calculate the probability of obtaining the human state according to this text, and consider the surface of "this great earth" as being just the surface of India, the odds would be once in a timespan of 5×10^{16} years (5 followed by 16 zeros). This is 5 million times the age of the universe.

Reincarnation in Taoism

Reincarnation is a teaching hard to find in the aphorisms of the *Tao-te Ching* (6th century BC), so it must have appeared later in Taoism. Although it is not specified what reincarnates, something has to pass from one life to another. An important scripture of Taoism, the *Chuang Tzu* (4th century BC), states:

> *Birth is not a beginning; death is not an end. There is existence without limitation; there is continuity without a starting point.*

> *Existence without limitation is space. Continuity without a starting point is time. There is birth, there is death, there is issuing forth, there is entering in. That through which one passes in and out without seeing its form, that is the Portal of God* (*Chuang Tzu 23*).

Reincarnation in Modern Thinking

Once the Eastern concept of reincarnation arrived in Europe, its meaning changed. During the Middle Ages it was a doctrine reserved for the initiates of some occult traditions such as Hermetism and Catharism, who had taken it over from Neo-Platonism. A wider acceptance of reincarnation was promoted in the Western world beginning only in the 19th century, by Theosophy, and later also by Anthroposophy. Then came the Eastern gurus, the New Age movement, and as a result we witness a wide acceptance of reincarnation in our society today. However, its modern version is substantially different from what Eastern religions affirmed. Far from being a torment out of which man has to escape by any price through abolishing personhood, New Age thinking sees reincarnation as an eternal progression of the soul toward higher levels of spiritual knowledge.

Thus what reincarnates is not the impersonal *atman*, but an entity which is currently called the soul, an entity which preserves the attributes of personhood from one life to the next. This compromise obviously emerged from the desire to adapt the reincarnation doctrine to Western thought. The concept of an impersonal *atman* reincarnating was too abstract to be easily accepted, so Westerners needed a milder version of this doctrine. Although this tendency may offer evidence for the soul's yearning for a personal destiny, it doesn't bear too much resemblance to classical Eastern spirituality, which rejects it as a perverted view.

The above information on the meaning of reincarnation in the Eastern religions and the nature of the entity which is reincarnating will be helpful in examining the modern proofs for it which are so popular today. While analysing them, we need to remember that according to the Eastern concept of reincarnation there cannot be any personal element that could travel from one life to the next.

Past-life Recall as Modern Proof for Reincarnation

Many people who accept reincarnation in the West today claim that it can be scientifically proven. They usually ground their belief on past-life recall experiences, which represent the ability of certain persons to recall facts of alleged previous lives. This phenomenon occurs under two distinct forms. One is observed under hypnosis, while regressing certain persons beyond the date of birth. The other is produced by some children who spontaneously remember a previous life identity, amasing their neighbours with specific details that match those of the life of a deceased person. Could these experiences really be proofs for reincarnation?

Hypnotic Regression as Proof for Reincarnation

Hypnosis can be defined as a method of inducing an altered state of consciousness, which causes a person to become very receptive to the hypnotist's suggestions. This method has been used in psychoanalysis for treating psychic diseases by evoking the painful events which caused them in the past (especially during childhood) and then by transmitting suggestions meant to heal them. Although there are some encouraging results in using it as a psychiatric therapy, it is a fact that hypnosis can mix fantasy with real memories or that it can even create entirely fictitious episodes. In deep states of hypnosis, some subjects have had out-of-body experiences and claimed to have travelled in mysterious spiritual realms. Others have had a mystical experience of oneness with the universe.

Hypnotic regression started to be used as a past-life recall method in 1952, when Ruth Simmons from Colorado, USA, was regressed "back in time" beyond the date of her birth. Suddenly she started to talk using a specific Irish accent, claiming that her name was Bridey Murphy and that she lived in Ireland in the year 1890. The few details she produced seemed to describe accurately the Irish society of the late 19th century. It was therefore believed that a scientific proof for reincarnation had been found. As a result, a growing number of hypnotists started to use the method in order to get information about alleged previous lives of their patients. Recently the method has gained a scientific aura, being used as therapy for releasing patients' fears and explaining certain personality tendencies as results of past-life experiences.

By simply being asked to go back in time beyond the date of their birth and describe their impressions, some patients tell impressive stories in which some characteristics match those of past and distant cultures of human history. They usually adopt a totally different personality, with a changed voice, behaviour and facial expression. All the information they produce is the result of a dialog between the hypnotist and his patient, in which the questions have to be easy and clear in order to get a proper answer. Since the information they produce couldn't have been normally learned during their lifespan, it is supposed that they really recall past lives. However, this conclusion raises some difficulties, as there are other possibilities to explain how the "novelties" are produced, without accepting the past-life recall hypothesis.

One possible explanation is cryptoamnesia. As hypnosis can be used in refreshing forgotten memories of one's past, facts that are no longer available to the conscious memory, in the same way can it be used for evoking information heard from other people, read in books, or seen in movies, in which the subject of hypnosis is involving himself as participant. His subconscious memory has kept this information stored and hypnosis determines its use in a completely fictitious scenario. Ian Stevenson, one of the important researchers of this phenomenon, mentions such a case:

> *There is another English case going back to the turn of the century that was studied by a Cambridge don, in which a young woman seemed to be describing the life of one Blanche Poynings, a person around the court of Richard II in the fourteenth century. She gave a lot of detail about the people concerned, including proper names and the sort of life she lived. The investigators kept on probing, and a little later they began asking her about sources of information. In her trancelike state the*

> *girl herself came out with a reference to a book, Countess Maud, published in the latter part of the nineteenth century, a classic Victorian novel all about a countess at the court of Richard II. The subject had modified it a little bit, but basically it was all in the novel, and it turned out that her aunt had a copy of the book. She didn't remember reading it, but she remembered turning the pages (Omni Magazine 10(4):76 (1988)).*

An intriguing aspect of the testimonies recorded under hypnosis is the fact that they depend heavily on the already existing data in current historic knowledge. In many cases, although the information corresponds to generally acknowledged historical data, further archaeological discoveries contradict them, casting serious doubts on the veracity of "past lives." Ian Wilson, another important researcher of this phenomenon, describes several such cases in his book *Reincarnation* (p. 88-90). One of them refers to a person who lived during the reign of the Egyptian pharaoh Ramses III. Instead of indicating the name No for the capital city, he used the name Thebes, given by the Greeks much later.

Moreover, a true ancient Egyptian could not have known the pharaoh's name by a number, as the numbering of pharaohs was adopted by Victorian Egyptologists during the 19th century. Another fault was mentioning the use of the *sestertius* coin, which was introduced by the Romans a thousand years later.

Another case reported Vikings making a landfall in North America in the 11th century. According to the description, they were wearing helmets with horns. In recent years, however, scholars have proved that this idea is false, as Vikings in fact wore conic, close-fitting caps. Horned helmets were worn only in religious ceremonies by individuals of high rank. This and other cases prove that past-life recall experiences depend heavily on the historical knowledge existing at the time the hypnotic regression was performed, and are often contradicted by later discoveries.

How could it be possible that the present perscnality could influence that of its "previous lives," some predating it by hundreds or thousands of years? How could people who lived four thousand years ago use the BC (before Christ) year numeration system? How can it be that some hypnotists can even "recall" future lives of their patients (which are obviously influenced by current science fiction literature)? These facts indicate that the alleged previous lives are culturally and religiously conditioned, casting serious doubts on their veracity. This is why writers who are favourable to rebirth stories usually avoid mentioning very specific data.

Another possible explanation that could overrule the veracity of past-life recall is the influence of the hypnotist, whose suggestion ability is a *sine qua non* for the effectiveness of hypnosis.

The other necessary factor is the receptivity of the patient to the hypnotist's suggestions. Although the two conditions determine the success of hypnosis when used as psychiatric treatment, when expecting to get information from alleged past lives, the suggestion ability of the hypnotist becomes an important hindrance in obtaining true information, since it can contaminate the patient's story. Ian Stevenson states:

> *In my experience, nearly all so-called previous personalities evoked through hypnotism are entirely imaginary and a result of the patient's eagerness to obey the hypnotist's suggestion. It is no secret that we are all highly suggestible under hypnosis. This kind of investigation can actually be dangerous. Some people have been terribly frightened by their supposed memories, and in other cases the previous personality evoked has refused to go away for a long time (Omni Magazine 10(4):76 (1988)).*

Under hypnosis, the subject is ready to accept all kinds of distortions, having his reality shaped according to the hypnotist's beliefs. Since in most cases the hypnotists expect confirmation of the reincarnation theory, at least subconsciously, they can, together with verbal suggestions inducing relaxation and different phases of regression, transmit their own convictions concerning past lives and custom scenarios of this kind. In many cases it is easy to discern the religious convictions of the hypnotists in the stories told by their patients.

The risk of inventing completely fictitious scenarios through hypnosis cannot be ignored. It actually has happened many times. Many cases have been reported of women who came for hypnotic treatment for their common problems, and over the course of therapy "discovered" incidents of sexual abuse by parents during childhood which proved to be false. Sigmund Freud abandoned hypnosis as a treatment method when he discovered so many cases of false memories. More than that, it was observed that the memories "discovered" under hypnosis can replace true memories after the hypnotic session is over and so completely distort one's personal life. This is called the false memory syndrome. Courts of law know these dangers and most do not accept testimonies produced under hypnosis or from witnesses that have previously been hypnotised. The same way as alleged sexual abuses in childhood discovered through hypnosis have been proved false, past lives (as well as "extraterrestrial abduction" stories) can also be fake scenarios.

Another compromising factor in getting true "past-life stories" is the preparation the patient undergoes before hypnosis. One is informed about its purpose, which induces in him or her a high expectancy state. The conscious desire to know the content of "previous lives" undoubtedly influences the response under hypnosis.

A third possible explanation of testimonies from alleged previous lives is given by psychiatry. The phenomenon of multiple personality is known as dissociative personality disorder. It causes somebody to exchange in a short period of time up to twenty distinct personalities, as if playing successive roles. These contradicting personalities have different mentalities, behaviours, voices and even sexes than the real person. Usually it happens that one of them knows and observes the acts and thoughts of the others, and is even able to speak in the name of all. From a psychiatrist's point of view, past-life testimonies may be the result of inducing dissociative personality disorder through hypnosis. This has actually happened in several cases of schizophrenia. Used to uncover covert personalities and reintegrate them with the main personality, many cases of hypnosis have produced new personalities that didn't manifest previously in one's normal state. They first appeared during hypnotic treatment, and then remained active after the session was over. So it really is possible to create new personalities through hypnosis and call them instances of "past-life recall".

However, there still remains an enigma to which the above naturalist-scientific interpretation doesn't have a satisfactory answer: How are the "past-life" personalities distributed in their roles, or who decides which one will be next in the show? It cannot be a random process. Ian Wilson writes in his book: "Somewhere, somehow, the show must have a 'director'. It is like watching a puppet show; we can see the puppets, see some of the strings by which they are made to work, but cannot see the puppet master." Who could be this hidden director of the multiple personality show?

The naturalistic explanation says that it must be in the person's mind, where consciousness is divided into separate entities, one of them taking the role of the director. The data supporting it is that under hypnosis a certain part of the mind stays conscious, continuing to receive data from the real world. But the unsolved problem concerns the motivation that such an entity (that remains conscious in the person's mind) could have to act like that. Why would it fool us about past lives?

Thus we come to another possible explanation of past-life recall. In parapsychology it is called channelling-the phenomenon of transmitting information generated by spiritual entities which are *external* to our world. They act through certain persons called mediums while they are in altered states of consciousness. The annihilation of normal consciousness through hypnosis creates optimal conditions for contacting such external entities, who can present themselves as personalities of one's past lives. The only reason for rejecting this hypothesis is the presumption that the entity which is communicating through the medium has no reason to lie when it claims to be a former personality and not an external spirit. However, channelling hasn't proved to be a reliable source of information about anything.

In conclusion, the only criterion left for establishing the veracity of "past-life recall" is our faith in the hypnotist and his reincarnationist interpretation.

Spontaneous Past-life Recall by Children as Proof for Reincarnation

Another category of experiences credited as proofs for reincarnation are cases of children, almost all under the age of 10, who spontaneously recall events of alleged past lives and insist that they are someone else who lived in the past. The details they mention concerning places, persons and happenings of the past, about which they could not normally know anything, prove to be true when investigations are performed in the indicated area. The extensive research of Dr. Ian Stevenson and his books on this topic are well known.

Although the cases of spontaneous past-life recall by children are much fewer than testimonies produced under hypnosis, they seem to be more convincing. The cases of the Indian girls Swarnlata and Shanti Devi are two of the most famous. At the ages of 3 (Swarnlata) and 4 (Shanti Devi) they both started to claim that they had lived previous lives as wives and mothers of two children, in a distant village. The most astounding element is that they mentioned specific facts about their alleged previous lives that have been verified by investigators. Imagine the scene: A married woman with several children dies and after four years a little girl knocks at the door and introduces herself as the deceased mother and wife. Emotional disturbances often develop in such cases. Stevenson comments: "These children become embroiled in divided loyalties. In many cases children have rejected their parents, saying they are not their real parents and have often started down the road toward their so-called real homes. In other cases, they insist on being reunited with their former husbands, wives, or children. One Indian boy was passionately attached to the woman he said had been his former mistress and was trying to get her back, causing himself and her real distress" (*Omni Magazine* 10(4):76 (1988)).

However, such stories can be explained in an alternative way, not necessarily as proof for reincarnation. There is the possibility that these children are contacting external spirits through channelling. In this case the medium would be the child, without necessarily being conscious of it. But since children lack the skills of mediums, a particular kind of channelling is required in their case. It is called *possession* of these children by external spiritual entities. In such cases the human person is forced to transmit the messages of a spirit without having any conscious contribution to the whole process. Spiritual possession as explanation for past-life recall by children is suggested by the fact that almost all such cases are produced by children who manifest them between the ages of two and five, when their spiritual discernment is almost nonexistent. As the children grow up, the entities lose their power of influence upon them, which could explain why the past-life memories are lost after the age of 10.

Cases that confirm the possession hypothesis are instances in which the possessing spirit enters the child's body a long time after he was born, and then produces a past-life recall experience which interferes with the already present personality of the child. There are enough such cases described in literature. Here is a brief description of two mentioned by Ian Stevenson, in his book *Twenty Cases Suggestive of Reincarnation*:

First, there is the case of an Indian boy named Jasbir, aged three and a half, who was very ill and lapsed into a coma which his family temporarily mistook for death. He revived a few hours later, and after several weeks displayed a completely transformed behaviour, claiming to be a Brahmin named Sobha Ram, who died in an accident while he (Jasbir) was sick. Since Sobha Ram died when Jasbir was already three and a half years old, his "past-life recall" obviously cannot be a proof of reincarnation. More than that, the "reincarnation" of Ram's soul must have taken place even before he had physically died, according to the timing of his accident and the illness of Jasbir. For the previous 3.5 years both persons lived physically in nearby villages. While speaking through Jasbir, the "reincarnated Mr. Ram" said that he was advised by a saint to take cover in Jasbir's body. As a result, at a certain moment there were present two personalities in Jasbir's body: the one of the child and the one of Mr. Ram. This suggests that it cannot be a case of reincarnation, but rather a possession of Jasbir's body by the so-called spirit of Mr. Ram.

Second, there is the case of Lurancy Vennum, a one-year-old girl who began to display the personality of Mary Roff when she (Mary Roff) died. This situation lasted several months, while Mary Roff claimed to have occupied the vacated body of the little girl. After this period Mary Roff departed and Lurancy Vennum resumed control. The overlapping of personalities and messages displayed during that period are strong indications of possession, excluding any possibility of reincarnation. Ian Stevenson admits in his book that "other cases of the present group of 20 cases may be instances of similar 'possessing influences' in which the previous personality just happened to die well before the birth of the present personality's body" (p. 381).

Third, there is the case of a Buddhist monk, Chaokhun Rajsuthajarn, who was born a day before the death of Nai Leng, the personality he claimed to have been in his previous life. Stevenson commented in an interview: "I studied this case with much care but couldn't find an explanation for the discrepancy" (*Omni Magazine* 10(4):76 (1988)).

Spirit influence could also explain another "proof" for reincarnation that is becoming increasingly popular: the correspondence between wounds that caused a person to die or other kinds of scars and birthmarks on children who are seen as being the reincarnation of that particular person. Not that a spirit influence could induce such physical abnormalities, but it could "suggest" a special origin to those who are born naturally with birthmarks and birth defects, especially in cultures where most physical and behavioural peculiarities are attributed to happenings in past lives (Southern Asia, the Druze in Lebanon, or Indians in North America). In the Western world birthmarks often are taken as a starting point in one's quest for finding his or her 'true' identity. As there is an increasing interest in reincarnation, the interpretation of birthmarks is often channelled towards acceptance of previous lives and as a personal proof of it.

A further indication for interpreting spontaneous past-life recall experiences by children is the fact that they are culturally dependent. Most cases are reported in India and other South Asian countries, where reincarnation is fully accepted. The Asian cases are always richer in details than the Western ones. Western children who have such experiences give only poor details that could permit verification. When checking some verifiable details is possible, they usually turn out to be past experiences of other members of the family. Cultural conditioning certainly plays an important role in these phenomena.

In the conclusion of his research, Ian Stevenson admitts in his book *Twenty Cases Suggestive of Reincarnation* that the cases he studied, as the very title indicates, are only *suggesting* reincarnation and cannot be considered proofs for it. Stevenson admitts: "All the cases I've investigated so far have shortcomings. Even taken together, they do not offer anything like proof" (*Omni Magazine* 10(4):76 (1988)).

Metaphysical Reasons for Rejecting Past-life Recall Experiences as Proofs for Reincarnation

Even if hypnotic regression and spontaneous recall of past lives by children were free of any contradiction, there still would be another major argument against their veracity: According to the classic doctrine of reincarnation, the entity which reincarnates is the impersonal self (*atman* or *purusha*), accompanied by the subtle body. Any psycho-mental element that defines personhood does not belong to the self or to the subtle body, and therefore ceases to exist at physical death. Memory is such an element. It acts only inside the limits of a physical life and vanishes at death. If things were different, if memory could pass to further lives through reincarnation, it could establish the veracity of reincarnation in less problematic ways.

The vehicle that carries the psychic impressions from one life to another is said to be the subtle body (*sukshma sharira* in Vedanta) or the karmic deposit (*karmashaya* in Samkhya-Yoga). Although some say that this vehicle acts as a kind of unconscious memory of previous lives, it cannot represent a third ontological category (different from both the self and the psycho-mental realm), which could play the role of a carrier of personal memory from one life to another. As mentioned in the previous article, the subtle body stores hidden tendencies or impressions (*samskara*) imprinted by karma that act as seeds which generate future behaviour and personal character. This kind of deposit merely serves as a mechanism for adjusting the effects of karma in one's life.

According to Samkhya and Yoga it dictates in an impersonal and mechanical manner the new birth, the length of life and the experiences that must accompany it. Karma represents an impersonal and mechanical law which functions with mathematical precision, so it cannot justify one's state at a certain moment. One cannot know his or her own karma, but only speculate what it could be, based on actual situations in life. Karma is simply pushing the self into a foreordained scenario, which one has to accept and adjust to.

Even though some special meditative techniques are mentioned which are said to provide limited information about past lives (for instance *Yoga-Sutra* 3.18 mentions the possibility of knowing the previous birth through practicing *samyama*), they are available only to the advanced Yogi. But even so, the veracity of the information acquired in altered states of consciousness is doubtful.

One's karmic debts could at best be imagined intuitively. For instance, it is supposed that a man who was murdered took his just reward for a murder he committed himself in a previous life. Past-life recall experiences do not provide any information about the "sins" one committed in a previous life, but only lead one to draw conclusions from when he or she allegedly was a victim or a simple observer of life.

These kinds of experiences do not attempt to prove the justice of karma, but only that past lives are real. In other words, the "recalled" scenarios do not indicate which facts of the previous life produced the present incarnation, but only try to prove that we lived previous lives, that reincarnation is true and has to be acknowledged.

Because of the metaphysical difficulties mentioned above, most Eastern masters do not consider experiences of past-life recall as valid proofs for reincarnation. At the time Stevenson was carrying out his studies among Indian children who remembered previous lives, he met an Indian swami of the Ramakrishna order. He commented on these cases: "Yes [reincarnation] is true, but it does not make any difference, because we in India have all believed in reincarnation and have accepted it as a fact, and yet it has made no difference. We have as many rogues and villains in India as you have in the West" (*Venture Inward Magazine*, September/October, 1995). These stories are appreciated mostly by Westerners, probably as a result of misunderstanding the original doctrine of reincarnation and also because of their pseudo-scientific outlook. A more important argument for reincarnation in the East has another nature and will be analysed next.

Reincarnation and Christianity

Today's religious syncretism not only accepts reincarnation as one of its basic doctrines but also tries to prove that it can be found in the Bible and that it was accepted by the early Church. We will therefore analyse the basic texts in the Bible which are claimed to imply belief in reincarnation, examine the position of some important Church fathers who are said to have accepted it, and emphasise the basic antagonism of this doctrine with Christian teaching.

Reincarnation and the Bible

Biblical texts that seem to imply belief in reincarnation.

The most "convincing" texts of this kind are the following:

(1) *Matthew* 11,14 and 17,12-13, concerning the identity of John the Baptist;

(2) *John* 9,2, "Who sinned, this man or his parents, that he was born blind?";

(3) *John* 3,3, "No one can see the kingdom of God unless he is born again";

(4) *James* 3,6, "the wheel of nature";

(5) *Galatians* 6,7, "A man reaps what he sows";

(6) *Matthew* 26,52, "all who draw the sword will die by the sword";

(7) *Revelation* 13,10, "If anyone is to go into captivity, into captivity he will go. If anyone is to be killed with the sword, with the sword he will be killed."

1. The first text concerns the identity of John the Baptist, supposed to be the reincarnation of the prophet Elijah. In *Matthew* 11,14 Jesus says: "And if you are willing to accept it, he (John the Baptist) is the Elijah who was to come." In the same Gospel, while answering the apostles about the coming of Elijah, Jesus told them: "But I tell you, Elijah has already come, and they did not recognise him, but have done to him everything they wished. In the same way the Son of Man is going to suffer at their hands." The commentary adds: "Then the disciples understood that he was talking to them about John the Baptist" (*Matthew* 17,12-13; *Mark* 9,12-13).

   At first sight, it may seem that these verses imply the reincarnation of the prophet Elijah as John the Baptist. The prophecy of the return of Elijah appears in the last verses of the Old Testament, in the book of the prophet *Malachi* (3,1; 4,5-6): "See, I will send you the prophet Elijah before that great and dreadful day of the Lord comes." In *Luke* 1,17 an angel announces the fulfilment of this prophecy at the birth of John the Baptist: "And he will go on before the Lord, in the spirit and power of Elijah, to turn the hearts of the fathers to their children and the disobedient to the wisdom of the righteous-to make ready a people prepared for the Lord." What could be the meaning of the words "in the spirit and power of Elijah"?

   First we must be aware that the Jews viewed 'spirit' and 'soul' as quite different things. The human person has a soul which will live on after physical death. The spirit is a kind of driving force, a motivation that makes people behave in one way or another. When a group of people are working to fulfil a common goal, they are said to be in the same spirit. Second, the text does not say that John the Baptist will go "in the soul of Elijah," but "in the spirit of Elijah." This means that John the Baptist and Elijah had the same "team spirit," not that one was the reincarnation of the other. John the Baptist was rather a kind of Elijah, a prophet who had to repeat the mission of Elijah in a similar context. The same as Elijah did nine centuries before him, John the Baptist had to suffer persecution from the royal house of Israel and act in the context of the spiritual degeneration of the Jewish nation. John had the same spiritual mission as the prophet Elijah, but not the same soul or self. For this reason the expression "in the spirit and power of Elijah" should not be interpreted as meaning the reincarnation of a person, but as a necessary repetition of a well-known episode in the history of Israel.

Other Gospel passages that refer to Elijah and John the Baptist confirm that this text cannot teach reincarnation. At the time John the Baptist began his public preaching, the priests in Jerusalem asked him about his identity: "Are you Elijah?" (*John* 1,21) John answered simply: "I am not." Another text that contradicts reincarnation as applying to this case is the story of Elijah's departure from this world. Elijah didn't die in the proper sense of the word, but "went up to heaven in a whirlwind" (*2 Kings* 2,11). According to the classic theory of reincarnation, a person has to die physically first in order that his self may be reincarnated in another body. In the case of Elijah this didn't happen. So it must be considered an exception both to the natural process of death, and to the rule of reincarnation. Finally, the three apostles at the Mount of Transfiguration said that they had seen Elijah, not John the Baptist, with whom they were familiar (*Matthew* 17,1-8, *Mark* 9,2-8; *Luke* 9,28-36).

2. The next disputed text is the introduction to the healing of the man born blind in *John* 9,2. Considering the apostles' question: "Rabbi, who sinned, this man or his parents, that he was born blind?", it is obvious that the first option (the man was born blind because of his sin) implies that he could sin only in a previous life. According to the classic theory of reincarnation, he might have been a cruel dictator who got the just reward for his bad deeds.

   However, the apostles' question about the possibility of having sinned before birth should not necessarily be judged as indicating an existing belief in reincarnation. It rather confirms that some religious factions believed that the fetus could somehow sin in its mother womb. If Jesus had considered reincarnation to be true, surely he would have used this opportunity, as was his custom, to explain to them how karma and reincarnation work in such a peculiar situation. Jesus never missed such opportunities to instruct his disciples on spiritual matters, and reincarnation would have been a crucial doctrine for them to understand.

   Nevertheless, in the answer Jesus gave, he rejected both options suggested by the apostles. Both ideas of sinning before birth and the punishment for the parents' sins were wrong. Jesus said: "Neither this man nor his parents sinned, but this happened so that the work of God might be displayed in his life" (*John* 9,3). "The work of God" is described in the next verses, when Jesus healed the blind man as a proof of his divinity (v. 39).

3. In the *Gospel According to John* Jesus said to Nicodemus: "I tell you the truth, no one can see the kingdom of God unless he is born again" (*John* 3,3). Out of its context, this verse seems to suggest that reincarnation is the only possibility for attaining spiritual perfection and admission into the "kingdom of God." Nicodemus' following question indicates that he understood by these words a kind of physical rebirth

in this life, and not classic reincarnation: "How can a man be born when he is old? Surely he cannot enter a second time into his mother's womb to be born!" (v. 4). Jesus rejected the idea of physical rebirth and explained man's need for *spiritual rebirth*, during this life, in order to be admitted into God's kingdom in the afterlife.

Jesus further explained the meaning of his words by referring to a well-known episode in Israel's history: "Just as Moses lifted up the snake in the desert, so the Son of Man must be lifted up" (*John* 3,14). That episode occurred while the Israelites were travelling in the wilderness toward the Promised Land under the command of Moses (*Numbers* 21,4-9). They spoke against God and against Moses, and God punished them by sending poisonous snakes against them. Grasping the gravity of the situation, they recognised their sin and asked for a saving solution. God's solution was that Moses had to make a bronze copy of such a snake and put it up on a pole. Those who had been bitten by a snake had to look at this bronze snake, believing that this symbol represented their salvation, and so were healed. Coming back to the connection Jesus made between that episode and his teaching, he said: "Just as Moses lifted up the snake in the desert, so the Son of Man must be lifted up, that everyone who believes in him may have eternal life" (*John* 3,14-15). In other words, as Moses lifted up the bronze snake 13 centuries earlier, in the same way was Jesus to be lifted up on the cross, in order to be the only antidote to the deadly bite of sin. As the Jews had to believe that the bronze snake was their salvation from death, the same way Nicodemus, his generation and the entire world had to believe that Jesus' sacrifice on the cross is the perfect solution provided by God for the sins of the world. Therefore the kind of rebirth Jesus was teaching was not the Eastern concept of reincarnation but a spiritual rebirth that any human can experience in this life.

4. A fourth text interpreted as indicative of reincarnation is found in the *Epistle of James* 3,6, where some translations (such as the American Standard Version) mention "the wheel of nature" which seems to be the equivalent of the cycle of endless reincarnations stated in Eastern religions. However, in this context the reference is made to the control of speech in order not to sin. The ASV translation states: "And the tongue is a fire: the world of iniquity among our members is the tongue, which defileth the whole body, and setteth on fire the wheel of nature, and is set on fire by hell." The tongue out of control is compared with a fire that affects all aspects of existence, thought and deed, in a vicious cycle. This means that sinful speech is at the origin of many other sins which are consequently generated. The NIV translation is clearer at this point: "The tongue also is a fire, a world of evil among the parts of the body. It corrupts the whole person, sets the whole course of his life on fire, and is itself set on fire by hell."
5. A classic example of suggesting karma and *samsara* in the Bible is often claimed to be represented by the words of the Apostle Paul in *Galatians*: "Do not be deceived: God cannot be mocked. A man reaps what he sows" (*Galatians* 6,7). This "sowing and reaping" process would allegedly represent someone's acts and their consequences as dictated by karma in further lives. However, the very next verse indicates that the point is judging the effects of our deeds from the perspective of eternal life, as stated in the Bible, without a further earthly existence being involved: "The one who sows to please his sinful nature, from that nature will reap destruction; the one who sows to please the Spirit, from the Spirit will reap eternal life" (6,8). "Reaping destruction" means eternal separation from God in hell, while "eternal life" represents eternal communion with God in heaven. In their given context, these verses cannot suggest the reincarnation of the soul after death. According to Christianity, the supreme judge of our deeds is God, and not impersonal karma.

6. After Peter had cut off the ear of the high priest's servant in his attempt to prevent Jesus' arrest in Gethsemane, Jesus rebuked him by saying: "All who draw the sword will die by the sword" (*Matthew* 26,52). Could this be the justice of karma in action?

   All four Gospels give the account of Jesus' rebuke to Peter's initiative. Although heroic, it went against God's plan ("How then would the Scriptures be fulfilled that say it must happen in this way?"–verse 54). In this case Peter was sinning and, according to the well-known Old Testament law of sin retribution, the sinner must be punished consistently ("Whoever sheds the blood of man, by man shall his blood be shed; for in the image of God has God made man"-*Genesis* 9,6; *Exodus* 21,23-25; *Leviticus* 24,19-20; *Deuteronomy* 19,21). However, throughout the Old Testament this law was referring solely to one's present physical life, by no means to future lives. Otherwise Jesus' words would lead to an absurd implication. If he meant that killing someone in this life with a sword would require that the doer would be literally killed at his turn with a sword in a future life, then his crucifixion (which followed soon after this episode) must have been a punishment for his own sins done in previous lives and not a solution for other people's sins, as he claimed.

7. "If anyone is to go into captivity, into captivity he will go. If anyone is to be killed with the sword, with the sword he will be killed" (*Revelation* 13,10). This verse belongs to a prophecy that speaks about the end times, when Satan and his subjects will have temporary power on earth. Adherents of reincarnation must be aware that it is a quotation from the Old Testament: "And if they ask you, 'Where shall we go?' tell them, 'This is what the LORD says: "Those destined for death, to death; those for the sword, to the sword; those for starvation, to starvation; those for captivity, to captivity" (*Jeremiah* 15,2). This sentence was spoken by Jeremiah just before the fall of Jerusalem and the Babylonian

exile (586 BC) and expresses God's punishment of a sinful Jewish nation which had rejected him. It is not the impersonal law of karma acting here but the will of the personal creator God. He chooses how to punish those who have rejected him. The author of Revelation used this quotation for assuring those involved in the events to come that God would do justice again, as he did in the ancient times. Therefore they should act in "patient endurance and faithfulness" as *Revelation* 13,10 adds.

As can be observed, in all situations where "Biblical proofs" for reincarnation are claimed, the context is always ignored. Other passages used as proofs of reincarnationist beliefs mean, in fact, the existence of Christ prior to his human birth (*John* 8,58), the continuity of the souls' existence after death (*John* 5,28-29; *Luke* 16,22-23; *2 Corinthians* 5,1), or the spiritual rebirth of believers in their present life (*Titus* 3,5; *1 Peter* 1,23), without giving any plausible indication for reincarnation.

Did the Clergy Rewrite the Bible, so that the Passages Teaching Reincarnation were Removed?

Another hypothesis is that the Bible contained many passages teaching reincarnation in an alleged initial form, but they were suppressed by the clergy at the fifth ecumenical council, held in Constantinople in the year AD 553. The reason for this would have been the spiritual immaturity of the Christians, who could not grasp the doctrine at that time, or the desire of the clergy to manipulate the masses. However, there is no proof that such "purification" of the Biblical text has ever occurred. The existing manuscripts, many of them older than AD 553, do not show differences from the text we use today. There are enough reasons to accept that the New Testament was not written later than the first century AD.

If the clergy had decided to erase from the Bible the "compromising" passages about reincarnation, why did they keep those mentioned above (concerning the identity of John the Baptist, etc.)? On the other hand, there are other passages in the Bible that clearly contradict the idea of reincarnation, explicitly or implicitly. (*Samuel* 12,23; 14,14, *Job* 7,9-10, *Psalm*

78,39, *Matthew* 25,31-46, *Luke* 23,39-43, *Acts* 17,31, 2 *Corinthians* 5,1;4;8, *Revelation* 20,11-15.) Here is one verse in the New Testament which contradicts reincarnation as clearly as possible:

> *Just as man is destined to die once, and after that to face judgment, so Christ was sacrificed once to take away the sins of many people; and he will appear a second time, not to bear sin, but to bring salvation to those who are waiting for him (Hebrews 9,27-28).*

That the Christian Church teaches that we live only once is beyond doubt, as surely as it teaches that Jesus had to die only once for our sins. In other words, the unique historical act of Jesus' crucifixion and the teaching that we live only once are equally affirmed and cannot be separated. The judgment that follows death is obviously not the judgment of the impersonal karma, but that of the personal almighty God, after which man either enters an eternal personal relation with him in heaven, or an eternal separation from him in hell.

Did the Early Church Fathers Believe in Reincarnation?

Early Christianity spread in a world dominated by Greek philosophy. Many important figures of the early church had this spiritual background when they became Christians. Could they have been influenced by the doctrine of reincarnation? In order to answer this, we first have to understand the actual teaching on reincarnation at that time in the Greek world.

Reincarnation According to Platonism

The dominant form of reincarnation known by Greek philosophy during the first three Christian centuries belongs to Platonism. Unlike the Eastern spiritual masters, Plato taught that human souls existed since eternity in a perfect celestial world as intelligent and personal beings. They were not manifested out of a primordial impersonal essence (such as Brahman) or created by a personal god. Although the souls lived there in a pure state, somehow the divine love grew cold in them and, as a result, they fell in physical bodies to this earthly, imperfect world. Plato writes in *Phaedrus* about this:

But when she (the celestial soul) is unable to follow, and fails to behold the truth, and through some ill-hap sinks beneath the double load of forgetfulness and vice, and her wings fall from her and she drops to the ground, then the law ordains that this soul shall at her first birth pass, not into any other animal, but only into man; and the soul which has seen most of truth shall come to the birth as a philosopher, or artist, or some musical and loving nature.

In the same work, Plato states that "ten thousand years must elapse before the soul of each one can return to the place from whence she came." Only the soul of the philosopher or of the lover can get back to its original state in less time (*i.e.*, in three thousand years). The souls that fail to aspire to perfection and live in ignorance are judged after their earthly life and then punished in "the houses of correction, which are under the earth." One lifetime is not enough to return to the original celestial state of purity.

For this reason "the soul of a man may pass into the life of a beast, or from the beast return again into the man." This is the Platonist idea of reincarnation. It does not represent a voyage of an impersonal essence (as *atman*) toward an impersonal union with the Absolute (Brahman), but only a temporary punishment on the way back towards a purified personal existence (the state of pure being). Between Platonism and Eastern religions there is a big difference concerning man's identity in general and reincarnation in particular. Plato's meaning of salvation is definitely personal, as can be understand from *Phaedo*:

Those also who are remarkable for having led holy lives are released from this earthly prison, and go to their pure home which is above, and dwell in the purer earth; and those who have duly purified themselves with philosophy live henceforth altogether without the body, in mansions fairer far than these, which may not be described, and of which the time would fail me to tell.

How did these ideas affect the beliefs of the early church fathers? We will now proceed to examine the most important cases of early church fathers accused of holding reincarnationist convictions.

Origen and Origenism

The most controversial early church father concerning his alleged beliefs on reincarnation is undoubtedly Origen (185-254). Many adherents of reincarnation mention him today as a classic example which proves the alleged early Christian belief in reincarnation, which is supposed to have been condemned and forbidden by the fifth ecumenical council (Constantinople, AD 553). Although it is a fact that Origen was strongly influenced by Platonism prior to his conversion to Christianity, the claim that he believed in reincarnation is absurd.

Before using any quotes from his writings, we strongly advise you to read the file Origen and Origenism in order to get a brief description of Origen's life, writings and teachings. This article will give you a sound perspective on what he actually taught and what was later condemned as Origenism. Then see the act of refuting Origenism by the fifth ecumenical council, *The 15 Anathemas Against Origen*.

As can easily be observed, there is no clear concept of reincarnation mentioned at this council of the early church, but only the Platonist ideas concerning the preexistence of souls, besides universalism and a wrong form of Christology, as main heresies to be rejected. Since Origenism had incorporated these Platonistic ideas, it was rejected at the council of Constantinople. But the issue was not any form of Eastern reincarnation, as it is claimed today. For instance, the fourth anathema states:

> *If anyone shall say that the reasonable creatures in whom the divine love had grown cold have been hidden in gross bodies such as ours, and have been called men, while those who have attained the lowest degree of wickedness have shared cold and obscure bodies and are become and called demons and evil spirits: let him be anathema.*

The condemned ideas are closely related to what Plato had stated in *Phaedrus*. Origenism did not teach a classic form of reincarnation. In fact, Origen rejected plainly this doctrine in his *Commentary on Matthew* (Book XIII,1), written in the last years of his life. He refutes the speculation of considering John the Baptist the reincarnation of Elijah (*Matthew* 11,14; 17,12-13), a text we mentioned earlier. Origen writes:

> *In this place it does not appear to me that by Elijah the soul is spoken of, lest I should fall into the dogma of transmigration, which is foreign to the church of God, and not handed down by the Apostles, nor anywhere set forth in the Scriptures; for it is also in opposition to the saying that "things seen are temporal," and that "this age shall have a consummation," and also to the fulfilment of the saying, "Heaven and earth shall pass away," and "the fashion of this world passeth away," and "the heavens shall perish," and what follows.*

In the same commentary, under the title *"The spirit and power of Elijah"-not the soul-were in the Baptist*, Origen adds: "For, observe, he did not say in the 'soul' of Elijah, in which case the doctrine of transmigration might have some ground, but 'in the spirit and power of Elijah.'" Origen's whole commentary on this text is a refutation of the reincarnation theory. Therefore it is obvious that he cannot be considered at all an "early Christian adherent of reincarnation."

Other early Church Fathers vs. Reincarnation

Here are some quotations from other early church fathers which express their opinion on reincarnation. They prove that it cannot have been one of their beliefs.

Justin Martyr (100-165)

His opinion on reincarnation is plainly stated in the following fragment of his *Dialogue with Trypho* 1,4 (AD 155), part one, chapter 4, where he discusses Platonism with Trypho the Jew:

The old man: "What, then, is the advantage to those who have seen [God]? Or what has he who has seen more than he who has not seen, unless he remember this fact, that he has seen?"

Justin: "I cannot tell," I answered.

The old man: "And what do those suffer who are judged to be unworthy of this spectacle?" said he.

Justin: "[According to Plato] They are imprisoned in the bodies of certain wild beasts, and this is their punishment."

The old man: "Do they know, then, that it is for this reason they are in such forms, and that they have committed some sin?"

Justin: "I do not think so."

The old man: "Then these reap no advantage from their punishment, as it seems: moreover, I would say that they are not punished unless they are conscious of the punishment."

Justin: "No indeed."

The old man: "Therefore souls neither see God nor transmigrate into other bodies; for they would know that so they are punished, and they would be afraid to commit even the most trivial sin afterwards. But that they can perceive that God exists, and that righteousness and piety are honourable, I also quite agree with you," said he.

Justin: "You are right," I replied.

Irenaeus (130-200)

In his well-known treatise *Against Heresies* (Book II), Irenaeus entitled the 33rd chapter "Absurdity of the Doctrine of the Transmigration of Souls." The whole chapter criticizes this doctrine, emphasising the futility of reincarnation devoid of any memory of past lives:

> *They (the souls) must of necessity retain a remembrance of those things which have been previously accomplished, that they might fill up those in which they were still deficient, and not by always hovering, without intermission, round the same pursuits, spend their labour wretchedly in vain.*

Tertullian (145-220)

In his *Treatise on the Soul*, Tertullian traces the origin of reincarnationist ideas down to Pythagoras. He writes:

If, indeed, the sophist of Samos is Plato's authority for the eternally revolving migration of souls out of a constant alternation of the dead and the living states, then no doubt did the famous Pythagoras, however excellent in other respects, for the purpose of fabricating such an opinion as this, rely on a falsehood, which was not only shameful, but also hazardous.

His conclusion is that "we must likewise contend against that monstrous presumption, that in the course of the transmigration beasts pass from human beings, and human beings from beasts."

Gregory of Nyssa (335-395)

Finally, one of the master theologians of early Christianity rejected in his turn any idea of predestination in his writing *Against Fate*, and also the concept of reincarnation in the 28th chapter of his treatise *On the Making of Man*:

Those who assert that the state of souls is prior to their life in the flesh, do not seem to me to be clear from the fabulous doctrines of the heathen which they hold on the subject of successive incorporation: for if one should search carefully, he will find that their doctrine is of necessity brought down to this. They tell us that one of their sages said that he, being one and the same person, was born a man, and afterwards assumed the form of a woman, and flew about with the birds, and grew as a bush, and obtained the life of an aquatic creature;- and he who said these things of himself did not, so far as I can judge, go far from the truth: for such doctrines as this of saying that one soul passed through so many changes are really fitting for the chatter of frogs or jackdaws, or the stupidity of fishes, or the insensibility of trees.

All these early church fathers lived before the fifth ecumenical council (Constantinople, AD 553), so it cannot be true that the doctrine of reincarnation was condemned and forbidden only as a result of that council, as a deceitful act of manipulating Christianity by the clergy. Although reincarnation was taught by some non-Christian movements of that time, such as the Gnostics and the Neo-Platonists, it had nothing in common with the teachings of the early church, being always rejected as a heresy by the early church fathers.

Why cannot Christianity Accept Reincarnation?

The idea of reincarnation has never been accepted by Christianity because it undermines its basic tenets. First, it compromises God's sovereignty over creation, transforming him into a helpless spectator of the human tragedy. But since he is sovereign and omnipotent over creation, God can punish evil and will do it perfectly well at the end of history (*Matthew* 25,31-46; *Revelation* 20,10-15). There is no need for the impersonal law of karma and for reincarnation to play this role.

Second, belief in reincarnation may affect one's understanding of morality and motivation for moral living. An extreme application of reincarnationist convictions could lead to adopting a detached stand to crime, theft and other social plagues. They could be considered nothing else but normal debts to be paid by their victims, which originated in previous lives.

Third, reincarnation represents a threat to the very essence of Christianity: the need for Christ's redemptive sacrifice for our sins. If we are to pay for the consequences of our sins ourselves in further lives and attain salvation through our own efforts, the sacrifice of Christ becomes useless and absurd. It wouldn't be the only way back to God, but only a stupid accident of history. In this case Christianity would be a mere form of Hindu *Bhakti-Yoga*.

As a result, no matter how many attempts are made today to find texts in the Bible or in the history of the Church that would allegedly teach reincarnation, they are all doomed to remain flawed.

2

The Metaphysics of Karmic Law

Introductory Statements

There is no greater evolutionary force in Creation than the karmic law of cause and effect. As the primary means by which souls evolve through all dimensions of apparent time-space, it is the prime mover in soul progression across all realms of incarnation.

It is itself a consequence and derivative of the grand Law of Free Will (the causative basis of manifest Creation) by which beings are given the right and, indeed the duty to continually choose their way. As its main function, the karmic law encourages and guides continual soul growth and the ineluctable progress of time-space itself. It is no less magnificent than this, and generates the very pathways of all-dimensional existence, being this close to the heart of the Creator-Logoi in fulfilment of their unknowable Cosmic Plan.

Reaping what we sow, creating our own reality, meeting projected fragmentary aspects of inner life on the canvas of so-called external activity—all this is guided by the majestic laws of karma. It is the process by which the aspected and apparently complex (*i.e.*, self-contradictory) personal self returns in form, energy and consciousness to a completed universal self. Without karmic operation, souls literally could not return to themselves.

In human life, we wonder why various circumstances come our way, why some of us enjoy streaming pleasure while others seem doomed to constant limitation—and yet, all this proceeds under ineluctable karmic law, not accidental in the least. The universe is not capricious; terran humanity simply doesn't comprehend the logic of soul progression along the long, multi-incarnational and multidimensional way of polarised manifestation.

Gautama Buddha explained it simply and for practical usage in his primary teachings. As a "way-shower," he pointed out that our virtuous thoughts and deeds are precursors to happiness, while selfishness in all forms is the progenitor of suffering. And yet, many souls of deep love and kindness in this world dc suffer greatly, while many of the most heinous (negatively polarised souls) on Earth reap untold wealth and influence, living in oases of luxury with continual options for further self-enhancement. This state of affairs simply cannot be understood without deep recognition of timeless reincarnation plans and the prevailing extra-dimensional laws and pre-incarnative life-design of souls.

This principle of higher-dimensional planning for incarnation is no less than the metaphysical basis for eventually coming to terms with the purpose of all form-based life itself. Though its complete dynamic cannot be fully understood with the current mind complex we use in the 3rd dimensional matrix, it can be penetrated in an elementary way by those who seek to know and gain wisdom. Such is the purpose of this writing.

PART I

Essential Principles

There can be no real understanding of karmic law without recognition of several main precedents, as noted below. These recognitions also provide a philosophic gateway to all durable, universally valid spiritual wisdom regarding karmic operation in our own lives. Attachment to such differentiated conception must, of course, one day be transcended, but it is deeply useful at our stage of development. These elementary precedents to comprehensive realisation of karmic law include the following:

(1) A relatively eternal, time/space independent soul (in the Buddhist approach, a non-solid/selfless yet continuing life-stream of mental tendencies);

(2) Multidimensional existence (the basic so-called "inner worlds" which are, in actuality, far more complex than the outer physical form-manifestation); and

(3) Intelligent guidance (equated with God, Logos, Creator, Higher Self, or simply a wholly lawful self-organising principle of Life and Mind itself).

I have no doubt that all we experience has been chosen at some level of our being. All the minutiae and larger situational experiences coming our way were created by us, either consciously or unconsciously. Thus, each of us absolutely and without exception 'deserve' and are due exactly and fully all that we experience, down to the length and shade of each hair on the body. Karmic law is profoundly complex and exacting in all its details.

It is said that, "God never gives us more than we can handle," and that, "all things exist for a purpose." Such statements reiterate this view, essential to spiritual wisdom and the cognitive foundation to eventual total self-responsibility—which is itself the basis of all durable self-healing and balancing.

Without such self-ownership of personal life details, we simply cannot make peace with ourselves, our fated life-components, and the current challenges we each individually face. This type of realisation is itself a gateway to accessing the fuller powers of self, via personal linkage to the Logoic will. Comprehending karmic law is, in deed, an exercise in plumbing the mind of God, and thereby, divine omnipotent power.

This type of metaphysical analysis also points to the specific functions of karmic law, though the law goes far deeper than personal process. We cannot make true peace with the countless, ever-shifting, challenging dynamics of personality life without recourse to appreciation of karmic law, its complexity and profound subtlety. Without such understanding, we remain in the position of Job, railing against the Creator for the experiences of suffering we ourselves have created.

Nor can we grasp the course and directions of group-soul progress (in our case, this pertains to earth human collective history and current manifestations), without deep consideration of karmic process over millennia and across dimensions. Again, we can only achieve a mere toe-in to this comprehension while still embodied in 3D form, but even our elementary exercise of such wisdom has great personal value as a means to greater mind complex clearance and activation.

Indeed, these are most serious matters, and thus it is said that some of the highest, eldest, most sublime beings still at work in manifest Creation oversee the complex minutiae of karmic dispensation, at both collective and individual levels. For it must be noted that there are both karmic streams of individuated souls on their own polarised path (pursuing either unity or separation, the so-called positive and negative orientations), as well as countless major groupings of souls, at all dimensional levels. For the so-called Lords of Karma, there is vast life to coordinate and assist in seven-dimensional spheres.

Both categories of consciousness groups (that of relatively simple units of body-mind-spirit complexes, what we call "souls," as well as the greater coordinated streams of associated units evolving en masse), demand highly complex karmic arrangements for their continued, proper evolution. Obviously, the spiritual growth of beings cannot be overseen and coordinated at the same level of their own learning—it can only be overseen by those finished with such progression—*i.e.*, those done with the entire circuit of octave evolution.

In human affairs, this is comparable to the maxim that a problem cannot be solved at the same level of its genesis nor its same field of operation. In a little-appreciated statement, Einstein once remarked something to the effect that, "the problems we face cannot be solved by the same minds that created them." This is even more so in the case of karmic operation, since the 'problems" in that field are truly multidimensional.

All such groups (individual souls and collective soul groups) traverse inconceivable eons of time-space through multiple densities, along the course of which they are required to perfectly 'balance out' the consequences of all experiences they have consciously chosen and self-created through ignorance, distortion, and incomplete awareness of perfect love-unity. As the path is circular, souls cannot return to their original true nature unless they have come back into energetic conformity with the nature of their essential starting-point.

All such personal knots and blockages—manifested in etheric energy fields as well as in apparent mental/cognitive confusion and imbalances—must be resolved, untangled, and harmonised along the way. Only then can souls and soul-groups fully return to the innate condition of perfect love-unity, that is both our source and our destination. Thus, metaphysical teachings refer to soul evolution as, "the path of return."

The supervised dispensation of karmic dues and the gradual and meticulously timed precipitation into manifest (apparently external) form of all that yet remains fragmented to evolving soul consciousness, can only be effected by beings who are themselves so far outside time-space as to be entirely free of all karmic necessity.

Rightly, oversight for karmic operation begins at the level of Higher Self in late-sixth density, so we are admittedly a bit over our heads here! Nevertheless, some Wanderers on Earth have come from this level of being, and can thus appreciate this perspective...

Those beings in oversight of karmic operation can be said to have absolute mastery over the boundless ramifications of an infinite variety of soul choices. They wield with impeccable wisdom and skill the potentia of manifold experiential forms and incarnative experience, all for the purpose of catalysing required re-balancing and soul orientation.

Obviously, this is no small matter, far, far beyond the comprehension of almost all Earth humans. The degree of intelligence required for administration of perfectly accurate karmic precipitation, for souls and soul-groups at all dimensional levels of Creation (simultaneously), is far beyond the human keen, to say the least.

Thus, RA noted that beings "from beyond the octave," beyond the sevenfold dimensional scheme of solar systems and individuated soul and group-soul evolution, fulfil such operative karmic functions. Only they are capable of such activity, and in the writings of Alice Bailey and the teacher Djwhal Khul, only these beings can rightly being called the "Lords of Karma." Down here on the ground, the most we can do (which is quite a task itself), is to process as best we can all such experiential distillates in personal life.

In line with this, the entire topic of karma was one of several themes Gautama Buddha deemed "the incomprehensibles." Such speculation for the monks of his day (even though many of them would be classed as advanced adepts, no small achievement) was deemed a fruitless topic for mental engagement. Still under the sway of apparently real, dualistic space-time conditions, and still subject to variable and ever-unstable personal becoming through mental grasping, there really is little on these matters that can be known—since, as stated before, we ourselves are certainly nowhere near beyond the operation of karmic law. Thus, it was deemed a waste of time to devote personal attention to mere speculation.

Nevertheless, in my view, there is value in attempting relative comprehension of the absolutely incomprehensible, especially if we are fully aware at the outset that the best we can hope for is but a tiny fraction of total gnosis. As RA said of soul work in physical 3rd density existence, it is wholly a task of, "working in darkness with a tiny candle." And yet, real growth can be made for those who accept the challenges of gross limitation, as we really can expand our access to the realm of knowable things.

And so, this essay is an exercise in bringing scant illumination to the 3rd dimensional mind complex of those who feel attraction to this rather advanced work. To know what is beyond us, even just a bit, refines and energizes our own development though long-term activation of greater spiritual seeking. To gain a bit more understanding of karmic law, its application to personal and collective life at this time in human history, and its nature and function in overall cosmic plan, is certainly worthy of our time and attention. Seeking that which is beyond seeking, if approached rightly, is highly effective catalyst for quickened soul growth.

PART II

Functions of Karmic Law

Overall, karma operates to accelerate soul and soul group evolution, namely, the dissolution of each and every mind/body/spirit distortion to total realisation of love-unity. Being "finished with karma" equates to completion of the long path of individuated light-spark soul progress, and occurs only with final fusion into the formless light of the One Infinite. Obviously, anyone who publicly claims such achievement is self-deluded.

Technically, this normally occurs late within what is called 7th density, which is akin to the achievement of "sat-chit-ananda" (truth-consciousness-bliss), the term used in the Hindu yogic system. It is comparable to the state of "avatara" and Buddha—complete and perfect enlightenment. Of course, it can be achieved here in 3D, but again, it is exceptionally rare to find such a one on the world stage.

Karmic law is at the heart of all evolutionary catalysis, as the primary force behind increasingly higher dimensional progress and consciousness expansion of all souls. Of course, the specific forms of karmic expression (and this entire discussion) become increasingly subtle and harmonious above 3rd density life. This is beyond the current level of discussion, of course.

Essentially, the ultimate goal of love-unity realisation requires dissolution of all fixed belief in substantial duality, and is accompanied by absolute mastery and freedom within all realms of the octave system. This can only be achieved when souls realise the true nature of all manifest catalyst to likewise be non-substantial (so-called "emptiness" or sunyata in the Buddhist system) and imbued with essential love (the quality of infinite light being absolute beneficence).

Such transmuted-being realisation defines the operative parameters of attaining return to the condition of oneness with all Creation and all forms of life. The existence of karmic law itself is an expression of boundless Logoic love, and its nature and function is to continually encourage realisation of the underlying, immanent unity of all being and becoming. Bringing this down to personal life, we find continual activity of karmic law in human affairs.

Normally, karma is only recognised as such when its expression surpasses a certain threshold of energetic charge to the individual. However, this tendency to focus on that which indicates "contrast' (bound up with perception of conflict and complexity) fails to see and appreciate the greater bulk of karmic operation in personal life.

As the teacher Djwhal Khul once noted, souls have far more "good karma" than "bad," though most of us pay far more attention to the latter, as contrast, conflict and complexity capture attention far more rapidly than harmony. Nevertheless, this 'negative focus' is the norm simply because the internal condition of soul itself is absolute harmony—thus the perception of non-harmony is internally incongruent with our true nature.

Of course, this innate harmony forms the subtle background-field against which all experience of apparent disharmony strikes a clear, discordant vibratory note. As the soul seeks to impress its own being upon the manifest body-mind-spirit (which is none other than itself, in final analysis), there is created a sort of non-echo in the soul-personality axis—which is the esoteric cause of all spiritual seeking, in the first place.

More practically, most souls recognise the operation of karmic law only according to the dichotomous experience of pleasure/pain, and thus remain bound to the limitations of this bipolar view. No doubt, such shallow comprehension of karmic operation also ensures a limited ability to work with the law and process karmic experience.

Perceiving the operation of karmic law only when life-catalyst elicits a certain intensity of personal reaction, then placing it simply into a static categorisation of pleasure/pain, indicates a somewhat early stage of realising karmic process.

A more advanced view eliminates this polarity altogether, and helps us appreciate that all experience (whether pleasant r otherwise) serves the purpose of encouraging soul chievement of complete non-distortion. Such a view recognises karmic law as an intrinsically impersonal universal force, and goes even further to acknowledges the existence of apparent causality itself but a perceptual 'trick' of limited mind development.

When consciousness is sufficiently enlightened by itself, apparent causality is resolved into complete omnipresent simultaneity. At that stage, souls are no longer bound by time-space and karmic law, and may enter the ranks of those who administer the operation of karma within such realms of apparent duality, an example of which is our 3rd dimension.

Furthermore, the distinction between "good karma" and "bad" is misleading because the determination of karmic law proceeds from levels of consciousness far beyond all such polarised judgement. Its practical operation really has little do with human conceptions of reward and punishment (as such deeper belief bases give rise to the "good/bad" dichotomy in the first place). Enormous confusion has been spawned by this particular interpretation, as evidenced by the distortions of all major religious teachings on heaven.

Plainly, the dispensation of soul and soul group karma is actually a morally neutral phenomenon. To the Logoi, there are no so-called "moral" valuations, only a straight recognition of metaphysical free will choice (that of the personality and its higher aspect which realises the complete Path to be trod). Beyond this, the Logoi provide the needed structuring of the laws of Creation (one of which is karmic law) to encourage further soul progress according to soul decision.

From the evolutionary perspective of Logos and Higher Self (the primary agents of our overshadowing self-luminous intelligence), what souls choose to do in response to karmic outpouring is really the central issue—not whether or not karmic down flow is deemed good or bad. The purpose of evolution and life itself is not enjoyment, though increased pleasure does result from wise soul choice along the path.

The Creator and Creation are not much interested in static rewards and punishment. What is achieved today may surely be reversed tomorrow, and what is useful catalyst to one soul may be absolutely invisible to another—all of which is as it should be. In light of this, it is quite short sighted to define karma in terms of good/bad, or pleasure/pain.

As the central and most important outcropping of the Law of Free Will, *the primary function of karmic law is to catalyze soul choice*, first and foremost, and from the evolutionary purist view, simply and only for its own sake. As "the purpose of Creation is that the Creator may experience Itself," freely established choice is the primary nutriment that feeds the boundless divine experience. From this perspective as well, terms such as "good karma" and "bad" have little importance and no use.

Returning to the more mundane, but no less important consideration of personal human life, it should be known that most instances of above-threshold karmic operation classed along the "good/bad" continuum are simply a return to the sender of energies and tendencies previously set in motion by that soul itself. Prior acts of the evolving and reincarnating mind/body/spirit complex, the personal triadic web of the soul field in time-space set all individual karmic streams in motion, which provide the main working field of our own growth.

Such karmic returns manifest several distinct operations, including:

(1) The precise quality of their originating self-generated energies cleverly transformed into apparently outer events;

(2) Various manifestations and changes of the body complex itself, as complex symbolic representations of inner personality imbalances, blockages, and conflicts; and

(3) Qualities of mind and emotion carried and offered by other souls in relationship to us, revealing aspects of as-yet unrecognised inner dynamics within us needing some degree of spiritual re-orientation; and

(4) Thought forms transmitted and received at mental-spiritual levels, material or subtle, which offer the catalyst of revealed options for such re-orientation itself.

What is classed as "good karma" is simply the set of reflections we favour, and the contrary for the "bad." Yet, in no case is it the intention of such karmic precipitation to lock us into fixed experiences of pleasure/pain. No matter how ghastly such circumstances may feel to the participant and appear to the onlooker, the mechanism of such experiential challenge proceeds only from divine beneficence. Of course, this may only be an article of faith for those of us without adequate gnosis, not having yet made direct contact with the essential impetus behind life-events.

PART III

Practical Considerations and Polarity

Along the personal subjective continuum, karmic precipitation that we generally class into the duality of pleasure/pain, actually serves to confirm, validate, mirror, express, and often challenge (particularly in the case of "bad karma") prevailing trends and tendencies already resident within the recipient soul to whom appears. We are only being given back discretely apportioned elements of ourselves, no matter how miserable it may feel.

As internal trends and tendencies of the personal human mind are generally poorly seen, known, and accepted (if not totally ignored) by souls in 3rd density fixation, the process of karmic precipitation serves *to reveal the deeper self to the conscious self.* This is both the path and fruit of the universal Way of Return: the return of conscious awareness to all-awareness, self to Self, god to God, and the lesser manifest light to the One infinite light.

Obviously, the axiom that "we create our own reality" is far more difficult to recognise, apply, and use constructively in the case of painful inbound catalyst (*i.e.*, so-called "bad karma)," which may be quite horrific in its appearance. For example, why was it that earth humanity suffered over 100 million wartime deaths in the 20th century? At our level of being, such represents incalculable personal tragedy, and yet, this was but the karmic result of innumerable causal sequences, some of which are significantly inter-dimensional in their origin.

It is not that the Creator ordained such primitive bloodletting, but it was certainly not stopped from occurring through intervention from higher levels of being. And yet, it did serve multiple spiritual re-orientation goals for both individual souls and the entire human soul group family on this planet. The specific purposes—including a needed "lightening of the astral plane," as stated by Djwhal Khul through Alice Bailey—are well known by those who guide our evolution.

Thus, whatever comes down the pike is just our own face in various guises. This can be considered (especially in San Francisco, my hometown) the Logos in drag, and a mirror-appearing opportunity for greater freedom from our unseen inner distortions. This is hard to realise, of course, when the incoming guest is violence and bloodshed.

And yet, despite the drama, souls are just being shown on the palette of 'external life' their own deeper aspects, patterns, layers, potentials, and general mind/spirit qualities. In the case of what we call "good karma," karmic law operates to give us what can be seen as *congratulatory support for further advance* upon that soul's own chosen path. In contrast to the inherent fixity of the "reward" view, karmic activity is in fact intensely, immensely dynamic and finely ever shifting, inconceivably sensitive to all minute shifts in soul consciousness and the actions that proceed therefrom.

In the case of those upon the positive path of service to others (which is the major way of soul evolution, directly seeking love-unity through truth, balance and non-grasping), the support granted by harmonious karmic inflow serves to reduce various kinds of personal limitation. It thus increases opportunity for further evolution (including opportunity for service to others) to the soul that has proven itself *capable of progressing in harmony*, not needing severe restraint for re-balancing and re-orientation.

Interestingly, the real benefit given by such beneficent physical, mental and spiritual conditions is the fact that such experiences and influences demand *no further attention*. The deeper value of so-called "good karma" is the fact that it releases and frees up soul attention and energy for increased work on matters of greater priority than simply dealing with the latest crises of the day. Various forms of "good karma" obviously feel like some kind of reward, and generally elicit pleasure, but in actuality, *the matrix of such august conditions is simply the removal of potential obstacles*. The dispensation of such conditional harmony was never meant to become a stopping point upon the ageless path of ceaseless growth. It is only humanity, which sees life through the lens of corporeal identification, that interprets karma in static terms implying some kind of "final resting place."

Clearly, when karmic law is seen strictly through the bi-focal lens of fixed reward-and-punishment, souls are more likely to pause, stop, and grow entangled in life conditions. Ironically, this involves emotional attachment to the very same outer and inner conditions that were only meant to be the basis for further *non*-attachment. This is quite interesting, and likely represents a successful ploy on the part of negative higher dimensional forces influencing religious notions of karma—seeking to retard human soul progression.

In another light, these pleasing outer/material karmic manifestations (including the so-called 'inner conditions" of radiant body and finely tuned mind by birth) simply all mirror the inward grace, harmony and beauty already achieved by that soul. This is echoed by Jesus's statement: "to him who has much, much shall be given." Harmony within certainly generates harmony without.

As a glimpse of glory (some semblance of perfection in form) and completion (primarily through the function of removing additional soul obstacles), such karmic dispensation is meant as a light above the path, leading that one on to the further greater light. From the perspective of karmic administration, the single motivation is always the intention to support further soul progress.

On the other side, considering those on the negatively oriented path of service to self (the minor way or left-hand path of seeking Oneness through separation via control), the process is somewhat reversed. For them, what we would consider good fortune (*i.e.*, harmonious karmic dispensation) is actually the ripened fruit due them by previously achieved 'evil.' Regardless of path, *harmonious karmic down flow results from efficient use of catalyst*, granting them a platform for quickened evolution and further progress according to their own chosen orientation.

Thus, successful use of catalyst on the negative path reaps fruit of the conqueror, and may be seen as karmic "rewards" that allow even greater polarity. Those at a high level on the negative path may be born with native strength and beauty of body (respectively for men and women); this serves the purpose of further drawing in other souls, so as to dominate them. They may have luxurious and abundant material conditions, great powers of logic and intelligence (though no degree of kindness), well-oiled social networks to aid further power aggrandizement (*i.e.*, "the right connections"), and well-honed instincts of smooth manipulation of others.

Possession of these qualities may be considered to be "karmic reward" by those on the left-hand path, but ironically, these conditions are highly valued by all Earth humanity. In this way, we can see how our planetary world culture can rightly be considered "leftward leaning," though not quite fully service to self.

Though the phrase, "successful evil" may seem paradoxical, it is not so from the view of Higher Self. In essence, what is deemed to be "efficient use of catalyst" (which is key to the quality of karmic dispensation programmed from higher being) on the negative path is exactly opposite from what it is on the positive path. It is not quite correct to say that such beings simply "need love and self-healing"—for those ingredients do not further at all their continued soul progression on the so-called "left-hand path."

For those of negative orientation, ever greater control of self and others is key, and is the measure and mark of efficient use of catalyst. Achieving greater external/social and internal/spiritual dominance is exactly their goal and just what they require to progress.

On the other hand, the key to the positive path is continued body/mind/spirit balancing in love-light manifestation, with increasingly demonstrated appreciation of unity. For while the path of self-service demands deception, the heart of the positive path is maintenance of evolving wholeness.

In both cases, what is considered "reward" or "good karma" is perfectly suited to further soul growth upon their chosen path, which is a far more dynamic process than the relative stasis assumed and imbedded in the dichotomous paradigm of reward and punishment. Humans may call it "good karma," but beyond the comfort and pleasure experienced, the essence of what makes it "good" is simply the potent support it grants for further soul polarisation.

Of course, well-processed and intelligently handled "bad karma" may also function to boost soul growth, which is also its native intention and purpose. In general, the value of conflict, pain and hardship comes through its power to shatter and interrupt certain ingrained patterns of mind-distortion (whether established in past lives or created in the current one).

Thus, Higher Self will not save us from the consequences of our own doing, though guidance and comfort are available. Interestingly, earth humans often seem to require (and thus perpetually recreate) painful circumstances to revitalise their soul growth.

Indeed, it is a very important achievement to recognise misfortune as opportunity, misery as self-created, the reception of human injustice as cosmic justice, and personal limitation as a wide-open door to further spiritual expansion. Of course, these are lovely phrases, but hard to realise amidst the intensity of disharmonious experiential catalyst. As RA once said, 3D human life provides "an adequate heaven, and a more than adequate hell."

Karma in Hinduism

Karma is a concept in Hinduism which explains causality through a system where beneficial effects are derived from past beneficial actions and harmful effects from past harmful actions, creating a system of actions and reactions throughout a person's reincarnated lives. Karma in Hinduism explains the problem of evil that persists in spite of an omniscient, omnipotent, benevolent God; it is thus related to theodicy.

Parts of the Mahabharata are sometimes anaylsed as a Karma story (the other parts being related to Moksha), a story where people received the reward of their actions, good and bad. The original Hindu concept of karma was later elaborated on by several other movements within the religion, most notably Vedanta, Yoga, and Tantra. The concept was adopted by other religions such as Buddhism and Jainism, whose views differ from Hinduism as the concept of Karma does not involve a personal supreme God. Karma has had a major influence on worldwide philosophy and spirituality.

Definition: "Karma" literally means "deed" or "act", and more broadly names the universal principle of cause and effect, action and reaction, which Hindus believe governs all life. It is believed that only beings that can distinguish right from wrong, such as adult humans, can accumulate Karma. Animals and young children are not considered to accumulate Karma as they are incapable of discriminating between right and wrong. However, all sentient beings can feel the effects of Karma, which are pleasure and pain.

Karma is not fate; humans are believed to act with free will, creating their own destinies. According to the Vedas, if an individual sows goodness, he or she will reap goodness; if one sows evil, he or she will reap evil. Karma refers to the totality of mankind's actions and their concommitant reactions in current and previous lives, all of which determine the future. However, many karmas do not have an immediate effect; some accumulate and return unexpectedly in an individual's later lives. The conquest of karma is believed to lie in intelligent action and dispassionate reaction.

Unkindness yields spoiled fruits, called *papa*, and good deeds bring forth sweet fruits, called *punya*. As one acts, so does he become: one becomes virtuous by virtuous action, and evil by evil action.

There are three types of karma in Hinduism:

1. sanchita karma, the sum total of past karmas yet to be resolved;
2. prarabdha karma, that portion of sanchita karma that is to be experienced in this life; and
3. kriyamana karma, the karma that humans are currently creating, which will bear fruit in future.

The Role of God

Although in Buddhism and Jainism, karma is seen as simply a law of nature, several different views exist in Hinduism. In Hinduism, many see God as playing some kind of role, for example, as the dispenser of the fruits of karma. Other Hindus consider the natural laws of causation sufficient to explain the effects of karma. Some interpretations of the Bhagavad Gita suggest an intermediate view, that karma is a law of cause and effect yet God can mitigate karma for His devotees. Another view holds that a Sadguru, acting on God's behalf, can mitigate or work out some of the karma of the disciple.

Thus, according to many Hindus, God does have hand in the process of karma. Unlike Buddhists and Jains who believe that Karma on its own joins the soul when it reincarnates, this Hindu belief describes the role of God in linking Karma to an individual.

In fact, Hinduism argues for the existence of an Omniscient God (Sanskrit: *Ishvara*) because the judgment of intelligent actions (*i.e.* Karma) requires intelligence on the part of the judge (*i.e.* God). Unintelligent nature by itself cannot judge the performance of actions of intelligent beings. Hence the intervention of an Omniscient God is required to dispense the fruits of Karma — which are rewards for good actions (in the form of pleasure) and punishments for evil actions (in the form of pain).

Two Examples from the Puranas: The story of Markandeya, who was saved from death by Shiva, illustrates that God's grace can overcome Karma and death for His beloved devotee.

The story of Ajamila in the Bhagavata Purana, also illustrates the same point. Ajamila had committed many evil deeds during his life such as stealing, abandoning his wife and children, and marrying a prostitute. But at the moment of death, he involuntarily chanted the name of Narayana and therefore received Moksha or union with God, and was saved from the messengers of Yama. Ajamila was actually thinking of his youngest son, whose name was also Narayana. But the name of God has powerful effects, and Ajamila was forgiven for his great sins and attained salvation, despite his bad Karma.

Views of Hindu Traditions on Karma

Advaita Vedanta: Swami Sivananda, an Advaita scholar, reiterates the same views in his commentary synthesising Vedanta views on the Brahma Sutras, a Vedantic text. In his commentary on Chapter 3 of the Brahma Sutras, Sivananda notes that karma is insentient and short-lived, and ceases to exist as soon as a deed is executed. Hence, karma cannot bestow the fruits of actions at a future date according to one's merit. Furthermore, one cannot argue that karma generates apurva or punya, which gives fruit. Since apurva is non-sentient, it cannot act unless moved by an intelligent being such as God. It cannot independently bestow reward or punishment.

There is a passage from Swami Sivananda's translation of the Svetasvatara Upanishad (4:6) illustrating this concept:

Two birds of beautiful plumage — inseparable friends — live on the same tree. Of these two one eats the sweet fruit while the other looks on without eating.

In his commentary, the first bird represents the individual soul, while the second represents Brahman or God. The soul is essentially a reflection of Brahman. The tree represents the body. The soul identifies itself with the body, reaps the fruits of its actions, and undergoes rebirth. The Lord alone stands as an eternal witness, ever contented, and does not eat, for he is the director of both the eater and the eaten.

Swami Sivananda also notes that God is free from charges of partiality and cruelty which are brought against him because of social inequality, fate, and universal suffering in the world. According to the Brahma Sutras, individual souls are responsible for their own fate; God is merely the dispenser and witness with reference to the merit and demerit of souls.

In his commentary on Chapter 2 of the Brahma Sutras, Sivananda further notes that the position of God with respect to karma can be explained through the analogy of rain. Although rain can be said to bring about the growth of rice, barley and other plants, the differences in various species is due to the diverse potentialities lying hidden in the respective seeds. Thus, Sivananda explains that differences between classes of beings are due to different merits belonging to individual souls. He concludes that God metes rewards and punishments only in consideration of the specific actions of beings.

Shaivism: Thirugnana Sambanthar writes about karma in his outline of Shaivism. He explains the concept of karma in Hinduism by distinguishing it from that of Buddhism and Jainism, which do not require the existence of an external being like God. In their beliefs, just as a calf among a large number of cows can find its mother at suckling time, so also does karma find the specific individual it needs to attach to and come to fruition. However Hindus posit that karma, unlike the calf, is an unintelligent entity. Hence, karma cannot locate the appropriate person by itself. Shri Sambantha concludes that an intelligent Supreme Being with perfect wisdom and power (Shiva, for example) is necessary to make karma attach to the appropriate individual. In such sense, God is the Divine Accountant.

Appaya Dikshita, a Saivite theologian and proponent of Shiva Advaita, states that Shiva (God) only awards happiness and misery in accordance with the law of karma. Thus persons themselves perform good or evil actions according to their own inclinations as acquired in past creations, and in accordance with those deeds, a new creation is made for the fulfilment of the law of karma. Shaivas believe that there are cycles of creations in which souls gravitate to specific bodies in accordance with karma, which as an unintelligent object depends on the will of Shiva alone. Thus, many interpret the caste system in accordance with karma, as those with good deeds are born into a highly spiritual family (probably the *brahmana* caste). Srikantha, another Saivite theologian, believes that individual souls themselves do things which may be regarded as the cause of their particular actions, or desisting from particular actions, in accordance with the nature of the fruition of their past deeds. Srikantha further believes that Shiva only helps a person when he wishes to act in a particular way or to desist from a particular action.

Satguru Sivaya Subramuniyaswami explains in the lexicon section of his book, *Dancing with Shiva*, that karma literally means "deed or act" and more broadly names the universal principle of cause and effect, action and reaction which governs all life. As he explains it, karma is not fate, for man acts with free will creating his own destiny. The Vedas tell us that if we sow goodness, we will reap goodness; if we sow evil, we will reap evil. Satguru Sivaya Subramuniyaswami further notes that karma refers to the totality of our actions and their concomitant reactions in this and previous lives, all of which determine our future. The conquest of karma lies in intelligent action and dispassionate reaction. Not all karmas rebound immediately. Some accumulate and return unexpectedly in this or other births.

Vaishnavism: Ramanuja attempts to fashion a solution to the problem of evil by attributing all evil things in life to the accumulation of evil karma of jivas (human souls), and maintains that God is amala or without any stain of evil.

Madhva, the founder of the Dvaita school, on the other hand, believes that there must be a root cause for variations in karma even if karma is accepted as having no beginning and being the cause of the problem of evil. Since jivas have different kinds of karma, from good to bad, all must not have started with same type of karma from the beginning of time. Thus, Madhva concludes that the jivas are not God's creation as in the Christian doctrine, but are rather entities coexistent with Vishnu, although under His absolute control. Souls are thus dependent on Him in their pristine nature and in all transformations that they may undergo.

According to Madhva, God, although He has control, does not interfere with Man's free will; although He is omnipotent, that does not mean that He engages in extraordinary feats. Rather, God enforces a rule of law and, in accordance with the just deserts of jivas, gives them freedom to follow their own nature. Thus, God functions as the sanctioner or as the divine accountant, and accordingly jivas are free to work according to their innate nature and their accumulated karma, good and bad. Since God acts as the sanctioner, the ultimate power for everything comes from God and the jiva only utilises that power, according to his/her innate nature.

Swami Tapasyananda further explains the Madhva view by illustrating the doctrine with this analogy: the power in a factory comes from the powerhouse (God), but the various cogs (*jivas*) move in a direction in which they are set. Thus he concludes that no charge of partiality and cruelty can be brought against God. The jiva is the actor and also the enjoyer of the fruits of his/her own actions. Madhva differed significantly from traditional Hindu beliefs, owing to his concept of eternal damnation. For example, he divides souls into three classes: one class of souls which qualify for liberation (Mukti-yogyas), another subject to eternal rebirth or eternal transmigration (Nitya-samsarins), and a third class that is eventually condemned to eternal hell or Andhatamas (Tamo-yogyas). No other Hindu philosopher or school of Hinduism holds such beliefs. In contrast, most Hindus believe in universal salvation: that all souls will eventually obtain Moksha, even if it is after millions of rebirths.

Gita Interpretations and Role of Guru

Some interpretations of certain verses in the Bhagavad Gita suggests an intermediate view, that karma is a law of cause and effect yet God can mitigate karma for His devotees. Another view holds that a Sadguru, acting on God's behalf, can mitigate or work out some of the karma of the disciple.

Caste and Karma

As stated earlier, there are cycles of creations in which souls gravitate to specific bodies in accordance with karma, which as an unintelligent object depends on the will of God alone. Thus, many interpret the caste system in accordance with karma, as those with good deeds are born into a spiritual family, which is synonymous with the *brahmana* caste. However, Krishna said in the Gita that characteristics of a brahmin are determined by behaviour, not by birth. A verse from the Gita illustrates this point: "The duties of Brahmins, Kshatriyas, Vaishyas as also of Sudras, O scorcher of foes, are distributed according to the gunas (behaviour) born of their own nature." (Chapter 18, verse 41)

Karma in Buddhism

Karma (Sanskrit *karman*) or *Kamma* (Pali) means "action" or "doing"; whatever one does, says, or thinks is a *karma*.

In Buddhism, the term *karma* is used specifically for those actions which spring from :

- Mental intent (Pali: *cetana*)
- Mental obsessions

Which bring about a fruit (Pali, *phala*) or result (vipaka), either within the present life, or in the context of a future rebirth. Karma is the engine which drives the wheel of sacsara for each being.

In a discourse (Anguttara Nikaya *Nibbedhika Sutta*) the Buddha said:

> *"Intention (*cetana*), monks, is kamma, I say. Having willed, one acts through body, speech and mind".*

Every time a person acts there is some quality of intention at the base of the mind and it is that quality rather than the outward appearance of the action that determines the effect. For example, a man walking in a forest encounters a deer that runs past him in distress. Subsequently, a man dressed in hunting gear with a gun also passes him asking which direction the deer went. The man misinforms the hunter sending him in a direction other than that in which the deer went. Although he has told a lie, he has acted out of compassion for the deer which forms the underlying intention behind his action. That volition (*cetana*) behind the action will be a cause for his own future well-being. On the other hand if a person professes piety and virtue but nonetheless acts with greed, anger or hatred (veiled behind an outward display of well-meaning intent) then the fruit of those actions will bear testimony to the fundamental intention that lay behind them and will be a cause for future unhappiness. In this sense the Buddha spoke of wholesome actions (*kusala-kamma*) and unwholesome actions (*akusala-kamma*).

Karma is thus used as an ethical principle, rather than a cosmological explanation for the world. Buddhists believe that the actions of beings determine their own future, and because of this there are no private actions: all actions have a consequence. The emphasis of karma in Buddhism is on cause, not on effect: Buddhists do not say "it was due to her karma that it happened to her"-indeed the karmic consequences of one's actions are dependent on sufficient conditions.

There is a further distinction between wholesome kamma that leads to more exalted and rarefied forms of samsaric happiness (birth in higher realms), to neutralising actions (called in Sanskrit and Pali *Kriya*-see Kriya Yoga) which lead to enlightenment: (nirvana). Therefore there is samsaric good karma, which leads to more fortunate rebirths (such as the human realm), and then there is liberating karma-which is supremely good. Nonetheless, the Buddha advocated the practise of wholesome actions: "Refrain from unwholesome actions/ Perform only wholesome ones/Purify the mind/This is the teaching of the Enlightened Ones." Dhp v.183.

Samsaric karma is typically divided into the three: good, neutral, and bad (in accordance with the degree of samsaric happiness or suffering that will mature as a consequence). Likewise, liberating karma is divided into three: according to whether it will mature the being as a uravakabuddha, pratyekabuddha, or a samyaksambuddha.

In Buddhism, the term *karma* is often used to refer only to *samsaric karma*, as indicated by the twelve nidanas of dependent origination.

The differentiation between "good" karma and "liberating" karma has been used by some scholars to argue that the development of Tantra depended upon Buddhist ideas and philosophies. Because of the inevitability of consequence, Karma entails the notion of Buddhist rebirth. However, karma is not the sole basis of rebirth.

The rebirths of eighth stage (and above) Bodhisattvas in the Mahayana tradition refers to those liberated beings who consciously choose to be reborn in a future life in order to help others still trapped in sacsara. Some people have problems with the teaching on karma, often of what exactly the Buddha is asking them to believe in when asking them to have conviction in karma.

- First, action really is happening—it's not an illusion.
- Second, you really are responsible for your actions. There's no outside force like the stars or some good or evil being acting through you. When you're conscious, you're the one who decides what to do.
- Third, your actions have results—you're not just writing on the water—and those results can be good or bad depending on the quality of the intention behind the act.

A very good example of the working of karma in real life is recorded by Mr. Yuan Liao-Fan, a sixteenth century high ranking government officer in China. He wrote the *Liao-Fan Four Lessons* with the hope that it would teach his son, Yuan Tian-Qi, how to understand the true nature of destiny.

Wrong Understandings of Karma

In Buddhism, Karma is not pre-determinism, fatalism or accidentalism, as all these ideas lead to inaction and destroy motivation and human effort that a human being can change for the better no matter what his or her past was and are designated as "wrong view" in Buddhism.

1. *Pubbekatahetuvada:* The belief that all happiness and suffering arise from previous karma (Past-action determinism).

2. *Issaranimmanahetuvada:* The belief that all happiness and suffering are caused by the directives of a Supreme Being (Theistic determinism).
3. *Ahetu-apaccayavada:* The belief that all happiness and suffering are random, having no cause (Indeterminism or Accidentalism).

"Bhikkhus, adhering to previously done kamma as the essence, there are neither motivation nor effort with what should be done and what should not be done... Not upholding ardently what should be done, nor abandoning what should be abandoned, those ascetics and Brahmins are as if deluded, lacking a control, incapable of having any true teaching. (Buddha) In Buddhism, Karma is simply there as a guide and an indication of what your present is and how one's future can be made better by self effort, otherwise, fatalism and pre-determinism is the anti-thesis of the notion of perfection or self-conquest-which is the primary aim of Buddhism. The Buddha asserts effort and motivation as the crucial factors in deciding the ethical value of these various teachings on kamma.(P.A. Payutto).

3

Salvation Versus Liberation

The approach to paradises or heavens presented here is a Mahayana Buddhist one. Buddhists generally do not recommend that individuals seek paradises following death for two reasons.

First, such places are believed to be temporary and do not give eternal salvation and happiness as is claimed by some religions. Second, paradises are believed to halt the spiritual development of those that reside there. In addition, paradises tend to also halt learning and creativity, and do not provide opportunities to help the suffering which is an important value for Mahayana Buddhists.

From a Buddhist perspective, there are many gods and many paradises and we will generalise about them rather than talking about a specific heaven or a specific deity.

The discussion presented here is based on intuition, and conversations with a Bhairava, or an inner spiritual Buddhist guide. However, in many ways, it echos the basic approach of Buddhists to paradises.

What is somewhat unique about the approach is that it clarifies the relationship of an individual's negative karma (or sin) to the paradise worlds.

The Bhairava describes the attributes of the paradise worlds by answering two questions.

Many Buddhists question what becomes of a person's karma when he or she enters a heaven world. In western terms, the question is more correctly stated: "Is it true that all sin is forgiven when an individual is admitted to a paradise?"

The Bhairava answers as follows:

Many paradise worlds revolve around deities who are powerful enough to create the world and are therefore also powerful enough to manipulate the karma of the souls who enter that world. Many paradises are made with a sort of coat closet at the entrance—a place to check your karma until you leave. The karma has not disappeared—it is just waiting in the coat closet. It is returned when the person or being leaves the paradise.

This approach emphasises that there is not really a "forgiveness of sins" when the individual enters the paradise as much as there is a suspension of karma where retribution is delayed perhaps for a very long time.

To the question, "Why not enter a paradise rather than seek Buddhist Nirvana?" the Bhairava responds:

In a paradise, the individual is a kind of slave to the deity. Many of the deities are quite nice, but there is no tolerance for rebellion. If you do not worship the deity, you are out. Some gods are notorious about requiring constant worship, and they are very sensitive about any concern for or loyalty to other gods.

The Buddhist paradises are more tolerant, but the individual is still expected to behave in a certain way. He or she should be meditating, or planning how to become a Bodhisattva. The individual in such a paradise can focus on mercy or emptiness but not on passion or creativity. Being in a paradise means you cannot even think about such things, or your karma will be thrown around your neck like iron chains, and you will be reborn.

Paradises are very good places to meditate and pray. However, they have limited options for creativity. These paradises already exist, and are decorated and furnished. They do not need creativity and change. And there are limited options for helping the suffering. Beings who suffer usually have karma too heavy to even consider paradises. If you are in a paradise, you cannot help them. You are too busy pleasing the deity or pleasing yourself. As Bhairavas, we value helping suffering beings, and we work in the worlds of form and formlessness.

People in paradises take the easy way out. They could be struggling and striving for enlightenment, and instead choose a feathered nest without responsibility or maturity. For the sake of temporary happiness, they renounce knowledge and freedom. They then have no choice but happiness. Their growth is stunted like a child who will never leave his mother's lap, no matter how old he gets.

From a certain perspective, the individual carries his karma like a knapsack full of stones. Most are heavy and dirty, but some are like bright jewels. These two classes of stones represent bad and good karma respectively.

Though the individual lays the bag at the coat check room in the paradise, some paradises require an entrance fee. It may be your total love and devotion, and it may be a renunciation of spiritual maturity. In some cases, the individual must offer those jewels of light-the light of his or her past kindness and good deeds. They are taken away as the individual enters, and if the individual should turn his or her back on the god, he will be left with nothing [*i.e.* no good karma]. It is like a woman giving up her dowry in marriage-she will have nothing to turn to if the marriage does not work out.

Liberation is not easy, but it is the birthright of every person. Frittering away time in the heaven worlds may be enjoyable, but it is a form of spiritual gluttony. You are fulfilling your own desires and those of a powerful and often egotistical deity, but what are you doing to help the universe?

Paradises are places for the weak and traumatised, who need shelter and cannot take life's intellectual challenges. This is why paradise deities emphasise love [as opposed to knowledge]. Only those who cannot go forward will choose to stay back forever. And paradises fulfil a valid need-the world is full of people seeking shelter.

The Bhairava because he focuses on wisdom has a somewhat harsh view of the paradise worlds. He does emphasise that some gods act out of compassion to create paradise worlds to help individuals purify themselves through meditation and prayer, and thus escape the worlds of incarnation and suffering.

He views Buddhism as a path towards spiritual maturity rather than towards happiness as an end in itself. In many ways, the debate about the fundamental values and goals of life is reflected in this opposition of seeking knowledge versus happiness.

The Bhairava's approach to paradises is generally consistent with the Buddhist worldview though many Buddhists believe that the individual who enters a paradise will eventually run out of good karma and be forced to reincarnate. The Bhairava takes the approach that individuals can stay in the paradises for eons, and may never be forced to reincarnate. Paradises can be virtually eternal for those that live according to the rules of the paradise world. However, any place where staying is contingent upon certain attitudes and actions which could cease is not truly eternal since at least theoretically, access to that paradise could end at any point in time.

A common notion is that good karma is basically a kind of currency. Being in a paradise is like living in a luxury hotel where because it is expensive to stay there, the guests will eventually run out of money, and need to reincarnate (leave the paradise) when they become destitute. However, a different approach to paradises is that once the individual enters one, there developes a self-sustaining system where the individual gives devotion to the deity and the deity gives grace in return. Here, we have a kind of perpetual motion machine which does not require good karma to sustain it. A certain amount of good karma is required to enter the paradise but not necessarily to stay there.

Ethic of Reciprocity

The *ethic of reciprocity* or *"The Golden Rule"* is a fundamental moral principle found in virtually all major religions and cultures, which simply means *"treat others as you would like to be treated."* It is arguably the most essential basis for the modern concept of human rights. Principal philosophers and religious figures have stated it in different ways:

- "Love your neighbour as yourself." — Moses (ca. 1525-1405 BCE) in the Torah, Leviticus 19:18

- "What you do not wish upon yourself, extend not to others." — Confucius (ca. 551–479 BCE)
- "It is impossible to live a pleasant life without living wisely and well and justly."-Epicurus (ca. 300 BCE)
- "What is hateful to you, do not to your fellow man." — Hillel (ca. 50 BCE-10 CE)
- "Do unto others as you would have them do unto you."— Jesus (ca. 5 BCE—33 CE) in the Gospels, Luke 6:31; Luke 10:27 (affirming of Moses)— Matthew 7:12
- "Hurt no one so that no one may hurt you." — Muhammad (c. 571 – 632 CE) in The Farewell Sermon.

Interpretation: The rule is meaningless without identifying the recipient and the situation. Otherwise, a depressed person who wishes to be killed would be morally obligated to kill others. It has to include an attempt to put yourself in the recipient's shoes and evaluate how you would wish to be treated if you were in their situation. Another way to rewrite the rule would be *"treat others as you would like to be treated, if you were them"*.

The ethic of reciprocity, or *Golden Rule* of ethics can further be understood in terms of what it is not.

Not Tit for Tat: The ethic of reciprocity should not be confused with tit for tat, revenge, an eye for an eye or retributive justice. A key element of the ethic of reciprocity is that a person attempting to live by this rule treats all people, not just members of his or her in-group, with consideration. Mahatma Gandhi famously said, "An eye for an eye makes the whole world blind".

Not Non-aggression: The ethics of reciprocity should not be confused with another major ethical principle, often known as Wiccan Rede, harm principle, or liberty principle (non-aggression principle) which is an ethical prohibition against aggression. This rule is also an ethical rule of "licence" or "right", that is people can do anything they like as long as it does not harm others. This rule does not compel one to help the other in need. On the other hand, "the golden rule is a good standard which is further improved by doing unto others, wherever possible, as *they* want to be done by." Karl Popper (*The Open Society and Its Enemies, Vol. 2)*

Criticism: Not a "Rule": The ethic of reciprocity or Golden Rule of ethics, should not be confused with a "rule" in the semantic or logical sense. A logical loophole in the positive form of Golden "rule" is that it would require a masochist to harm others, even without their consent, if that is what the masochist would wish for himself. This loophole can be addressed by invoking a supplementary rule, which is sometimes called the silver rule. This states "treat others in the way that they wish to be treated".

The silver rule could demand that the golden rule be rewritten as "Do unto others as they would have done unto them". However, the golden rule may create another logical loophole. In a situation where an individual's background or belief may offend the sentiment of the majority, the golden rule may imply ethical majoritarianism if the Golden rule was to be enforced as if it were a law. An absurd example may be Adolf Hitler's reference to Otto Weininger, which was something in the effect of "There was only one decent Jew, and he killed himself." Weininger was a Christian convert with a Jewish background who was well known for his view about supposed superiority of Christianity and Christian character over Judaism and Jewishness.

Tolerance: Ethical teaching interprets the Golden Rule as mutual respect for one's neighbour (rather than as a deontological or consequentialist rule.) Most of us know that different people have different faiths or ideological beliefs, different preferences concerning sex or other matters, and may belong to a different cultural heritage. George Bernard Shaw once said that "The golden rule is that there are no golden rules".

Religion

Universal Command: Older Eastern culture formulations (Confucius, Hillel) tend to be passive or negative, while in Western culture, it is most commonly rendered as an active or proscriptive form, beginning with "do", "love" or "treat." This traditional guiding rule was (and is) so highly valued that it has for centuries been known in English as the "Golden Rule." Major religions give the Golden Rule as a universal moral command or religious duty. Most religious expressions of the Golden Rule explicitly state a positive moral command (or imply a religious duty) as a virtue to love others or treat others as oneself. *e.g.*, *Moses* in the Torah recorded the command *"Love your neighbour as your self."* (Leviticus 19:18)

Jesus affirmed Moses by giving the equivalent Golden Rule *"Do unto others as you would have them do unto you."* (Matthew 7:12) Jesus also reaffirmed Hillel's commentary on Moses' command-"Love your neighbour as yourself"-identifying it as the Second Command. (Matthew 22:39) The original meaning of *neighbour* was *fellow Jew*, but when asked who counted as a neighbour, Jesus extended the meaning with his parable about a Samaritan helping a Jew. In those days, it was not uncommon for Jews and Samaritans to add many miles to their journeys in order to travel around the next door tribe, rather than passing through the lands owned by the opposing tribe. (Luke 10:25-37) Jesus then affirmed Hillel's statement that supreme love for God and the Golden Rule sums up or is "the Law and the Prophets." (Matthew 7:12)

Subsidiary to Love for God

The Monotheistic Religions Judaism and Christianity teach that the Golden Rule and other moral commands on human relations are subsidiary to commands relating to God. *e.g.*, Jesus explicitly identified the Great Commandment as supreme love for God,. affirming the Torah. (Mark 12:30 Deuteronomy 6:5) (Jesus gave the supreme command-"Love one another as I have loved you"-equivalent to Moses' Great Commandment) (John 13:34) By categorising "Love your neighbour as yourself" as the Second command, Jesus placed the Golden Rule and human relationships as subsidiary to one's relationship to God.

Equal to Love for Oneself: In Judaism and Christianity, the Golden Rule stipulates that one should love others *as* oneself. This clearly means "not less," but does not clearly include "and not more." So the Judeo-Christian Golden Rule may be considered silent on the subject of self-sacrifice; it neither mandates nor clearly forbids it.

Hinduism: The true rule of life is to guard and do by the things of others as they do by their own.

"This is the sum of the Dharma: Do naught unto others which would cause you pain if done to you" (Mahabharata 5:15:17)

"One should not behave towards others in a way which is disagreeable to oneself. This is the essence of morality. All other activities are due to selfish desire."—Mahabharata, *Anusasana Parva,* 113.8

Wound not others, do no one injury by thought or deed, utter no word to pain thy fellow creatures. (The Ordinances of Manu)

The Golden Rule has many similarities to the Hindu belief in karma.

Sikhism: "As you see yourself, see others as well; only then will you become a partner in heaven." Bhagat Kabir GGS 480:

"Compassion-mercy and religion are the support of the entire world". Japji Sahib GGS

"Don't create enmity with anyone as God is within everyone." Guru Arjan Devji GGS 259

"No one is my enemy, none a stranger and everyone is my friend." Guru Arjan Dev GGS 1299

"We obtain salvation by loving our fellow man and God." (Granth Japji 21)

Note:GGS is an acronym for Guru Granth Sahib, the Sikh Holy Scriptures.

Buddhism: Ethics of reciprocity is fundamental to Buddhism. This is partly due to the fact that Buddhism, unlike theistic religions, does not rely on divine revelation. Therefore, in Buddhism, all aspects of teaching are regarded as wisdom rather than supernaturally derived and are to be undertaken voluntarily rather than as "commandments." For example, the first of the Five Precepts (Panca-sila) of Buddhism is to abstain from destruction of life. The justification of the precept is given in Chapter 10 of the Dhammapada, which states:

"Everyone fears punishment; everyone fears death, just as you do. Therefore do not kill or cause to kill."

According to the second of Four Noble Truths of Buddhism, egoism (desire, craving or attachment) are rooted in ignorance and is considered as the cause of all suffering. Consequently, kindness, compassion and equanimity is regarded as the untainted aspect of human nature.

"One should seek for others the happiness one desires for one's self."

"Hurt not others in ways that you yourself would find hurtful." (Udana-Varga 5:18)

"I will act towards others exactly as I would act towards myself." (The Siglo-Vada Sutta, about 500 BCE).

"Comparing oneself to others in such terms as 'Just as I am so are they, just as they are so am I,' he should neither kill nor cause others to kill." (Sutta Nipata 705)

"In five ways should a clansman minister to his friends and familiars,.... by treating them as he treats himself." (Sigalovada Sutta 31)

"Is there a deed, Rahula, thou dost wish to do? Then bethink thee thus: Is this deed conducive to my own harm, or to others harm, or to that of both? Then is this a bad deed entailing suffering. Such a deed must thou surely not do." (Majjhima Nikaya 1.415)

"The Ariyan disciple thus reflects, Here am I, fond of my life, not wanting to die, fond of pleasure and averse from pain. Suppose someone should rob me of my life... it would not be a thing pleasing and delightful to me. If I, in my turn, should rob of his life one fond of his life, not wanting to die, one fond of pleasure and averse from pain, it would not be a thing pleasing or delightful to him.

For a state that is not pleasant or delightful to me must also be to him also; and a state that is not pleasing or delightful to me, how could I inflict that upon another? As a result of such reflection he himself abstains from taking the life of creatures and he encourages others so to abstain, and speaks in praise of so abstaining." (Samyutta Nikaya v.353)

Judaism: Here, the Golden Rule, as it became known to later Western tradition, finds its origin. The Hebrew Bible, states:

"Thou shalt not avenge, nor bear any grudge against the children of thy people, but thou shalt love thy neighbour as thyself: I am the LORD." Leviticus 19:18.

This is one of the most famous and oft-quoted principles from the entire Bible. While this statement sounds universal in its scope to modern ears, the term "neighbour" meant roughly "kinsman."

"Take heed to thyself, my child, in all thy works; and be discreet in all thy behaviour. And what thou thyself hatest, do to no man." (Tobit 4:14-15)

Another significant statement in Judaism concerning the Ethic of reciprocity is uttered by Hillel the Elder (Talmud, Shabbat 31a) as the essence of Judaism (literally worded "on one foot").

"A certain heathen came to Shammai and said to him, "Make me a proselyte, on condition that you teach me the whole Torah in the time I can stand on one foot." Thereupon he repulsed him with the rod which was in his hand. When he went to Hillel, Hillel said to him, 'What is hateful to you, do not do to your neighbour: that is the whole Torah; all the rest of it is commentary; go and learn." (Talmud, Shabbat 31a)

Christianity: Part of the Lord's Prayer:

Forgive us our [debts], as we forgive our [debtors]. (Some translations of Matthew 6:12 have debts or trespasses, while Luke 11:4 has sins)

"Love your neighbour as yourself" (Matthew 19:19; Matthew 22:39) (Mark 12:31) (Luke 10:27) (Romans 13:9) (James 2:8)

"So in everything, do to others what you would have them do to you, for this sums up the Law and the Prophets." (Matthew 7:12)

"Therefore all things whatsoever ye would that men should do to you, do ye even so to them: for this is the law and the prophets." (Matthew 7:12)

"For all the law is fulfilled in one word, even in this; Thou shalt love thy neighbour as thyself." (Galatians 5:14)

"Teacher, which is the great commandment in the law?" Jesus said to him, "You shall love the Lord your God with all your heart, and with all your soul, and with all your mind. This is the great and first commandment. And a second is like it, You shall love your neighbour as yourself. On these two commandments depend all the law and the prophets." (Matthew 22:36-40)

"Give to everyone who asks you, and if anyone takes what belongs to you, do not demand it back. And as ye would that men should do to you, do ye also to them likewise." (Luke 6:30-31)

"...and don't do what you hate...", (Gospel of Thomas)

"And, behold, a certain lawyer stood up, and tempted him, saying, Master, what shall I do to inherit eternal life? He said unto him, What is written in the law? how readest thou? And he answering said, Thou shalt love the Lord thy God with all thy heart, and with all thy soul, and with all thy strength, and with all thy mind; and thy neighbour as thyself. And he said unto him, Thou hast answered right: this do, and thou shalt live." (Luke 10:25-28)

"Owe no man anything, but to love one another: for he that loveth another hath fulfilled the law. For this, Thou shalt not commit adultery, Thou shalt not kill, Thou shalt not steal, Thou shalt not bear false witness, Thou shalt not covet; and if there be any other commandment, it is briefly comprehended in this saying, namely, Thou shalt love thy neighbour as thyself. Love

worketh no ill to his neighbour: therefore love is the fulfilling of the law."
(Romans 13:8-10)

In his parable of the Good Samaritan (Luke 10:25-37), Jesus expanded the concept of "neighbour" beyond its traditional meaning as "kinsman."

Islam

"No one of you is a believer until he desires for his brother that which he desires for himself." (Sunnah. Forty Hadith of an-Nawawi 13)

"None of you [truly] believes until he wishes for his brother what he wishes for himself." (Number 13 of Imam "Al-Nawawi's Forty Hadiths." 7th Century CE)

"... regard the life and property of every Muslim as a sacred trust. Return the goods entrusted to you to their rightful owners. Hurt no one so that no one may hurt you." — Muhammad, The Farewell Sermon.

If anyone harms (others), God will harm him, and if anyone shows hostility to others, God will show hostility to him." Sunan of Abu-Dawood, Hadith 1625.

Confucianism

"What you do not wish upon yourself, extend not to others."—Analects of Confucius, Chapter 15, Verse 3, *c. 500 B.C.*

According to Wing-tsit Chan's *A Source Book in Chinese Philosophy*, the ethic of reciprocity appears in the Analects of Confucius, Chapter 4, in the discussion of *i-kuan* (pinyin: *yi guan*), the "one thread" that combines *chung* (altruism) and *shu* (conscientiousness):

Confucian teachings may be summed up in the phrase "one thread" (*i-kuan*), but Confucianists have not agreed on what it means....All agree, however on the meanings of *chung* and *shu*, which are best expressed by Chu Hsi, namely, *chung* means the full development of one's [originally good] mind and *shu* means the extension of that mind to others. As Ch'eng I put it, *chung* is the Way of Heaven, whereas *shu* is the way of man; the former is substance, while the latter is function. Liu Pao-nan is correct in equating *chung* with Confucius' saying, "Establish one's own character," and *shu* with "Also establish the character of others." Here is the positive version of the Confucian golden rule.

Liu Pao-nan is citing *Analects* 6:28, but according to Dr. Chan, the same principle appears in *Analects* 14:45: "To cultivate oneself so as to give all people security and peace, even Yao and Shun found it difficult to do."

> *"Tzu-kung asked, 'Is there one word that can serve as a principle of conduct for life?' Confucius replied, 'It is the word 'shu'—reciprocity. Do not impose on others what you yourself do not desire." (Analects 15.23)*
>
> *"Try your best to treat others as you would wish to be treated yourself, and you will find that this is the shortest way to benevolence." (Mencius VII.A.4)*

Surely it is the maxim of loving-kindess: Do not do unto others what you would not have them do unto you. (Analects 15:23 about 500 BCE). When one cultivates to the utmost the principles of his nature, and exercises them on the principle of reciprocity, he is not far from the path. What you do not like when done to yourself, do not do to others. Doctrine of the Mean 13.3 (Li Ki 28.1.32, SBE 38.305)

What a man dislikes in his superiors, let him not display in the treatment of his inferiors; what he dislikes in inferiors, let him not display in the service of his superiors; what he hates in those who are before hi, let him not therewith precede those who are behind him; what he hates in those who are behind hi, let him not therewith follow those who are before him; what he hates to receive on the right, let him not bestow on the left; what he hates to receive on the left, let him not bestow on the right: this is what is called "The principle with which, as with a measuring-square, to regulate one's conduct." (The Great Learning 10.2)

Bahaí

> *"Ascribe not to any soul that which thou wouldst not have ascribed to thee, and say not that which thou doest*

not. Blessed is he who prefers his brother before himself" Bahaullah Tablets of Bahaullah 6.71

"And if thine eyes be turned towards justice, choose thou for thy neighbour that which thou choosest for thyself." (Epistle to the Son of the Wolf. Bahaullah Tablets of Bahaullah 6.64)

"Wish not for others what you wish not for yourselves" Bahaullah Aqdas 148.73

"The seeker should not wish for others that which he does not wish for himself, nor promise that which he does not fulfil" Bahaullah Kitab-i-Iqan 194, Gleanings from the Writings of Bahaullah 125.266

"Lay not on any soul a load which ye would not wish to be laid upon you, and desire not for anyone the things ye would not desire for yourselves" Bahaullah, Summons of the Lord of Hosts 544 & Gleanings from the Writings of Bahaullah 66.128

"Wherefore must the loved ones of God associate in affectionate fellowship with stranger and friend alike, showing forth to all the utmost loving-kindness, disregarding the degree of their capacity, never asking whether they deserve to be loved. In every instance let the friends be considerate and infinitely kind. Let them never be defeated by the malice of the people, by their aggression and their hate, no matter how intense. If others hurl their darts against you, offer them milk and honey in return; if they poison your lives, sweeten their souls; if they injure you, teach them how to be comforted; if they inflict a wound upon you, be a balm to their sores; if they sting you, hold to their lips a refreshing cup."

Other Examples

- "Selfishness is not living as one wishes to live, it is asking others to live as one wishes to live."

While this inverted formulation does not encompass the entire concept of the golden rule, it does have the advantage of emphasising respect for others' identity and ideals, which is included in most other forms but is easily be ignored if the golden rule is considered exclusive to the physical elements of human interaction, rather than being inclusive of all elements of human interaction.

- "Treat your inferiors as you would be treated by your superiors."
- "All human morality is contâined in these words: make others as happy as you yourself would be, and never serve them more ill than you would yourself be served."

  "It is not fair to ask of others what you are unwilling to do yourself." (Anna Eleanor Roosevelot)

  "We should bear ourselves toward others as we would desire they should bear themselves toward us." (Aristotle)

  "What you would avoid suffering yourself, seek not to impose on others." (Epictetus, circa 100 CE)

  "You should always ask yourself what would happen if everyone did what you are doing." (Jean-Paul Sartre)

  "May I do to others as I would that they should do unto me." (Plato)

  "Each man takes care that his neighbour shall not cheat him. But a day comes when he begins to care that he does not cheat his neighbour. Then all goes well-he has changed his market-cart into a chariot of the sun." (Ralph Waldo Emerson)

  "One of the most potent of the weapons of influence around us is the rule for reciprocation. The rule says that we should try to repay, in kind, what another person has provided us." (Robert B Cialdini)

  "Whatever is disagreeable to yourself do not do unto others." (Shayast)

  "Do not do to others that which would anger you if others did it to you."

  "What stirs your anger when done to you by others, that do not do to others." (Socrates)

History

- ~1970-1640s BCE "This is an ordinance: Act for the man who acts, to cause him to act. This is thanking him for what he does."-*The Tale of the Eloquent Peasant* In line B1 142 page 64 of The Tale of Sinuhe and Other Ancient Egyptian Poems, tr. R.B. Parkinson OUP.
- ~1280-650 BCE "You shall not take vengeance or bear a grudge against your countrymen. Love your fellow as yourself: I am the LORD."-Moses, Tanakh, new JPS translation, Leviticus (Leviticus 19:18), Judaism.
- ~700 BCE "That nature only is good when it shall not do unto another whatever is not good for its own self."-Dadistan-i-Dinik 94:5, Zoroastrianism.
- ? BCE "Whatever is disagreeable to yourself do not do unto others."-Shayast-na-Shayast 13:29, Zoroastrianism.
- ~500 BCE "Hurt not others in ways that you yourself would find hurtful."-Udana-Varga 5:18, Buddhism.
- ~500 BCE "The Sage...makes the self of the people his self." *Tao Te Ching* Ch 49, tr. Ch'u Ta-Kao, Unwin Paperbacks, 1976. Daoism
- ~500 BCE "What you do not want done to yourself, do not do to others." *Analects of Confucius* 15:24, Confucianism, tr. James Legge.
- ~500 BCE "Now the man of perfect virtue, wishing to be established himself, seeks also to establish others; wishing to be enlarged himself, he seeks also to enlarge others. To be able to judge of others by what is near in ourselves; this may be called the art of virtue." *Analects of Confucius* 6:30, Confucianism, tr. James Legge.
- ~500 BCE "One word that can serve as a principle of conduct for life [is] reciprocity. Do not impose on others what you yourself do not desire."-Doctrine of the Mean 13.3, Confucianism.
- ~500 BCE "Therefore, neither does he cause violence

to others nor does he make others do so."-Acarangasutra 5.101-2, Jainism.

- ~300 BCE "One should not behave towards others in a way which is disagreeable to oneself. This is the essence of morality. All other activities are due to selfish desire."-*Mahabharata, Anusasana Parva* 113.8, Hinduism
- ~300 BCE "It is impossible to live a pleasant life without living wisely and well and justly (agreeing 'neither to harm nor be harmed'). And it is impossible to live wisely and well and justly without living a pleasant life."-Epicurus
- ~180 BCE "What you hate, do not do to anyone."-The Book of Tobit 4:15, NRSV translation, Judaism.
- ~150 BCE "This is the sum of duty: Do naught unto others which would cause you pain if done to you."-*Mahabharata* 5:1517, Brahmanism and Hinduism.
- ~100 CE "What you feel painful to yourself, do not do to others."-Tiruvalluvar, Tirukkural 316.
- ~100 CE "What is hateful to you, do not to your fellow man. This is the law: all the rest is commentary."-Hillel the Elder; Talmud, Shabbat 31a, Judaism.
- ~30 CE "So in everything, do unto others as you would have them do unto you, for this sums up the law and the prophets." Jesus-Sermon on the Mount, Gospel of Matthew (Matthew 7:12 NIV), Christianity
- ~100 CE "What you would avoid suffering yourself, seek not to impose on others."-Epictetus.
- ~600 CE "Hurt no one so that no one may hurt you." — Muhammad in The Farewell Sermon.
- 1785: "Act as if the maxim of thy action were to become by thy will a universal law of nature."-Kant's categorical imperative.
- ~1808 "Identity is the identity of identity and non-identity."-Hegel's reflexive, antisymmetric identity, X = not(X), at foundation of all moral systems.

- ~1870 "He should not wish for others what he does not wish for himself."-Bahaullah, *Kitab-i-Aqdas 148.73* Bahaí Faith.
- ~1890 "And if thine eyes be turned towards justice, choose thou for thy neighbour that which thou choosest for thyself."-Epistle to the Son of the Wolf, 30, Bahaí Faith.
- ~1940 "An eye for an eye makes the whole world blind."-Gandhi
- 1945: "The golden rule... is further improved by doing unto others, wherever possible, as they want to be done by."-Karl Popper (The Open Society and Its Enemies, Vol. 2)
- 1999: "Don't do things you wouldn't want to have done to you."-British Humanist Association, Humanism.

Effects of the Golden Rule on Politics

The Golden Rule, as taught by Confucius, was also referred to in Capra's Why We Fight series. China was portrayed as a free nation of peaceful people fighting against Axis aggression and oppression. It is said that China, in its long history, did not concern itself much with the expansion of its national boundaries due to this devotion to the Golden Rule. The more accurate reason for this course of action throughout China's history is because China sees itself as one big family and every other nation outside of that. Since many things in Chinese culture depend on relations (at least, they used to), and since other nations are isolated from these relations, China didn't see other nations to be of interest. It would be seen as a full family getting another set of parents, and adopting several children when they already have some unnecessary.

Reciprocal Altruism and Tit for Tat

In evolutionary biology, reciprocal altruism is a form of altruism in which one organism provides a benefit to another in the expectation of future reciprocation. This is equivalent to the Tit for tat strategy in game theory for the iterated prisoner's dilemma. Four main conditions of the strategy are:

1. Unless provoked, the agent will always cooperate
2. If provoked, the agent will retaliate
3. The agent is quick to forgive
4. The agent must have a chance of competing against the opponent more than once.

For several decades tit-for-tat was the most effective strategy for playing the game, winning in annual automated tournaments against (generally far more complex) strategies created by teams of computer scientists, economists, and psychologists. Moreover, tit-for-tat still is the most effective strategy if one compares the average performance of each competing team. Game theorists informally believed the strategy to be optimal (although no proof was presented).

This implies that ethics of reciprocity may be somewhat compatible with both reciprocal altruism and cooperative egoism providing philosophical middle ground between ethical altruism and ethical egoism. However, in the game of iterated prisoner's dilemma, each players are set as equal. If one player is dominant in the game from the outset, it may be advantageous for such a player to abandon the cooperation and betray other players, resulting in a suboptimal outcome from the collective point of view.

The ethics of reciprocity, on the other hand, presuppose from the outset that everyone is equal, no matter what. However, many actual articulations of ethics of reciprocity in history provide an exemption in the context of the violation of cooperation from the other party. This indicates that the golden rule may have had significant utilitarian justification as well as deontological justification.

As applied in Bambi, the ethics of reciprocity include abstaining from speech in the case that one has nothing nice to say.

4

Vedic Tradition in New Age

srutam etan maya purvam
jnanam vijnana-samyutam
dharmam bhagavatam suddham
naradad deva-darsanat

Prahlada Maharaja continued: I received this knowledge from the great saint Narada Muni, who is always engaged in devotional service. This knowledge, which is called bhagavata-dharma, is fully scientific. It is based on logic and philosophy and is free from all material contamination. (Srimad Bhagavatam 7.6.28)

Vedic Tradition-Short Definition

Vedic tradition (different from so-called "Hinduism") consists of philosophy, culture and civilization based on Vedic scriptures (Shastra), it is revealed by God (avaroha-pantha, or descending knowledge; to understand it both by one's own endeavour and mercy of the Lord) after the creation of the universe, and it contains all knowledge, both material (apara-vidya) and transcendental (para-vidya). The correct understanding of Shastra is possible only with the help of a guru from genuine parampara (spiritual lineage or succession). It's three main branches are Vaisnava (worship of Visnu), Saiva (worship of Shiva) and Sakta (worship of Shakti, Durga).

The scriptures consist of sabda (transcendental sound) in the form of mantras with purifying effect (practical realisation). They are self-evident pramana (evidence). This means they do not need any other support, on the other hand they support other evidences-pratyaksa (sense perception) and anumana (logical analysis). Vedic sastras are called "manuals for using this world". Vedic philosophy is authorised and authoritative. Therefore it can assure elevation.

Analogy: authorised products have homologation certificates, warranties, user manuals, support and service, and collection system of used ones. Unauthorised products, although usually cheaper, have no such benefits.

Vedic education begins with acknowledgement of four errors of every conditioned living being (illusion, imperfect senses, making mistakes, cheating) and realisation that Shastra is not influenced by them. It leads to jnana, or knowledge of meanings, differences and relationships among five categories of reality (tattva)-isvara, jiva, prakrti, kala, karma-and enables differentiation between material and transcendental reality. Otherwise there is a danger of confusing them, *e.g.* jiva with body or mind.

Jnana leads to vijnana (realised knowledge) and life in harmony with cosmic order (dharma) which brings minimal karma.

yamaduta ucuh
veda-pranihito dharmo
hy adharmas tad-viparyayah
vedo narayanah saksat
svayambhur iti susruma

The Yamadutas replied: That which is prescribed in the Vedas constitutes dharma, the religious principles, and the opposite of that is irreligion. The Vedas are directly the Supreme Personality of Godhead, Narayana, and are self-born. This we have heard from Yamaraja. (SB 6.1.40)

Bhakti is the peak and the goal of jnana and vijnana, it is beyond material intelligence:

bahunam janmanam ante
jnanavan mam prapadyate
vasudevah sarvam iti
sa mahatma su-durlabhah

After many births and deaths, he who is actually in knowledge surrenders unto Me, knowing Me to be the cause of all causes and all that is. Such a great soul is very rare. (BG 7.19)

Bhakti (sanatana-dharma, para-dharma) is devotion expressed in actions. It is both means and end of itself. Bhakti is elaborated on in confidential sastras (BG, SB, sattvika Upanisads, Puranas and Tantras, writings of Vaisnava acaryas) and taught within four Vaisnava sampradayas (philosophical schools, or traditions).

Sastras present four divisions or paths: karma, jnana, yoga, bhakti. Karma and jnana form apara-vidya, knowledge enabling life in this world in harmony with dharma. It creates karma and should be therefore minimised.

Yoga (impersonal) and bhakti (personal) form para-vidya, knowledge enabling to leave this world and live in the transcendental realm. It does not create karma (akarma).

New Age-Definition

New Age is a mixture of various religious, philosophical and other teachings, some with very ancient roots. By no means it can be judged (accepted or rejected) as a homogeneous doctrine.

The New Age boom started in sixties and especially increased during last 10-20 years thanks to the media (TV, movies, videos, computer games, books).

There are prophecies from various traditions awaiting new era characterised by profound spiritual restoration. They speak about an advent of an empowered personality (*e.g.* Maitreya Buddha in Mahayana Buddhism) and mention other specific signs (*e.g.* Miracle, white buffalo born in Wisconsin, August 1994 was an important sign for Prairie Indians).

Formerly used term "Age of Aquarius" (*e.g.* in musical Hair) is incorrect-astronomically it will begin after 450 years. It is so called after the zodiac sign in which the sun rises during the vernal equinox. This sign changes approximately every 2100 years because of earth axis precession, whole cycle lasts 25 600 years (so-called Platonic year).

Vedic version of new era:

Sastras like Brahma-vaivarta Purana 4.129, SB 1.5.11, Bhagavata Mahatmya of Padma Purana, Bhavisya Purana, Divyaprabandha, Caitanya-bhagavata 4.126 (prthivite ache yata...), Caitanya-mangala, and great spiritual masters like Ramanuja, Madhva and Bhaktivinod Thakur (pioneer of this era) speak about coming Vedic spiritual restoration in this age, or more specifically, about 10,000 years of golden age in this Kali-yuga characterised by spreading of bhagavata-dharma based on chanting of holy names of Lord. Its beginning is ascertained as 5,000 years of Kali-yuga (which started on Feb 18, 3102 BC. The means circa year 1900 which is the time of spiritual renaissance of Gaudiya Vaisnavism started by Bhaktivinod Thakur and Bhaktisiddhanta Sarasvati Thakur. A.C. Bhaktivedanta Swami Prabhupada, founder-acarya of Hare Krsna movement was born at this time.

Characteristics of New Age Teachings

1. *apara vidya (material knowledge, how to live in this world of three gunas)*

The main subjects of interest are medicine/healing, astrology, music, martial arts, worship of demigods as independent on Krsna (Asatru, worship of Goddess and Mother Earth/Gaia-tendency to elevate Shakti over saktiman, feminism).

2. *aroha-pantha (ascending knowledge, endeavour to elevate and perfect oneself by one's own power regardless of God)*
3. *heterogeneity, syncretism (artificial mixing of various teachings)*

There are many different sources / teachings included under New Age label:

-natural religions (paganism-druidism, wicca, shamanism, satanism-as opposition to "institutionalised" ones)

-secret teachings of Egypt (hermetism), Judaism (kabala), Christianity (gnosticism), etc.

-healing (natural, energetic, psychic)

-Eastern philosophy ("Hinduism", Buddhism, Taoism, Shintoism) and its derivations (theosophy, anthroposophy)

4. *confusion of spirit and matter (mind and other subtle material energies are considered immaterial), matter claimed to be the source of creation*

It seems that modern materialism got this idea from various ancient esoteric philosophies like nirisvara (atheistic) Sankhya (Caitanya-caritamrta Adi 6.18).

Vedanta-sutra 2.2.1-10 refutes this idea by showing that the pradhana (unmanifest material energy), being unconscious and therefore unintelligent, cannot be the creator of the universe. It can't be shown how and why the passive dead matter started to act. Rather, matter tends to disintegrate (Second Law of Thermodynamics). "Ultimate reality" in the form of impersonal energy will therefore not create anything-it lacks impulse to do so. Similarly, matter is dull (jada) and cannot create.

"Within the effect (world) the cause (Brahman) can be seen just as cobweb makes one think of a spider." (Vedanta-sutra 2.2.15 paraphrased)

"This material nature, which is one of My energies, is working under My direction, O son of Kunti, producing all moving and nonmoving beings. Under its rule this manifestation is created and annihilated again and again." (BG 9.10)

"By His glance, the Supreme Personality of Godhead enables the modes of material nature to act as the causes of universal creation, maintenance and destruction. The Supreme Soul is unlimited and beginningless, and although He is one, He has manifested Himself in many forms. How can human society understand the ways of the Supreme?"

(SB 5.25.9, similar verses: 3.20.12, 3.26.19, 5.18.38, 10.46.31, 10.85.6-8, Caitanya-caritamrta Adi 5.59-61, 6.16-20, CC Madhya 20.259-262, etc.)

This is a problem of all Western philosophies including Christianity (Thomas Aquinas) reflecting in many spheres of life, *e.g.* language. Reputed Bible translator Eugene Nida said that Holy Spirit in some Bible translations may look as an evil demon due to lack of proper synonyms.

"Everything is God" "Everything is God's energy" (SB 3.21.19, Isopanisad 1) Not everything can act like God. Sunrays are not as powerful as the sun.

5. *impersonal nature (God and His energies considered to be without personal identity, "all paths are the same"- yatha mata tatha pata)*

vadanti tat tattva-vidas
tattvam yaj jnanam advayam
brahmeti paramatmeti
bhagavan iti sabdyate

Learned transcendentalists who know the Absolute Truth call this nondual substance Brahman, Paramatma or Bhagavan. (SB 1.2.11) Brahman is a lower aspect of God.

Characteristics of New Age Followers

1. *endeavour for power over matter and other beings, often regardless of dharma and karma (magic, modern science and technology)*

Aham-mameti, or purusa-abhimana ("Ye shall be as gods", Genesis 3:5) is the main disease of conditioned jiva who turned from God and tries to become Him.

In the Western philosophy first seen in works of Roger Bacon (13th century) and Francis Bacon (1561-1626), especially in his Novum Organum Scientiarum (1620). Science is newly emerging discipline endeavoring to subdue the 'inimical' nature and separating man from it. Research is based on pratyaksa and anumana. Among its pioneers are Rene Descartes, and Isaac Newton. Philosopher David Hume comes up with so-called "problem of evil". This ushers in an era of an attack on Christian paradigm in form of materialistic philosophies and profound secularisation of Western society. This society is very proud of its scientific achievements and power to change the world but suffers of subconscious fear of God and nature (natural disasters are perceived as reminders of their power). This leads to unnatural hiding of reality of suffering-poverty, hunger, disease, physical handicaps, old age and death. There is a great contrast in this regard with countries like India where these phenomena are accepted as normal part of life.

Impersonalism is a common feature of all New Age doctrines. Although some acknowledge existence of superhuman beings (devas, angels) they reject personal God.

2. *indiscrimination in accepting authorities*

Naivete and lack of knowledge leads to uncritical acceptance of "spiritual guides" of problematical character (cheaters, false avataras) or even unknown origin (channelling). Rejection of authority-one's ego becomes authority instead. Non-philosophical attitude-preference of secondary meaning of scriptures (gauna-vrtti) when primary one (mukhya-vrtti) doesn't fit one's ideas.

[About mukhya and gauna vrtti CC Adi 7.110, p., CC Madhya 20.146. Saksad upadesas tu srutih-"The instructions of the sruti-sastra should be accepted literally, without fanciful or allegorical (gauna or laksana-vrtti) interpretations." (Jiva Gosvami, Krsna-sandarbha 29.26-27)]

3. *speculativeness, adjusting and watering down of existing systems*

Trans-Saturnian planets (Uranus, Neptune, Pluto) discovered by modern astronomers were incorporated into modern Western astrology. Although some astrologers objected to it (see Ponde, Shil, 1939, Hindu Astrology, Joytisha[sic] Shastra, New York, NY: Larwood Publishers) the "progress" prevailed.

4. *purposeless sensationalism and love of mysteriousness (exploited by the individuals and media to make huge profits)*

As examples may serve paranormal phenomena like OBE, NDE or alien abductions, Nostradamus' prophecies (their cryptic character enables unlimited speculation), etc.

5. *wrong understanding of karma and reincarnation*

From Tibetan Buddhism comes the idea that from certain advanced human level (rinpocche) one allegedly cannot fall into lower species. This is refuted in BG 9.20-21, 24, 25; 14.14-18, 16.6, 16.19-21, etc. More at The New Age misconception of samsara.

New Age Practices with Vedic Origin

Some traditional sciences and practices were 'adopted' by New Age and molded according to its image-*i.e.* mainly diluted and commercionalised. Thus nowadays they are seen as a part of New Age and share its criticism.

1. *yoga*

Usually is called hatha-yoga and is limited to asana and pranayama; its goal is health improvement. Its original form, astanga-yoga, comes from sage Patanjali. Astanga means "8 limbs" and is divided into hatha (first 5) and raja (other 3). The term "hatha" according to Hatha-yoga-pradipika by Swami Atmarama is composed of syllables "ha" (sun) and "tha" (moon).

Hatha-yoga is sometimes called kriya-yoga. Real kriya-yoga is defined in Padma Purana, Kriya-yogasara 3.4-5, where Vyasa speaks to Jaimini:

ganga-sri-visnu-puja ca danani dvijasattama
brahmananam tatha bhaktir bhaktir ekadasi-vrate
dhatri-tulasyor bhaktis ca tatha catithi-pujanam kriya-yogangabhutani proktaniti samasatah

Kriya-yoga consists of worship of: Ganga, Sri (Laksmi), Visnu, generosity, devotion to brahmanas, observance of the Ekadasi-vrata, devotion to the Dhatri tree and the Tulasi plant, and hospitality to guests.

2. *pranic healing (cchi-kung, reiki)*

Prana is a subtle material energy in microcosm (body) and macrocosm (universe).

Comparison of concepts in Ayurveda and Chinese philosophies:

pitta = yang

kapha = yin
vata/prana = cchi/ki

3. *martial arts (wu-shu)*

Origin of martial arts comes from Dhanurveda, one of Upavedas. It involved operation of hi-tech weapons and war machines as well as techniques of individual combat with and without weapons. Monk Bodhidharma came from India to China around 6th century CE and founded the original Shao-lin temple. He brought techniques of personal combat which were developed into famous chuan-fa (kung-fu) system. From it stemmed Korean, Japanese and other systems. Term wu-shu denotes all of these systems. Martial arts history overview is described in the article From Vedic martial arts to Aikido.

Martial arts endeavour to unify body and mind/soul by control of prana to achieve superhuman feats. This is however opposed to the goal of para-vidya, ultimate liberation from the material body.

4. *astrology (vedanga-jyotisa vs. Western astrology)*

Trans-Saturnian planets (Uranus, Neptune, Pluto) discovered by modern astronomers were incorporated into modern Western astrology. Although some astrologers objected to it (Ponde, Shil, 1939, Hindu Astrology, Joytisha[sic] Shastra, New York, NY: Larwood Publishers) the "progress" prevailed.

5. *gemology (ratna-Shastra)*

Gems are often used in astrology to mitigate negative influences although the faultless ones are very expensive. Immense business profits made at the cost of uninformed people who do not know that other much less costly means can be used for the same end.

Philosopher's stone (cintamani) is one of the goals of alchemy. The name "alchemy" is derived from the Arabic el-kimya, Khem being the name for Egypt where it was practiced even before the Christian era. It blended with the magic and mysticism of the legendary Hermes Trismegistus which became known as the Hermetic philosophy.

In the fourth century A.D. alchemy evolved to its historical form. Its tradition reached Europe through Muslim alchemists in Spain in the twelfth century.

Medieval alchemy contained Gnostic elements. In its popularised form it is considered the art of mutation of metals. Yet, it went deeper than that. It issued from the assumption that matter is alive and may grow (abiogenesis) and with the right rituals matter could be influenced to transmute into higher forms.

This is the view of materialistic version of Sankhya philosophy mentioned in CC Adi 6.18. It is shared by various esoteric philosophies, both Eastern and Western, and lead to modern materialistic philosophy. Vedanta understanding is that matter is jada-tattva, unconscious substance-CC Madhya 20.260: "Without the Supreme Personality of Godhead's energy, dull matter cannot create the cosmic manifestation. Its power does not arise from the material energy itself but is endowed by Sankarsana."

Under the cover of semi-scientific experiments some of its practitioners followed a secret tradition. Thus, in its deeper mystical sense, alchemy was not a search for the philosopher's stone for the transmutation of metals into gold but a search for purification and mystical transmutation of the mind necessary for obtaining direct divine knowledge.

yatha kancanatam yati
kamsyam rasa-vidhanatah
tatha diksa-vidhanena
dvijatvam jayate nrnam

As bell metal is turned to gold when mixed with mercury in an alchemical process, so one who is properly trained and initiated by a bona fide spiritual master becomes a brahmana immediately. (Tattva-sagara, quoted in Hari-bhakti-vilasa 2.12)

6. *kama-sastra*

It is a part of pravrtti-marga, path of sense gratification regulated by sastric injunctions. Pravrtti-marga consists of four goals of human life (purusartha)-dharma, artha, kama and moksa. In the context of varnasrama it is followed by grihasthas, whereas brahmacaris, vanaprasthas and sannyasis follow nivrtti-marga, path of detachment from material enjoyment. These paths are mentioned for example in SB 3.32.35, 4.29.13, 6.1.1, or 7.15.47. Famous Kama-sutra is only a part of the body of texts in the kama-sastra system and even this is too much to follow for Westerners who try it.

7. *tantra*

For most people in the West the term "tantra" blends with "sexual exercises". It means "thread" (in a reference to the subtle structure of universe) or "ritual". Tantras are called agama and Vedas are called nigama. Tantras are classified according to three gunas. Sattvika-tantras are Pancaratra, Gautamiya-tantra, Urdhvamnaya-tantra, etc. They deal with the worship of Lord Visnu/Krsna and His saktis.

New Age Influences on Society

1. *Positive:*

It is an alternative to Western philosophies and religions which more or less exhausted their potential. Introduces missing concepts like karma, reincarnation, etc., and answers important existential questions (personal identity, nature and meaning of life and suffering, life in this universe and beyond-Brahman, etc.). It has raised an interest in environment and inspired an endeavour to protect it although the goal is just sense gratification. Increased interest in vegetarianism, natural healing, paranormal phenomena and alternative explanations of history ("forbidden archaeology" phenomena-Daeniken, Sitchin, Hancock, Thompson & Cremo) can be ascribed to it. This is undermining the authority of materialistic science by attacking its linchpin, evolution theory.

2. *Negative*

- It brought incorrect or wrong understanding of philosophical concepts and impersonalism undermining the position of theistic religions with society values and structure (family) they upheld.
- There is a tendency to make profit by any means (like misusing astrology for doomsday predictions)

which gives bad name to all alternative paths and teachings. (*e.g.* Declaration of War Against Exploiters of Lakota Spirituality)

- Violent and catastrophic scenes in movies often including inimical aliens are meant to invoke fear for easy manipulation of people (*e.g.* millennium phenomena).
- Negative vibrations polluting consciousness.

3. *Important Features and Names:*

Orson Welles (radio play War of the Worlds, 1938), first alien movie "When the Earth Stood Still", Star Trek, Star Wars, Steven Spielberg (Close Encounters of the Third Kind, E.T., etc.), Alien 1-4, apocalyptical movies at the end of nineties (Deep Impact, Harmaggedon).

Cult of human power, violence and technology (purusa-abhimana) in action movies (Stallone, Schwarzenegger). Action movies with Eastern martial arts. The pioneer was Bruce Lee at the end of sixties but the boom was at the end of eighties which lead to an upsurge of interest in wu-shu and Eastern philosophies.

Movie Highlander (Ch. Lambert) was based on combination of mortal combats with immortality phenomena (movie covered several hundred years). Later it was followed by at least two TV series.

Movies Ghost, Poltergeist, Halloween featured ghosts, magic and evil powers, and ways how to face them. "Ghost" was obviously inspired by Vedic resources, probably Prabhupada's books (Yamadutas), movie Fluke about reincarnation of a man into a dog, too.

Movie series Matrix employ the analogy of maya as well as a host of other religious and other analogies. The idea of Matrix previously appeared in William Gibson's sci-fi classic Neuromancer. The end of the first movie presents a Mayavadi/New Age idea when Neo overcomes the illusion of Matrix he finds himself to be all-powerful and able to do anything he likes. This is something like 'thetan' in Scientology, in other words purusa-abhimana (isvaro 'ham) syndrome of false ego.

Combination of satanism with heavy-metal. Satanistic symbolism in texts and gestures. One member of an Italian metal group in eighties lost his sanity because of satanistic rituals.

Mass suicides of fanatical members of sects like Heaven's Gate. It was influenced by a false story about aliens in cosmic ship within the Hale-Bopp comet coming to save them from impending earth catastrophe. Compare it with the effect of Orson Welles' "War of the Worlds" radio play from 1938. The whole New York and surrounding areas were in panic that inimical aliens landed. Allegedly it was mass mind control experiment. On the other hand some contactees propagate meditation and pure lifestyle.

Conclusion

Vedic, and especially Vaisnava tradition, offers knowledge (especially para-vidya) to everyone. Bhagavata-dharma should be established in the West as authority on both apara-and para-vidya, replacing current so-called authorities for the sake of sincere seekers. Vaisnavas don't use much their potential in presentation of their tradition by non-traditional ways, *e.g.* in connection with the New Age phenomena, to make it accessible to those who now end up with New Age. In ISKCON there are few exceptions in fields of astronomy & astrology, ayurveda, forbidden archaeology, etc.

The New Age Misconception of Samsara

Many New Age followers uphold an idea that there is no degradation to the lower species from the human form of life and "all paths are the same". They think that if one acts wrongly he will be at worst born few times as a human being and then he will continue to be elevated. They think that the only purpose of this life is to get rid of one's hangups and gain some experience, and ultimately to become God, the common desire of all pseudo spiritualists. (One group with partially Christian background believes in a variation of this idea-the soul eternally develops so in the future we will become as powerful as God. But God also develops so He is always ahead...)

This idea is found in the Tibetan Buddhism which teaches that after one becomes a so-called Rinpocche, one cannot degrade to the subhuman species regardless of how he behaves. It is based on the misunderstanding of the Upanisads. Kausitaki Upanisad 2.1 says: "All who leave this world go to Candraloka (moon) [one of the heavenly planets]."

The wrong conclusion is that they will remain there eternally, enjoying the heavenly life. This desire for higher standard of material enjoyment is common to all materialists, religious or not.

The Vedic scriptures provide many quotes and examples to refute this idea. Some are:

Bhagavad-gita As It Is, 9.20-21:

trai-vidya mam soma-pah puta-papa
yajnair istva svar-gatim prarthayante
te punyam asadya surendra-lokam
asnanti divyan divi deva-bhogan

Those who study the Vedas and drink the soma juice, seeking the heavenly planets, worship Me indirectly. Purified of sinful reactions, they take birth on the pious, heavenly planet of Indra, where they enjoy godly delights.

te tam bhuktva svarga-lokam visalam
ksine punye martya-lokam visanti
evam trayi-dharmam anuprapanna
gatagatam kama-kama labhante

When they have thus enjoyed vast heavenly sense pleasure and the results of their pious activities are exhausted, they return to this mortal planet again. Thus those who seek sense enjoyment by adhering to the principles of the three Vedas achieve only repeated birth and death.

Srimad Bhagavatam 3.32.20-21:

daksinena patharyamnah
pitr-lokam vrajanti te
prajam anu prajayante
smasananta-kriya-krtah

Such materialistic persons are allowed to go to the planet called Pitrloka by the southern course of the sun, but they again come back to this planet and take birth in their own families, beginning again the same fruitive activities from birth to the end of life.

tatas te ksina-sukrtah
punar lokam imam sati
patanti vivasa devaih
sadyo vibhramsitodayah

When the results of their pious activities are exhausted, they fall down by higher arrangement and again come back to this planet, just as any person raised to a high position sometimes all of a sudden falls.

BG 9.24:

aham hi sarva-yajnanam
bhokta ca prabhur eva ca
na tu mam abhijananti
tattvenatas cyavanti te

I am the only enjoyer and master of all sacrifices. Therefore, those who do not recognise My true transcendental nature fall down.

Purport: Here it is clearly stated that there are many types of yajna performances recommended in the Vedic literatures, but actually all of them are meant for satisfying the Supreme Lord. Yajna means Visnu. In the Third Chapter of Bhagavad gita it is clearly stated that one should only work for satisfying Yajna, or Visnu. The perfectional form of human civilization, known as varnasrama-dharma, is specifically meant for satisfying Visnu. Therefore, Krsna says in this verse, "I am the enjoyer of all sacrifices because I am the supreme master." Less intelligent persons, however, without knowing this fact, worship demigods for temporary benefit. Therefore they fall down to material existence and do not achieve the desired goal of life. If, however, anyone has any material desire to be fulfilled, he had better pray for it to the Supreme Lord (although that is not pure devotion), and he will thus achieve the desired result.

9.25:

yanti deva-vrata devan
pitrn yanti pitr-vratah
bhutani yanti bhutejya
yanti mad-yajino 'pi mam

Those who worship the demigods will take birth among the demigods; those who worship the ancestors go to the ancestors; those who worship ghosts and spirits will take birth among such beings; and those who worship Me will live with Me.

Purport: If one has any desire to go to the moon, the sun or any other planet, one can attain the desired destination by following specific Vedic principles recommended for that purpose, such as the process technically known as darsa-paurnamasi. These are vividly described in the fruitive activities portion of the Vedas, which recommends a specific worship of demigods situated on different heavenly planets.

Similarly, one can attain the Pita planets by performing a specific yajna. Similarly, one can go to many ghostly planets and become a Yaksa, Raksa or Pisaca. Pisaca worship is called "black arts" or "black magic." There are many men who practice this black art, and they think that it is spiritualism, but such activities are completely materialistic. Similarly, a pure devotee, who worships the Supreme Personality of Godhead only, achieves the planets of Vaikuntha and Krsnaloka without a doubt.

It is very easy to understand through this important verse that if by simply worshipping the demigods one can achieve the heavenly planets, or by worshipping the Pitas achieve the Pita planets, or by practicing the black arts achieve the ghostly planets, why can the pure devotee not achieve the planet of Krsna or Visnu? Unfortunately many people have no information of these sublime planets where Krsna and Visnu live, and because they do not know of them they fall down. Even the impersonalists fall down from the brahmajyoti. The Krsna consciousness movement is therefore distributing sublime information to the entire human society to the effect that by simply chanting the Hare Krsna mantra one can become perfect in this life and go back home, back to Godhead.

14.14:

yada sattve pravrddhe tu
pralayam yati deha-bhrt
tadottama-vidam lokan
amalan pratipadyate

When one dies in the mode of goodness, he attains to the pure higher planets of the great sages.

14.15:

rajasi pralayam gatva
karma-sangisu jayate
tatha pralinas tamasi
mudha-yonisu jayate

When one dies in the mode of passion, he takes birth among those engaged in fruitive activities; and when one dies in the mode of ignorance, he takes birth in the animal kingdom.

Purport: Some people have the impression that when the soul reaches the platform of human life it never goes down again. This is incorrect. According to this verse, if one develops the mode of ignorance, after his death he is degraded to an animal form of life. From there one has to again elevate himself, by an evolutionary process, to come again to the human form of life. Therefore, those who are actually serious about human life should take to the mode of goodness and in good association transcend the modes and become situated in Krsna consciousness. This is the aim of human life. Otherwise, there is no guarantee that the human being will again attain to the human status.

14.16:

karmanah sukrtasyahuh
sattvikam nirmalam phalam
rajasas tu phalam duhkham
ajnanam tamasah phalam

The result of pious action is pure and is said to be in the mode of goodness. But action done in the mode of passion results in misery, and action performed in the mode of ignorance results in foolishness.

14.18:

urdhvam gacchanti sattva-stha
madhye tisthanti rajasah
jaghanya-guna-vrtti stha
adho gacchanti tamasah

Those situated in the mode of goodness gradually go upward to the higher planets; those in the mode of passion live on the earthly planets; and those in the abominable mode of ignorance go down to the hellish worlds.

16.16:

aneka-citta-vibhranta
moha-jala-samavrtah
prasaktah kama-bhogesu
patanti narake 'sucau

Thus perplexed by various anxieties and bound by a network of illusions, they become too strongly attached to sense enjoyment and fall down into hell.

16.19:

tan aham dvisatah kruran
samsaresu naradhaman
ksipamy ajasram asubhan
asurisv eva yonisu

Those who are envious and mischievous, who are the lowest among men, I perpetually cast into the ocean of material existence, into various demoniac species of life.

Purport: In this verse it is clearly indicated that the placing of a particular individual soul in a particular body is the prerogative of the supreme will. The demoniac person may not agree to accept the supremacy of the Lord, and it is a fact that he may act according to his own whims, but his next birth will depend upon the decision of the Supreme Personality of Godhead and not on himself.

In the Srimad-Bhagavatam, Third Canto, it is stated that an individual soul, after his death, is put into the womb of a mother where he gets a particular type of body under the supervision of superior power. Therefore in the material existence we find so many species of life—animals, insects, men, and so on. All are arranged by the superior power. They are not accidental. As for the demoniac, it is clearly said here that they are perpetually put into the wombs of demons, and thus they continue to be envious, the lowest of mankind. Such demoniac species of men are held to be always full of lust, always violent and hateful and always unclean. The many kinds of hunters in the jungle are considered to belong to the demoniac species of life.

16.20:

asurim yonim apanna
mudha janmani janmani
mam aprapyaiva kaunteya
tato yanty adhamam gatim

Attaining repeated birth amongst the species of demoniac life, O son of Kunti, such persons can never approach Me. Gradually they sink down to the most abominable type of existence.

Purport: It is known that God is all-merciful, but here we find that God is never merciful to the demoniac. It is clearly stated that the demoniac people, life after life, are put into the wombs of similar demons, and, not achieving the mercy of the Supreme Lord, they go down and down, so that at last they achieve bodies like those of cats, dogs and hogs. It is clearly stated that such demons have practically no chance of receiving the mercy of God at any stage of later life.

In the Vedas also it is stated that such persons gradually sink to become dogs and hogs. It may be then argued in this connection that God should not be advertised as all-merciful if He is not merciful to such demons. In answer to this question, in the Vedanta-sutra we find that the Supreme Lord has no hatred for anyone. The placing of the asuras, the demons, in the lowest status of life is simply another feature of His mercy.

Sometimes the asuras are killed by the Supreme Lord, but this killing is also good for them, for in Vedic literature we find that anyone who is killed by the Supreme Lord becomes liberated. There are instances in history of many asuras—

Ravana, Kamsa, Hiranyakasipu—to whom the Lord appeared in various incarnations just to kill them. Therefore God's mercy is shown to the asuras if they are fortunate enough to be killed by Him.

16.21:

tri-vidham narakasyedam
dvaram nasanam atmanah
kamah krodhas tatha lobhas
tasmad etat trayam tyajet

There are three gates leading to this hell—lust, anger and greed. Every sane man should give these up, for they lead to the degradation of the soul.

Srimad-Bhagavatam 4.9.10:

ya nirvrtis tanu-bhrtam tava pada-padma-
dhyanad bhavaj jana-katha-sravanena va syat
sa brahmani sva-mahimany api natha ma bhut
kim tv antakasi-lulitat patatam vimanat

My Lord, the transcendental bliss derived from meditating upon Your lotus feet or hearing about Your glories from pure devotees is so unlimited that it is far beyond the stage of brahmananda, wherein one thinks himself merged in the impersonal Brahman as one with the Supreme. Since brahmananda is also defeated by the transcendental bliss derived from devotional service, then what to speak of the temporary blissfulness of elevating oneself to the heavenly planets, which is ended by the separating sword of time? Although one may be elevated to the heavenly planets, he falls down in due course of time.

SB 4.29.29:

kvacit puman kvacic ca stri
kvacin nobhayam andha-dhih
devo manusyas tiryag va
yatha-karma-gunam bhavah

Covered by the mode of ignorance in material nature, the living entity is sometimes a male, sometimes a female, sometimes a eunuch, sometimes a human being, sometimes a demigod, sometimes a bird, an animal, and so on. In this way he is wandering within the material world. His acceptance of different types of bodies is brought about by his activities under the influence of the modes of nature.

The Process of Elevation

The Vedas describe two paths of elevation-devayana (the path of gods) and pitryana (the path of ancestors). They are mentioned for example in the Bhagavad-gita 8.24-25 and Chandogya Upanisad 5.10.3-5. Interestingly, other world cultures (like the original inhabitants of North America) also know these paths.

In the Srimad Bhagavatam 8.5.36 the devayana path is called arci-radi-vartma. Sun god marks this paths by his rays (arcis, the name of the deity of the sun rays). This deity who appears to the dying pious person is the "light being" described by the people who underwent the near-death-experience (NDE). The deities (12 or 13) on this path are mentioned in the SB 7.15.53-54 beginning with the Arcis deity. They gradually lead a person upward to his karmic destination.

In the jnana-yoga process these deities are worshiped to help one to pass further on this path and to allow one to enjoy on the heavenly planets. But these worshipers generally cannot go beyond Candraloka (moon) and have to return to the earth as previously mentioned. The devotees of Visnu, or Krishna travel on the devayana path in a different way. Amanava purusa, "non human being", known from the Upanisads and Vedanta-sutra and in the Puranas called Visnudutas (plural; SB 4.12.20-25, 6.1.30-37, 6.3.18), leads them to the spiritual world passing the planets on the way like a special passes the whistle stops. As they are leaving the material universe they gradually shed their bodily coverings, from the grossest to the subtlest (SB 2.2.28-30).

This path is always the same, but the means of travel differ according to the particular yuga-dharma: SB 2.2.15-31 describes it from the point of view of yoga (Satya-yuga-dharma), SB 7.15.54-55 from the point of view of yajna (Treta-yuga-dharma), BG 8.23-27 from the point of view of demigod worship, or upasana (Dvapara-yuga-dharma) and Brhad-bhagavatamrta, part 2, by Srila Sanatana Goswami, from the point of view of harinama-sankirtana, chanting the holy names of God (Kali-yuga-dharma).

This travel cannot be understood from the point of view of linear cosmic space. The Vedas usually describe the universe from a multidimensional point of view: Samsara.

The relevant texts (paraphrases) of the Vedanta-sutra:

> *"The first stage of the devayana path to the spiritual world is called arcis (ray). The soul attains arcis as it departs the chamber of the heart by way of the susumna-nadi.* *(Vs 4.3.1)*
>
> *"The arciradi-vartma includes the stages of day (dina), white fortnight (suklapaksa), northern course of the sun (uttarayana), year (samvatsara), heaven (devaloka), wind (vayu), sun (aditya), moon (candra), lightning (vidyut), water (varuna), Indra and Caturmukha Brahma. This list of stages is collated from various upanisadic texts. No one text enumerates them all.* *(Vs 4.3.2-3)*
>
> *"The arciradi vartma is called devayana because at each stage the soul is guided by an ativahika-deva to the next higher stage. (Ati means 'great', vah means 'carry'.) After guiding the soul out of the heart, the arcis-deva turns him over to the dina-deva, who turns him over to the sukla-deva, etc.* *(Vs 4.3.4-5)*

Ekanath das: Baladeva, in his introductory words to his commentary on Vs 4.3.5 explains that Ajamila had seen such "associates", coming from above the earth, down to where he was.

Srinivasa in his Vedanta-kaustubha commentary quotes from Chandogya 4.15.5, where the conductor on the path is described as "tat puruso 'manavah" and he also quotes from a very similar passage from Brhadaranyaka 6.2.15-"tan puruso manasah."

The translator says "a non-human person", in the first case, and "a person consisting of mind", in the second case.

"The servants of the Supreme Lord, who are called amanava-purusa or non-mortal persons, conduct the devotees who have surpassed the moon (i.e. who are not attracted by the pleasures of heaven). Sometimes they save a fallen devotee, as in the case of Ajamila.

(Vs 4.3.6)

"Srila Vyasadeva declares that three kinds of devotees (svanistha, parinistha and nirapeksa), who directly meditate upon the transcendental form of the Supreme Lord, are guided by the amanava-purusa to the Lord Himself. The worshipers of five fires (pancagni) enter the planet of Caturmukha Brahma, to go with him to the Supreme after the dissolution of the universe. The indirect worshipers of the Lord, who worship Him symbolically, attain relative perfections in the material world. *(Vs 4.3.15)*

"Scripture reveals that certain nirapeksa devotees who wholeheartedly surrendered to the Lord in the midst of extreme suffering were delivered from material existence by the Supreme Lord Himself. *(Vs 4.3.16)*

"Many upanisadic passages describe liberation as the absorption of the soul into Brahman. This initial stage of the soul's entry into the effulgent Brahman sphere is called sayujya-mukti. Having attained the spiritual world, the soul may attain four higher kinds of mukti, all of which share the quality of unity established in sayujya-mukti. *(Vs 4.4.4)*

"The liberated soul is an enjoyer. In sayujya-mukti, the soul enjoys transcendental bliss without a spiritual body like a sleeping person enjoys dreams. The bliss of personal liberation, in which the soul manifests a spiritual body, is far greater. The desire of the liberated soul to enjoy is not materially motivated, for his pleasure is the mercy of the Supreme Lord." *(Vs 4.4.13-14)*

5

Sarvanandanatha

The Sarvollasa, a copy of which came into my possession some three years ago, is a rare MS. It is a Samgraha by the Sarvavidyasiddha Sarvanandanatha who, though celebrated amongst the Bengal followers of the Agama, is I should think, almost unknown to the general public. There is a life in Sanskrit of Sarvanandanatha entitled Sarvanandataramgini by his son Shivanatha in which an account of the attainment of his Siddhi is given and I am indebted in respect of this article to a short unpublished memoir by Sj. Dinesha Candra Bhattacaryya, formerly Research Scholar, who as a native of Tipperah has had the desire to see Sarvanandanatha's place in the History of the so-called "Tantricism" in Bengal duly recognised.

It is said that Sarvananda had striven for Siddhi for seven previous births and a verse preserves the names of the places where he died in these successive lives. His grandfather Vasudeva originally lived at Purvasthali in the Burdwan district but was led by a divine call to Mehar in Tipperah where in ages past Matanga Muni had done Tapas. A deep hole is still shown as being of Matanga's time. It is also said that round about the place where Sarvanandanatha performed his Shavasadhana, adept Sadhakas even now discover the hidden Linga established by Matanga marked out by equally hidden barriers or Kilakas.

Vasudeva then went to Kamakhya where he died after undergoing severe Tapas. He left his son at Mehar who himself afterwards had a son, the grandson of Vasudeva. In fact it is said that the grandfather Vasudeva was reborn as the son of his own son, that is, as Sarvananda. In early life the latter was stupid and illiterate. He was sharply rebuked by the local Rajah for his ignorance in proclaiming a New Moon day to be Full Moon day. Being severely punished by his relatives he determined to begin his letters and went out to search for the necessary palm-leaves. There in the jungle he met a Samnyasi, who was Mahadeva himself in that form and who whispered in his ears a Mantra and gave him certain instructions. His servant Puna was an advanced Sadhaka, who had been psychically developed under Vasudeva. Puna separating the subtle (Sukshmadeha) from the gross body, served as a corpse on the back of which Sarvananda performed Shavasadhana and attained Siddhi that same new moon night on which to the amazement of all a perfect moon shone over Mehar. This full moon episode is popularly the most famous of Sarvananda's wonders.

Some time after Sarvananda left Mehar after having given utterance to the curse that his own family would die out in the 22nd, and that of the local chief in the 15th generation. This last announcement is said to have come true as the Rajah's descendant in the fifteenth generation actually died without issue, though the family survives through his adopted son. Sarvananda started for Benares but stopped at Senhati in Jessore where he was compelled to marry again and where he lived for some years. His place of worship at Senhati is still shown. At the age of 50 he went to Benares with his servant Puna and nephew Sadananda. At Benares the Shaiva Dandins were then, as now, predominant. He quarreled with them, or they with him, on account of his doctrines and practice.

In return for their treatment of him, he to their awe and possibly disgust, converted (so it is said) their food into meat and wine. Of course the Benares Dandins, as is usual in such cases, give a different account of the matter. Their tradition is that, after a Shastric debate, Sarvananda was convinced by the Dandins that the Siddhi which he boasted of was no real Siddhi at all and was then made a convert to their own doctrines, which is the most satisfactory of all results for the men of piety who wrangle with others and try to make them come over to their views. It is worthy of note how quarrelsome in all ages many of the pious and wonder-workers have been. But perhaps we do not hear so much of the quieter sages who lived and let others live, diffusing their views not amongst those who were satisfied with what they knew or thought they knew, but among such as had not found and therefore sought.

After this event Sarvananda disappeared from Benares which rather points to the fact that the Dandins did not acquire a distinguished adversary for their community. Tradition is silent as to what happened to him later and as to the date and place of his end.

Dinesh Chandra Bhattacarya has made for me a calculation as to the date of Sarvananda's Siddhi which fell on a Pausha Samkranti corresponding to Caturdasi or Amavasya falling on a Friday. Between 1200 and 1700 A.D. there are three dates on which the above combination took place, *viz.*, 1342, 1426 and 1548 A.D. The first date is toe early as 15 or 16 generations, to which his family descends at present, does not carry us so far back. The last date seems too late. For according to tradition Janakivallabha Gurvvacarya, himself a famous Siddha, and fifth in descent from Sarvananda, was a contemporary of one of the "twelve Bhuiyas" of Bengal late in the reign of Akbar (*circ.* 1600 A.D.). The date 1426 A.D. is therefore adopted. It will thus appear that he lived about a century before the three great Bengal Tantrikas, namely, Krishnananda, Brahmananda and Purnananda, all of whom are of the 16th century. But this calculation has still to be verified by data culled from an examination of the Sarvollasa such as the authorities which its author cites.

This last work, I am told, is that by which he is best known. Two other short Tantrika works are ascribed to a Sarvananda though whether it is the same Siddha is not certain. There is, I am told, a Navarnapujapaddhati by Sarvanandanatha in a MS dated 1668 Vikramabda in the Raghunath Temple Library in Kashmir, and another work the Tripurarcanadipika is reported from the Central Provinces.

As is usual in such cases there is a legend that Sarvananda is still living by Kayavyuha in some hidden resort of Siddha-purushas. The author of the memoir, from which I quote, tells of a Sadhu who said to my informant that some years ago he met Sarvanandanatha in a place called Campakaranya but only for a few minutes, for the Sadhu was himself miraculously wafted elsewhere.

Some very curious reading of deep interest to the psychologist, the student of psychic phenomena and the historian of religions is to be found in the stories which are told of Sadhus and Siddhas of Sarvananda's type who, whether they did all that is recounted of them or not, yet lived so strangely, as for instance, to take another case, that of Brahmananda the author of the Shaktanandatarangini who going in his youth in quest of a prostitute, found in the house he entered and in the woman who came to him his own mother, herself the victim of a Mussulman ravisher. It was the horror of this encounter which converted his mind and led him to become a Sadhu, during which life he did Dhyana in the body of a dead and rotting elephant and the other things related of him. They await collection. But when their value has been discovered possibly these traditions may have disappeared. Even if all the facts related of these Sadhus and Siddhas were the work of imagination (and whilst some of them may be so, others are in all probability true enough) they are worth preservation as such. The history of the human mind is as much a fact as anything which is reverenced because it is "objective". This last class of fact is generally only the common experience. It is attractive, yet sometimes fearsome, to follow the mind's wanderings both in the light and in that curious dark, which only explorers in these paths know. If one does not lose one's way (and in this lies a peril) we emerge with a confidence in ourselves at having passed a test—a confidence which will serve our future. In any case as I have said there is an opportunity of research for those whose workings are in the outer crust of mere historical fact.

Cit-Shakti (The Consciousness Aspect of the Universe)

Cit-Shakti is Cit, as Shakti, that is as Power, or that aspect of Cit in which it is, through its associated Maya-Shakti, operative to create the universe. It is a commonly accepted doctrine that the ultimate Reality is Samvid, Caitanya or Cit.

But what is Cit? There is no word in the English language which adequately describes it. It is not mind: for mind is a limited instrument through which Cit is manifested. It is that which is behind the mind and by which the mind itself is thought, that is created. The Brahman is mindless (Amanah). If we exclude mind we also exclude all forms of mental process, conception, perception, thought, reason, will, memory, particular sensation and the like. We are then left with three available words, namely, Consciousness, Feeling, Experience. To the first term there are several objections.

For if we use an English word, we must understand it according to its generally received meaning. Generally by "Consciousness" is meant self-consciousness, or at least something particular, having direction and form, which is concrete and conditioned; an evolved product marking the higher stages of Evolution. According to some, it is a mere function of experience, an epiphenomenon, a mere accident of mental process. In this sense it belongs only to the highly developed organism and involves a subject attending to an object of which, as of itself, it is conscious. We are thus said to have most consciousness when we are awake (Jagrat avastha) and have full experience of all objects presented to us; less so when dreaming (Svapna avastha) and deep anesthesia in true dreamless sleep (Sushupti). I may here observe that recent researches show that this last state is not so common as is generally supposed.

That is complete dreamlessness is rare; there being generally some trace of dream. In the last state it is commonly said that consciousness has disappeared, and so of course it has, if we first define consciousness in terms of the waking state and of knowledge of objects. According to Indian notions there is a form of conscious experience in the deepest sleep expressed in the well-known phrase "Happily I slept, I knew nothing". The sleeper recollects on waking that his state has been one of happiness. And he cannot recollect unless there has been a previous experience (Anubhava) which is the subject-matter of memory. In ordinary parlance we do not regard some low animal forms, plants or mineral as "conscious".

It is true that now in the West there is (due to the spread of ideas long current in India) growing up a wider use of the term "consciousness" in connection not only with animal but vegetable and mineral life, but it cannot be said the term "consciousness" has yet generally acquired this wide signification. If then we use (as for convenience we do) the term "Consciousness" for Cit, we must give it a content different from that which is attributed to the term in ordinary English parlance. Nextly, it is to be remembered that what in either view we understand by consciousness is something manifested, and therefore limited, and derived from our finite experience.

The Brahman as Cit is the infinite substratum of that. Cit in itself (Svarupa) is not particular nor conditioned and concrete. Particularity is that aspect in which it manifests as, and through, Maya-Shakti. Cit manifests as Jnana-Shakti which, when used otherwise than as a loose synonym for Cit, means knowledge of objects. Cit-Svarupa is neither knowledge of objects nor self-consciousness in the phenomenal sense. Waking, dreaming and dreamless slumber are all phenomenal states in which experience varies; such variance being due not to Cit but to the operation or cessation of particular operation of the vehicles of mind (Antahkarana) and sense (Indriya). But Cit never disappears nor varies in either of the three states, but remains one and the same through all. Though Cit-Svarupa is not a knowledge of objects in the phenomenal sense, it is not, according to Shaiva-Shakta views (I refer always to Advaita Shaiva-darshana), a mere abstract knowing (Jnana) wholly devoid of content.

It contains within itself the Vimarsha-Shakti which is the cause of phenomenal objects, then existing in the form of Cit (Cidrupini). The Self then knows the Self. Still less can we speak of mere 'awareness" as the equivalent of Cit. A worm or meaner form of animal may be said to be vaguely aware. In fact mere "awareness" (as we understand that term) is a state of Cit in which it is seemingly overwhelmed by obscuring Maya-Shakti in the form of Tamoguna. Unless therefore we give to "awareness," as also to consciousness, a content, other than that with which our experience furnishes us, both terms are unsuitable. In some respects Cit can be more closely described by Feeling, which seems to have been the most ancient meaning of the term Cit. Feeling is more primary, in that it is only after we have been first affected by something that we become conscious of it. Feeling has thus been said to be the raw material of thought, the essential element in the Self, what we call personality being a particular form of feeling.

Thus in Samkhya, the Gunas are said to be in the nature of happiness (Sukha), sorrow (Dukha) and illusion (Moha) as they are experienced by the Purusha-Consciousness. And in Vedanta, Cit and Ananda or Bliss or Love are one. For Consciousness then is not consciousness of being (Sat) but Being-Consciousness (Sat-Cit); nor a Being which is conscious of Bliss (Ananda) but Being-Consciousness-Bliss (Sacchidananda). Further, "feeling" has this advantage that it is associated with all forms of organic existence even according to popular usage, and may scientifically be aptly applied to inorganic matter. Thus whilst most consider it to be an unusual and strained use of language, to speak of the consciousness of a plant or stone, we can and do speak of the feeling or sentiency of a plant.

Further the response which inorganic matter makes to stimuli is evidence of the existence therein of that vital germ of life and sentiency (and therefore Cit) which expands into the sentiency of plants, and the feelings and emotions of animals and men. It is possible for any form of unintelligent being to feel, however obscurely. And it must do so, if its ultimate basis is Cit and Ananda, however veiled by Maya-Shakti these may be. The response which inorganic matter makes to stimuli is the manifestation of Cit through the Sattvaguna of Maya-Shakti, or Shakti in its form as Prakriti-Shakti.

The manifestation is slight and apparently mechanical because of the extreme predominance of the Tamoguna in the same Prakriti-Shakti. Because of the limited and extremely regulated character of the movement which seems to exclude all volitional process as known to us, it is currently assumed that we have merely to deal with what is an unconscious mechanical energy. Because vitality is so circumscribed and seemingly identified with the apparent mechanical process, we are apt to assume mere unconscious mechanism. But as a fact this latter is but the form assumed by the conscious Vital Power which is in and works in all matter whatever it be.

To the eye, however, unassisted by scientific instruments, which extend our capacity for experience, establishing artificial organs for the gaining thereof, the matter appears Jada (or unconscious); and both in common English and Indian parlance we call that alone living or Jiva which, as organised matter, is endowed with body and senses. Philosophically, however, as well as scientifically, all is Jivatma which is not Paramatma: everything in fact with form, whether the form exists as the simple molecule of matter, or as the combination of these simple forms into cells and greater organisms. The response of metallic matter is a form of sentiency—its germinal form—a manifestation of Cit intensely obscured by the Tamoguna of Prakriti-Shakti.

In plants Cit is less obscured, and there is the sentient life which gradually expands in animals and men, according as Cit gains freedom of manifestation through the increased operation of Sattvaguna in the vehicles of Cit; which vehicles are the mind and senses and the more elaborate organisation of the bodily particles. What is thus mere incipient or germinal sentiency, simulating unconscious mechanical movement in inorganic matter, expands by degrees into feeling akin, though at first remotely, to our own, and into all the other psychic functions of consciousness, perception, reasoning, memory and will.

The matter has been very clearly put in a Paper on "The Four Cosmic Elements" by C. G. Sander which (subject to certain reservations stated) aptly describes the Indian views on the subject in hand. He rightly says that sentiency is an integrant constituent of all existence, physical as well as metaphysical and its manifestation can be traced throughout the mineral and chemical as well as vegetable and animal worlds. It essentially comprises the functions of relationship to environment, response to stimuli, and atomic memory in the lower or inorganic plane; whilst in the higher or organic planes it includes all the psychic functions such as consciousness, perception, thought, reason, volition and individual memory. Inorganic matter through the inherent element of sentiency is endowed with aesthesia or capacity of feeling and response to physical and chemical stimuli such as light, temperature, sound, electricity, magnetism and the action of chemicals.

All such phenomena are examples of the faculty of perception and response to outside stimuli of matter. We must here include chemical sentiency and memory; that is the atom's and molecule's remembrance of its own identity and behaviour therewith. Atomic memory does not, of course, imply self-consciousness, but only inherent group-spirit which responds in a characteristic way to given outside stimuli. We may call it atomic or physical consciousness. The consciousness of plants is only trance-like (what the Hindu books call 'Comatose') though some of the higher aspects of sentiency (and we may here use the word 'consciousness') of the vegetable world are highly interesting: such as the turning of flowers to the sun; the opening and shutting of leaves and petals at certain times, sensitiveness to the temperature and the obvious signs of consciousness shewn by the sensitive and insectivorous plants, such as the Sundew, the Venus Flytrap, and others. The micro-organisms which dwell on the borderland between the vegetable and animal worlds have no sense organs, but are only endowed with tactile irritability, yet they are possessed of psychic life, sentiency, and inclination, whereby they perceive their environment and position, approach, attack and devour food, flee from harmful substances and reproduce by division.

Their movements appear to be positive, not reflex. Every cell, both vegetable and animal, possesses a biological or vegetative consciousness, which in health is polarised or subordinate to the government of the total organism of which it forms an integral part; but which is locally impaired in disease and ceases altogether at the death of the organism. In plants, however, (unlike animals) the cellular consciousness is diffused or distributed amongst the tissues or fibers; there being apparently no special conducting or centralising organs of consciousness such as we find in higher evolutionary forms. Animal consciousness in its highest modes becomes self-consciousness.

The psychology of the lower animals is still the field of much controversy; some regarding these as Cartesian machines and others ascribing to them a high degree of psychic development. In the animals there is an endeavour at centralisation of consciousness which reaches its most complex stage in man, the possessor of the most highly organised system of consciousness, consisting of the nervous system and its centres and functions, such as the brain and solar plexus, the site of Ajna and upper centres, and of the Manipura Cakra. Sentiency or feeling is a constituent of all existence. We may call it consciousness however, if we understand (with the author cited) the term "consciousness" to include atomic or physical consciousness, the trance consciousness of plant life, animal consciousness and man's completed self-consciousness.

The term Sentiency or Feeling, as the equivalent of manifested Cit, has, however, this disadvantage: whereas intelligence and consciousness are terms for the highest attributes of man's nature, mere sentiency, though more inclusive and common to all, is that which we share with the lowest manifestions. In the case of both terms, however, it is necessary to remember that they do not represent Cit-Svarupa or Cit as It is in itself. The term Svarupa (own form) is employed to convey the notion of what constitutes anything what it is, namely, its true nature as it is in itself. Thus, though the Brahman or Shiva manifests in the form of the world as Maya-Shakti, its Svarupa is pure Cit.

Neither sentiency nor consciousness, as known to us, is Cit-Svarupa. They are only limited manifestations of Cit just as reason, will, emotion and memory, their modes are. Cit is the background of all forms of experience which are its modes, that is Cit veiled by Maya-Shakti; Cit-Svarupa is never to be confounded with, or limited to, its particular modes. Nor is it their totality, for whilst it manifests in these modes It yet, in Its own nature, infinitely transcends them. Neither sentiency, consciousness, nor any other term borrowed from a limited and dual universe can adequately describe what Cit is in Itself (Svarupa). Vitality, mind, matter are its limited manifestations in form. These forms are ceaselessly changing, but the undifferentiated substratum of which they are particularised modes is changeless. That eternal, changeless, substratum is Cit, which may thus be defined as the *changeless principle of all our changing experience.* All is Cit, clothing itself in forms by its own Power of Cit-Shakti and Maya-Shakti: and that Power is not different from Itself. Cit is not the subject of knowledge or speech. For as the *Varaha Upanishad* (Chap. IV) says it is "The Reality which remains after all thoughts are given up." What it is in Itself, is unknown but to those who become It.

It is fully realised only in the highest state of Ecstasy (Samadhi) and in bodiless liberation (Videha Mukti) when Spirit is free of its vehicles of mind and matter. A Modern Indian Philosopher has ("Approaches to Truth" and the "Patent Wonder" by Professor Pramathanatha Mukhyopadhyaya) very admirably analysed the notion of the universal Ether of Consciousness (Cidakasha) and the particular Stress formed in it by the action of Maya-Shakti. In the first place, he points out that logical thought is inherently dualistic and therefore pre-supposes a subject and object. Therefore to the pragmatic eye of the western, viewing the only experience known to him, consciousness is always particular having a particular form and direction. Hence where no direction or form is discernible, they have been apt to imagine that consciousness as such has also ceased.

Thus if it were conceded that in profounded sleep there were no dreams, or if in perfect anesthesia it were granted that nothing particular was felt, it was thereby considered to be conceded that consciousness may sometimes cease to exist in us. What does in fact cease is the consciousness of objects which we have in the waking and dreaming states. Consciousness as such is neither subjective nor objective and is not identical with intelligence or understanding—that is with directed or informed consciousness. Any form of unintelligent being which feels, however chaotically it may be, is yet, though obscurely so (in the sense here meant) conscious. Pure consciousness, that is consciousness as such, is the background of every form of experience.

In practical life and in Science and Philosophy when swayed by pragmatic ends, formless experience has no interest, but only certain forms and tones of life and consciousness. Where these are missed we are apt to fancy that we miss life and feeling-consciousness also. Hence the essential *basis* of existence or Cit has been commonly looked upon as a very much specialised and peculiar manifestation in nature.

On the contrary, Cit is Being or Reality itself. Cit as such is identical with Being as such. The Brahman is both Cit and Sat. Though in ordinary experience Being and Feeling-Consciousness are essentially bound up together, they still seem to diverge from each other. Man by his very constitution inveterately believes in an objective existence beyond and independent of his self. And this is so, so long as he is subject to the veil (Maya-Shakti). But in that ultimate basis of experience which is the Paramatma the divergence has gone; for the same boundless substratum which is the continuous mass of experience is also that which is experienced. The self is its own object. To the exalted Yogin the whole universe is not different from himself as Atma. This is the path of the "upward-going" Kundali (Urddhva-Kundalini).

Further, there has been a tendency in fact to look upon consciousness as a mere function of experience; and the philosophy of unconscious ideas and mind-stuff would even go so far as to regard it as a mere accident of mental process. This is to reverse the actual facts.

Consciousness should rather be taken as an original datum than as a later development and peculiar manifestation. We should begin with it in its lowest forms, and explain its apparent pulse-life by extending the principle of veiling (Maya-Shakti) which is ceaselessly working in man, reducing his life to an apparent series of pulses also. An explanation which does not start with this primordial extensity of experience cannot expect to end with it. For if it be not positive at the beginning, it cannot be derived at the end.

But what, it may be asked, is the proof of such pure experience? Psychology which only knows changing states does not tell us of it. This is so. Yet from those states, some of which approach indifferentiation, inferences may be drawn; and experience is not limited to such states, for it may transcend them.

It is true that ordinarily we do not meet with a condition of consciousness which is without a direction or form; but tests drawn from the incidents of ordinary normal life are insufficient, it has been argued, to prove that there is no consciousness at all when this direction and form are supposed to have gone. Though a logical intuition will not tell its own story, we can make reflection on intuition render us some sort of account, so that the intuitive fact appears in review, when it will appear that consciousness is the basis of, indeed, existence itself, and not merely an attendant circumstance. But the only proof of pure consciousness is an instance of it.

This cannot be established by mere reflection. The bare consciousness of this or that, the experience of just going to sleep and just waking, and even the consciousness of being as such, are but approximations to the state of consciousness as such, that is pure consciousness, but are not identical with it. Then, what evidence, it may be asked, have we of the fact that pure consciousness is an actual state of being? In normal life as well as in abnormal pathological states, we have occasional stretches of experience in which simplicity of feature or determination has advanced near to indifferentiation, in which experience has become almost structureless.

But the limit of pure experience is not there reached. On the other hand, there is no conclusive proof that we have ever had a real lapse of consciousness in our life, and the extinction of consciousness as such is inconceivable in any case. The claim, however, that consciousness as such exists, rests not so much on logical argument as on intuitive grounds, on revelation (Shruti) and spiritual *experience* of the truth of that revelation.

According to Indian Monism, a Pure Principle of Experience not only is, but is the one and only ultimate permanent being or reality. It does not regard Cit as a mere function, accident, or epiphenomenon, but holds it to be the ever existing *plenum* which sustains and vitalizes all phenomenal existence, and is the very *basis* on which all forms of multiple experience, whether of sensation, instinct, will, understanding, or reason, rest. It is, in short, the unity and unchanging Reality behind all these various changing forms which, by the veil or Maya-Shakti, Jiva assumes.

The Cit-Svarupa, inadequately described as mere blissful awareness of feeling, exists, as the basis and appears in the form of, that is clothed with, mind; a term which in its general sense is not used merely in the sense of the purely mental function of reason but in the sense of all the forms in which consciousness is displayed, as distinguished from Cit Itself, which is the unity behind all these forms whether reason, sensation, emotion, instinct, or will. All these are modes wherein the plastic unformed clay of life is determined. For every conception or volition is essentially an apparent circumscription or limitation of that Sat which is the basis of phenomenal life.

Professor P. N. Mukhyopadhyaya has described pure consciousness to be an infinitude of "awareness," lacking name and form and every kind of determination, which is a state of complete quiescence where the potential is zero or infinity—a condition without strain or tension which is at once introduced when the slightest construction is put upon it, resulting in a consciousness of bare "this" and "that". It is not a consciousness of anything. It is an experience of nothing *in particular*.

But this must not be confounded with *no* experience. The former is taken to be the latter because life is pragmatic, interest being shown in particular modes of awareness. To man's life, which is little else than a system of partialities, pure experience in which there is nothing particular to observe or shun, love or hate seems practically to be no experience at all. Pure Consciousness is impartial. There is no difference (Bheda) so far as pure Awareness is concerned. Pure Consciousness is a kind of experience which stands above all antithesis of motion and rest.

It does not know Itself either as changing or statical, since it is consciousness *as such* without any determinations or mode whatever. To know itself as changing or permanent, it must conceal its illogical and unspeakable nature in a veil (Maya). Every determination or form makes experience a directive magnitude. Consciousness then assumes a direction or special reference. It is not possible to direct and refer in a special way without inducing such a feeling of strain or tension, whether the conditions be physiological or psychological. Pure consciousness has, thus, been compared to an equipotential surface of electrical distribution.

There is no difference of potentials between any two points A and R over this surface. It is a stretch of consciousness, in which there is, apparently, no sensible diversity of features, no preference, no differential incidence of subjective regard. Like the equipotential surface, such consciousness is also quiescent. To secure a flow on it there must be a difference of potentials between any two points. Similarly, to have a reference, a direction, a movement of attention, there must be a determination in the total experience of the moment in the given mass of consciousness. Absolute quiescence is a state of consciousness which is pure being with no special subjective direction and reference; with no difference of level and potential between one part of the experience and another. Experience will show special subjective direction and reference if it assumes at least form or determination, such as "this" or "that"; to have no difference of level or potential, experience must be strictly undifferentiated—that is to say, must not involve the least ideal or representative structure. Absolute quiescence exists only with that Consciousness which is pure Being, or Paramatma.

With regard, however, to all descriptions of this state, it must be borne in mind that they only negatively correspond with their subject-matter by the elimination of characteristics which are peculiar to, and constitute the human consciousness of, the Jiva, and are therefore alien to the Supreme Consciousness. They give us no positive information as to the nature of pure Cit, for this is only known in Yoga by the removal of ignorance (Avidya) under which all logical thinking and speaking is done. This "ignorance" is nothing but a term for those limitations which make the creature what he is.

It is a commonplace in Indian religion and philosophy that the Brahman as It exists in itself is beyond all thought and words, and is known only by the Samadhi of Yoga. As the *Mahanirvana Tantra* says (III. V. 6 *et seq.):* "The Brahman is known in two ways: from His manifestations which are the object of Sadhana or as It is in itself in Samadhiyoga": for, as Ch. XIV, V. 135 *Ibid.,* says, Atmajnana is the one means of liberation in which Its nature is realised. It is, perhaps in part at least, because the merely negative and imperfect character of such description is not sufficiently noted that pure consciousness, as the author cited points out, has in general awakened no serious interest in the practical West; though it has been the crown of glory for some of, what have been said to be, the stateliest forms of Eastern thought, which asserts itself to be in possession of an *experimental* method by which the condition of pure consciousness may be realised.

The question is, thus, not one of mere speculation, but of *demonstration.* This state, again, is believed by the East to be not a dull and dreary condition, a dry abstraction or *reductio ad absurdum* of all which imparts to our living its worth and significance. Not at all; since it is the first Principle in which as Power all existence is potential and from which it proceeds. It is reasonable, therefore, it is contended, to assume that all which life possesses of real worth exists in the Source of life itself. Life is only a *mode* of infinite Supremacy with beatitude, which is Being and Consciousness in all its metaphysical grandeur, an absolutely understandable condition which no imagination can depict and no categories can reach and possess.

Owing to the necessarily negative character of some of the descriptions of the Supreme Brahman we find such questions "How can it differ from a nullity?" (Dialogues on Hindu Philosophy, 259, by Rev. K. M. Banerjee): and the statement of the English Orientalist Colonel Jacob (whose views are akin to those of others) that "Nirvana is an unconscious *(sic)* and stone-like *(sic)* existence". Such a misconception is the more extraordinary in that it occurs in the work of an author who was engaged in the translation of a Vedantic treatise.

These and many similar statements seem to establish that it is possible to make a special study of Vedanta and yet to misunderstand its primary concepts. It is true that the Brahman is unconscious in the sense that It is not our consciousness; for, if so, It would be Jiva and not Paramatma. But this is only to say that it has not our limitations. It is unlimited Cit. A stone represents its most veiled existence. In its Self it is all light and self-illumining (Svaprakasha). As Shruti says *(Katha Up.* 5-15) "All things shed luster by His luster. All things shine because He shines." All things depend on It: but It has not to depend on anything else for Its manifestation. It is therefore better to say with the Hamsopanishad and the Christian Gospel that It is the Peace beyond all understanding. It has been dryly remarked that "The idea that Yoga means a dull state is due, perhaps, to the misunderstanding of Patanjali's definition of it.

Man, however, ordinarily and by his nature craves for modes and forms (Bhaumananda); and though all enjoyment comes from the pure Supreme Consciousness, it is supposed that dualistic variety and polarity are necessary for enjoyment. What, thus, in its plenitude belongs to the sustaining spirit of all life is transferred to life alone. All knowledge and existence are identified with variety, change, polarity. Whilst skimming over the checkered surface of the sea, we thus, it is said, ignore the unfathomed depths which are in response and which nothing stirs, wherein is the Supreme Peace (Santa) and Bliss (Paramananda).

The *Brihadaranyaka Upanishad* says: "Other beings live on a fraction of this great Bliss." The Bliss of Shiva and Shakti are one, for they are inseparate. Hence she is called (Trishati II. 32) Ekabhoga: for Eka = Ishvara and Bhoga = Svasvarupananda.

Nyaya and Samkhya say that the chief end of man is the absolute cessation of pain, but Vedantins, going beyond this negative definition, say that, all pain having surceased on Unity with the Supreme, the chief end is that positive Bliss which is of its essence. The Devi Kalyani, the Mother of all, is Herself Bliss—that is, all bliss from earthly bliss (Bhaumananda) to Brahman-Bliss (Brahmananda). As the Commentator Shamkara in his commentary on the Trishati says (citing Shruti): "Who else can make us breathe, who else can make us live, if this blissful Ether were not?"

If, further, it be asked *what* is pure Experience which manifests itself in all these diverse forms, it must be said that from Its very definition pure Cit, or the Supreme Brahman (Parabrahman), is that about which nothing in particular can be predicated: for predication is possible only in relation to *determinations* or modes in consciousness. And in this sense *Yogatattva Upanishad* says that those who seek a knowledge of it in Shastras are deluded; "How can that which is self-shining be illuminated by the Shastras? Not even the Devas can describe that indescribable state." The *Mandukya Upanishad,* speaking of the fourth aspect (Pada) of Atma, says that it is the non-dual Shiva which is not an object which can be sensed, used, taken, determined (by any marks), or of which an account can be given, but is unthinkable and knowable only by the realisation of Atma. Negative predication may, however, clear away improper notions.

It is really inscrutable Being upon which no category can be fastened. This must always be borne in mind in any attempted definition of this transcendent state. It is of a self-existent (Niradhara), unending (Nitya), changeless (Avikari), undifferentiated (Abhinna), spaceless (Purna), timeless (Shasvata), all-pervading (Sarvatravastha), self-illumining (Svayamjyotih), pure (Shuddha) experience. As the *Kularnava Tantra* says (I—6, 7): "Shiva is the impartite Supreme Brahman, the all-knowing Creator of all." He is the stainless One and the Lord of all. He is one without a second (Advaya). He is light itself. He changes not, and is without beginning or end. He is without attribute and above the highest. He is Being (Sat), Consciousness (Cit), and Bliss (Ananda).

As Sat, It is unity of being beyond the opposites of "this" and "that". "here and there," "then and now". As Cit, It is an experiencing beyond the opposites of worldly knowledge and ignorance. As Supreme Ananda, It is the Bliss which is known upon the dissolution of the dualistic state which fluctuates between, and is composed of, happiness and sorrow; for created happiness is only an impermanent change of state (Vikara) or Becoming, but the Supreme Bliss (Paramananda) endures. Bliss is the very Nature (Svarupa) of this Supreme Consciousness, and not, as with the creature, a mere changing attribute of some form of Becoming. Supreme Being (Sat) is a unity without parts (Nishkala). Supreme Feeling-Consciousness (Cit) is immediacy of experience.

In the Jiva, Consciousness of Self is set over against the not-Self; for logical thought establishes a polarity of subject. Thus the undifferentiated Supreme Consciousness transcends, and the Supreme Bliss (Paramananda) is beyond, the changing feelings of happiness and sorrow. It is the great Peace (Santa) which, in the words of the *Hamsopanishad* (V. 12, Ed. Anandashrama, XXIX, p. 593) as of the New Testament, passes all worldly understanding. Sacchidananda, or Pure Being, persists in all the states of Becoming which are its manifestation as Shakti.

It may be compared to a continuous, partless, undifferentiated Unity universally pervading the manifested world like ether or space, as opposed to the limited, discontinuous, discrete character of the forms of "matter" which are the products of its power of Shakti. It is a state of quiescence free of all motion (Nishpanda), and of that vibration (Spandana) which operating as the Primordial Energy, evolves the phenomenal world of names and forms. It is, in short, said to be the innermost Self in every being—a changeless Reality of the nature of a purely experiencing principle (Caitanyam Atma) as distinguished from whatever may assume the form of either the experienced, or of the means of experience. This Cit in bodies underlies as their innermost Self all beings. The Cit or Atma as the underlying Reality in all is, according to Vedanta, one, and the same in all: undivided and unlimited by any of them, however much they may be separated in time and space. It is not only all-pervading, but all-transcending.

It has thus a two-fold aspect: an immanent aspect as Shakti (Power), in which It pervades the universes (Saguna Brahman);

and a transcendental aspect, in which It exists beyond all Its worldly manifestations (Nirguna Brahman). Cit, as it is in itself, is spaceless and timeless, extending beyond all limitations of time and space and all other categories of existence. We live *in* the Infinite. All limits exist *in* Cit. But these limits are also another aspect of *It* that is Shakti. It is a boundless tranquil ocean on the surface of which countless varied modes, like waves, are rising, tossing and sinking. Though It *is* the one Cause of the universe of relations, in itself It is neither a relation nor a totality of relations, but a completely relationless Self-identity unknowable by any logical process whatever.

Cit is the boundless permanent *plenum* which sustains and vitalizes everything. It is the universal Spirit, all-pervading like the Ether, which is, sustains, and illumines all experience and all process in the *continuum* of experience. In it the universe is born, grows and dies. This *plenum* or *continuum is* as such all-pervading, eternal, unproduced, and indestructible: for production and destruction involve the existence and bringing together and separation of parts which in an absolute partless *continuum* is impossible.

It is necessarily in itself, that is as Cit, motionless, for no parts of an all-filling *continuum* can move from one place to another. Nor can such a *continuum* have any other form of motion, such as expansion, contraction or undulation, since all these phenomena involve the existence of parts and their displacement. Cit is one undifferentiated, partless, all-pervading, eternal, spiritual substance. In Sanskrit, this *plenum* is called Cidakasha; that is, just as all material things exist in the all-pervading physical Ether, so do they and the latter exist in the infinitely extending Spiritual "Ether" which is Cit.

The Supreme Consciousness is thought of as a kind of permanent spiritual "Space" (Cidakasha) which makes room for and contains all varieties and forms appearing and disappearing. Space itself is an aspect of spiritual substance. It is a special posture of that stress in life which takes place in unchanging consciousness (P. Mukhyopadhyaya "The Patent Wonder," 21—24). In this Ocean of Being-Consciousness we live, move and have our being. Consciousness as such (that is as distinguished from the products of Its power or Shakti), is never finite. Like space, it cannot be limited, though, through the operation of its power of self-negation or Maya-Shakti, it may appear as determined.

But such apparent determinations do not ever for us express or exhaust the whole consciousness, any more than space is exhausted by the objects in it. Experience is taken to be limited because the Experiencer is swayed by a pragmatic interest which draws his attention only to particular features in the *continuum.* Though what is thus experienced is a part of the whole experience, the latter is felt to be an infinite expanse of consciousness or awareness in which is distinguished a definite mass of especially determined feeling.

As Cit is the infinite *plenum,* all limited being exists *in* it, and it is in all such beings as the Spirit or innermost Self and as Maya-Shakti it is their mind and body. When the existence of anything is affirmed, the Brahman is affirmed, for the Brahman is Being itself. This pure Consciousness or Cit is the Paramatma Nirguna Shiva who is Being-Consciousness-Bliss (Sacchidananda). Consciousness is Being. Paramatma, according to Advaita Vedanta, is not a consciousness of being, but Being-Consciousness. Nor is it a consciousness of Bliss, but it is Bliss.

All these are one in pure Consciousness. That which is the nature of Paramatma never changes, notwithstanding the creative ideation (Srishtikalpana) which is the manifestation of Shakti as Cit-Shakti and Maya-Shakti. It is this latter Shakti which, according to the Sakta Tantra, evolves. To adopt a European analogy which is yet not complete, Nishkala Paramatma is Godhead (Brahmatva), Sakala, or Saguna Atma, is God (Ishvara). Each of the three systems Samkhya, Mayavada Vedanta, and Sakta monism agrees in holding the reality of pure consciousness (Cit). The question upon which they differ is as to whether unconsciousness is a second independent reality, as Samkhya alleges; and, if not, how the admitted appearance of unconsciousness as the Forms is to be explained consistently with the unity of the Brahman.

Such then is Cit, truly known as it is in Itself only in completed Yoga or Moksha; known only through Its manifestations in our ordinary experience, just as to use the simile of the Kaivalya Kalika Tantra, we realise the presence of Rahu or Bhucchaya (the Eclipse) by his actions on the sun and moon. The Eclipse is seen but not the cause of it. Cit-Shakti is a name for the same changeless Cit when associated in creation with its operating Maya-Shakti. The Supreme Cit is called Parasamvit in the scheme of the Thirty-six Tattvas which is adopted by both the Shaiva and Shakta Agamas.

According to Shamkara, the Supreme Brahman is defined as pure Jnana without the slightest trace of either actual or potential objectivity. The Advaita Shaiva-Shaktas regard this matter differently in accordance with an essential principle of the Agamic School with which I now deal.

All occultism whether of East or West posits the principle that there is nothing in any one state or plane which is not in some other way, actual or potential, in another state or plane. The Western Hermetic maxim runs "As above, so below". This is not always understood. The saying does not mean that what exists in one plane exists *in that form* in another plane. Obviously if it did the planes would be the same and not different. If Ishvara thought and felt and saw objects, in the human way, and if he was loving and wrathful, just as men are, He, would not be Ishvara but Jiva.

The saying cited means that a thing which exists on one plane exists on all other planes, according either to the form of each plane, if it be an intermediate causal body (Karanavantarasharira) or ultimately as the mere potentiality of becoming which exists in Atma in its aspect as Shakti. The Hermetic maxim is given in another form in the Visvasara Tantra: "What is here is elsewhere. What is not here is nowhere" *(Yadihasti tad anyatra. Yannehasti na tat kvacit).* Similarly the northern Shaiva Shastra says that what appears *without* only so appears *because* it exists *within.* One can only take out of a receptacle what is first assumed to be within it. What is in us must in some form be in our cause.

If we are living, though finite forms, it is because that cause is infinite Being. If we have knowledge, though limited, it is because our essential substance is Cit the Illuminator. If we have bliss, though united with sorrow, it is because It is Supreme Bliss. In short, our experience must exist in germ in it. This is because in the Sakta Agama, there is for the worshipper a real creation and, therefore, a real nexus between the Brahman as cause and the world as effect. According to the transcendent method of Shamkara, there is not in the absolute sense any such nexus. The notion of creation by Brahman is as much Maya as the notion of the world created.

Applying these principles we find in our dual experience an "I" (Aham) or subject which experiences an object a "This" (Idam): that is the universe or any particular object of the collectively which composes it. Now it is said that the duality of "I" and "This" comes from the One which is in its essential nature (Svarupa) an unitary experience without such conscious distinction. For Vedanta, whether in its Mayavada or Sakta form, agrees in holding that in the Supreme there is no consciousness of objects such as exists on this plane. The Supreme does not see objects outside Itself, for it is the whole and the experience of the whole as Ishvara. It sees all that is as Itself.

It is Purna or the Whole. How then, it may be asked, can a supreme, unchanging, partless, formless, Consciousness produce from Itself something which is so different from Itself, something which is changing, with parts, form and so forth. Shamkara's answer is that transcendentally, it does not produce anything. The notion that it does so is Maya. What then is his Maya? This I have more fully explained in my papers on "Maya-Shakti" and on "Maya and Shakti". I will only here say that his Maya is an unexplainable (anirvacaniya) principle of unconsciousness which is not real, not unreal, and partly either; which is an eternal falsity (Mithyabhuta sanatani), which, though not Brahman, is inseparably associated with It in Its aspect as Ishvara; which Maya has Brahman for its support (Maya Brahmashrita); from which support it draws appearance of separate independent reality which in truth it does not possess. The Parabrahman aspect of the One is not associated with Maya.

According to the Sakta exposition of Advaitavada, Maya is not an unconscious (jada) principle but a particular Shakti of Brahman. Being Shakti, it is at base consciousness, but as Maya-Shakti it is Consciousness veiling Itself. Shakti and Shaktiman are one and the same: that is, Power and its Possessor (Shaktiman). Therefore Maya-Shakti is Shiva or Cit in that particular aspect which He assumes as the material cause (Upadanakarana) in creation. Creation is real; that is, there is a direct causal nexus between Shiva as Shakti (Cit-Shakti and Maya-Shakti) and the universe. In short Shiva as Shakti is the cause of the universe, and as Shakti, in the form of Jiva (all manifested forms, He actually evolves. Comparing these two views;—Shamkara says that there is in absolute truth no creation and therefore there can be no question how it arose. This is because he views the problem from the transcendental (Paramarthika) standpoint of self-realisation or Siddhi. The Sakta Shastra, on the other hand, being a practical Sadhana Shastra views the matter from our, that is the Jiva, standpoint.

To us the universe and ourselves are real. And Ishvara the Creator is real. Therefore there is a creation, and Shiva as Shakti creates by evolving into the Universe, and then appearing as all Jivas. This is the old Upanishadic doctrine of the spider actually evolving the web from itself, the web being its substance in that form. A flower cannot be raised from seed unless the flower was in some way already there. Therefore as there is an "Aham" and "Idam" in our experience, in some way it is in the supreme experience of Parashiva or Parasamvit. But the Idam or Universe is not there as with us; otherwise It would be Jiva. Therefore it is said that there are two principles or aspects in the Brahman, namely, that Prakasha or Cit aspect, and Vimarsha Shakti, the potential Idam, which in creation explicates into the Universe. But in the supreme experience or Amarsha, Vimarsha Shakti (which has two states) is in Its supreme form.

The subtler state is in the form of consciousness (Cidrupini); the gross state is in the form of the Universe (Vishvarupini). The former is beyond the universe (Vishvottirna). But if

Vimarsha Shakti is there in the form of consciousness (Cidrupini), it is one with Cit. Therefore it is said that the Aham and Idam, without ceasing to be in the supreme experience, are in supreme Shiva in undistinguishable union as Cit and Cidrupini. This is the Nirguna state of Shivashakti. As She is then in undistinguishable union with Shiva, She is then also simple unmanifested Cit. She is then Caitanya-rupa or Cidrupini: a subtle Sanskrit expression which denotes that She is the same as Cit and yet suggests that though in a present sense She is one with Him, She is yet in a sense (with reference to Her potentiality of future manifestation) different from Him.

She is Sacchidanandamayi and He is Sacchidananda. She is then the unmanifested universe in the form of undifferentiated Cit. The mutual relation, whether in manifestation or beyond it, whether as the imperfect or Ideal universe, is one of inseparable connection or inherence (Avinabhava-sambandha, Samanvaya) such as that between "I-ness" (Ahanta) and "I" (Aham), existence and that which exists (Bhava, Bhavat), an attribute and that in which it inheres (Dharma, Dharmin), sunshine and the sun and so forth. The Pancaratra School of the Vaishnava Agama or Tantra, speaking of the Mahashakti Lakshmi says, that in Her supreme state She is undistinguishable from the "Windless Atmosphere" (Vasudeva) existing only as it were in the form of "darkness" and "emptiness" (that is of unmanifested formlessness).

So the *Mahanirvana Tantra* speaks of Her "dark formlessness". In the *Kulacudamani Nigama,* Devi says (I. 16-24)—"I, though in the form of Prakriti, rest in consciousness-bliss' (Aham prakritirupa cet cidanandaparayana). Raghava Bhatta in his commentary on the *Sharada Tilaka* (Ch. I) says, "She who is eternal existed in a subtle (that is unmanifested) state, as consciousness, during the final dissolution" (Ya anadirupa caitanyadhyasena mahapralaye sukshma sthita).

It would be simpler to say that She is then what She is (Svarupa) namely Consciousness, but in creation that consciousness veils itself. These terms "formless," "subtle," "dark," "empty," all denote the same unmanifested state in which Shakti is in undistinguishable union with Shiva, the formless consciousness. The Pancaratra (Ahirbudhnya Samhita, Ch. IV), in manner similar to that of the other Agamas, describes the supreme state of Shakti in the dissolution of the Universe as one in which manifested Shakti "returns to the condition of Brahman" (Brahmabhavam brajate). "Owing to complete intensity of embrace" (Atisankleshat) the two all-pervading ones, Narayana and His Shakti, become as it were a single principle (Ekam tattvam iva). This return to the Brahman condition is said to take place in the same way as a conflagration, when there is no more combustible matter, returns to the latent condition of fire (Vahni-bhava).

There is the same fire in both cases but in one case there is the activity of combustion and in the other there is not. It follows from this that the Supreme Brahman is not a mere knowing with out trace of objectivity. In It the Aham is the Self as Cit and the Idam is provided by Cidrupini-shakti. There is Atmarama or play of the Self with the Self in which the Self knows and enjoys the Self, not in the form of external objects, but as that aspect of consciousness whose projection all objects are. Shakti is always the object of the Self and one with it. For the object is always the Self, since there is nothing but the Self. But in the supreme experience the object is one in nature with Shiva being Caitanya-rupa; in the universe the object seems to the Jiva, the creation of and subject to Maya, to be different from the Self as mind and matter.

The next point is the nature of creation or rather emanation (Abhasa) for the former term is associated with dualistic notions of an extra-Cosmic God, who produces a world which is as separate from Himself as is the pot from the potter. According to this doctrine there is an Evolution of Consciousness or Cit-Shakti (associated with Maya-Shakti) into certain forms. This is not to say that the Brahman is wholly transformed into its emanations, that is exhausted by them. The Brahman is infinite and can never, therefore, be wholly held in this sense in any form, or in the universe as a whole.

It always transcends the universe. Therefore when Consciousness evolves, it nevertheless does not cease to be what it was, is, and will be. The Supreme Cit becomes as Shakti the universe but still remains supreme Cit. In the same way every stage of the emanation-process prior to the real evolution (Parinama of Prakriti) remains what it is, whilst giving birth to a new Evolution. In Parinama or Evolution as known to us on this plane, when one thing is evolved into another, it ceases to be what it was. Thus when milk is changed into curd, it ceases to be milk. The Evolution from Shiva-Shakti of the Pure Tattvas is not of this kind. It is an Abhasa or "shining forth," adopting the simile of the sun which shines without (it was supposed) change in, or diminution of, its light. This unaffectedness in spite of its being the material cause is called in the Pancaratra by the term Virya, a condition which, the Vaishnava Lakshmi Tantra says, is not found in the world "where milk quickly loses its nature when curds appear."

It is a process in which one flame springs from another flame. Hence it is called "Flame to Flame". There is a second Flame but the first from which it comes is unexhausted and still there. The cause remains what it was and yet appears differently in the effect. God is never "emptied" as it is said wholly into the world. Brahman is ever changeless in one aspect; in another It changes, such change being as it were a mere point of stress in the infinite Ether of Cit. This Abhasa, therefore, is a form of Vivartta, distinguishable however from the Vivartta of Mayavada, because in the Agama, whether Vaishnava, or Shakta, the effect is regarded as real, whereas according to Shamkara, it is only empirically so.

Hence the latter system is called Sat-karanavada or the doctrine of the reality of the original source or basis of things, and not also of the apparent effects of the cause. This Abhasa has been called Sadrisha Parinama (*Introduction to Principles of Tantra,* Part II), a term borrowed from the Samkhya but which is not altogether appropriate. In the latter Philosophy, the term is used in connection with the state of the Gunas of Prakriti in dissolution when nothing is produced. Here on the contrary we are dealing with creation and an evolving Power-Consciousness. It is only appropriate to this extent that, as in Shadrisa Parinama there is no real evolution or objectivity, so also there is none in the evolution of the Tattvas until Maya intervenes and Prakriti really evolves the objective universe.

This being the nature of the Supreme Shiva and of the evolution of consciousness, this doctrine assumes, with all others,. a transcendent and a creative or immanent aspect of Brahman. The first is Nishkala Shiva; the second Sakala Shiva; or Nirguna Saguna; Parama, Apara (in Shamkara's parlance); Paramatma, Ishvara; and Paramabrahman, Shabdabrahman. From the second or changing aspect the universe is born. Birth means 'manifestation'. Manifestation to what'? The answer is to consciousness. But there is nothing but Cit. Creation is then the evolution whereby the changeless Cit through the power of its Maya-Shakti appears to Itself in the form of limited objects. All is Shiva whether as subject or object.

This evolution of consciousness is described in the scheme of the Thirty-six Tattvas.

Shamkara and Samkhya speak of the 24 Tattvas from Prakriti to Prithivi. Both Shaivas and Shaktas speak of the Thirty-six Tattvas, showing, by the extra number of Tattvas, how Purusha and Prakriti themselves originated. The northern or Advaita Shaiva Agama and the Sakta Agama are allied, though all Shaiva Scriptures adopt the same Tattvas. In all the Agamas whether Vaishnava, Shaiva, or Shakta, there are points of doctrine which are the same or similar. The Vaishnava Pancaratra, however, moves in a different sphere of thought. It speaks in lieu of the Abhasa here described of four Vyuha or forms of Narayana, *viz.*, Vasudeva, Samkarshana, Pradyumna and Aniruddha. The Thirty-six Tattvas are the 24 from Prithivi to Prakriti together with (proceeding upwards) Purusha, Maya and the five Kancukas (Kala, Kala, Niyati, Vidya, Raga), Shuddhavidya (or Sad-vidya), Shakti, Shiva. These are divided into three groups named Shiva Tattva, Vidya Tattva, Atma Tattva, and Shuddha, Shuddhashuddha, Ashuddha Tattvas.

The Shuddha or Pure Tattvas are all the Tattvas from *Shiva-Shakti* Tattvas to and including Sadvidya Tattva. The Pure-Impure or Mixed (Shuddha-ashuddha) Tattvas are those between the first and third group which are the Impure Tattvas (Ashuddha Tattva) of the world of duality, namely, the 24

Tattvas from Prakriti to Prithivi. The other group of three is as follows: Shiva Tattva includes Shiva Tattva and Shakti Tattva, Vidya Tattva includes all Tattvas from Sadashiva to Sadvidya, and Atma Tattva includes all Tattvas from Maya and the Kancukas to Prithivi. The particular description here of the 36 Tattvas, held by both Shaivas and Shaktas, is taken from the northern Shaiva Kashmir philosophical school, itself based on the older Agamas such as Malinivijaya Tantra and others.

It is common doctrine of Advaitavada that the One is of dual aspect; the first static (Shiva) and the other kinetic (Shakti). This doctrine of aspects is a device whereby it is sought to reconcile the fact that there is changelessness and change. Philosophically it is an evasion of the problem and not a solution. The solution is to be found in revelation (Veda) and in direct Spiritual Experience (Samadhi). These states vary in different men and in different races and creeds. But in support of Advaitavada, reliance may be placed on the fact that Samadhi or ecstasy, in all parts of the world and in all faiths, *tends* towards some kind of unity, more or less complete. All seek union with God. But the dispute is as to the nature of that union. Pure Advaitavada is complete identity. The scheme now outlined shows how that unitary experience, without ceasing to be what it is, assumes limited forms.

Parasamvit shown on top of the Diagram is Nishkala Shiva or the changeless Brahman aspect; and Shiva-Shakti below is the aspect of the supreme Brahman from which change comes and which appears as its products or changing forms. Both are Shiva-Shakti. When, however, Shiva is kinetic, He is called Shakti. Regarding the matter from the Shakti aspect both are Shakti. Neither ever exists without the other, though Shakti is in one aspect Cidrupini, and in the other in the form of the Universe (Vishvarupini). In themselves and throughout they are one.

The divergence takes place in consciousness, after it has been subjected to the operation of Maya, the effect of which is to polarise consciousness into an apparently separate "I" and "This". Parasamvit is not accounted a Tattva, for It is beyond all Tattvas (Tattvatita). Shiva Tattva and Shakti Tattva are counted separately, though Shakti Tattva is merely the negative aspect of Shiva Tattva. Shiva Tattva and Shakti Tattva are not produced. They thus are, even in dissolution. They are Saguna-Brahman; and Parasamvit is the Nirguna-Brahman. The first evolved Tattva is Sadashiva of Sadakhya Tattva of which the meaning is Sat akhya yatah, or that state in which there is the first notion of Being; for here is the first incipiency of the world-experience as the notion "I am this" which ultimately becomes a separate "I" and "This". In my *Garland of Letters* I have with more technical detail described the evolution of Jiva-consciousness. Here I will only shortly summarise the process.

As already stated, the Aham and Idam exist in an unitary state which is indescribable in Parasamvit. Shakti Tattva is called negative because negation is the function of Shakti (Nishedha-vyapara-rupa Shaktih). Negation of what P The answer is negation of consciousness. The universe is thus a product of negation. Where there is pure experience there is no manifested universe. Shakti negates the pure experience or consciousness to the extent, that it appears to itself limited. Shakti disengages the unified elements (Aham and Idam) which are latent in the Supreme Experience as an undistinguishable unity. How? The answer is one of great subtlety.

Of the Shiva-Shakti Tattvas, Shiva represents the Prakasha and Shakti the Vimarsha aspect, which contains potentially within it, the seed of the Universe to be. The result is that the Prakasha aspect is left standing alone. The Shiva Tattva is Prakasha-matra, that is, to use the imagery of our plane, an "I" without a "This". This is a state in which the unitary consciousness is broken up to this extent, that it is no longer a Perfect Experience in which the Aham and Idam exist in undistinguishable union, but there is one Supreme Aham Consciousness only, which is the root of all limited subjectivity To this Aham or Shiva Tattva, Shakti gradually unveils Herself as the Idam or Vimarsha aspect of consciousness.

The result is that from Shiva and Shakti (in which the latter takes the playful part) there is evolved the first produced consciousness called Sadakhya Tattva. There is then an Aham and Idam aspect of experience. But that experience is not like the Jiva's, which arises at a later stage after the intervention of Maya-Shakti. In the Jiva consciousness (Jivatma) the object (Idam) is seen as something outside and different from itself. In Sadakhya Tattva and all the subsequent pure Tattvas, that is Ishvara Tattva and Shuddhavidya Tattva, the "This" is experienced as part of the Self and not as separate from it. There is (as will appear from the Diagram) no outer and inner. The circle which represents the one Consciousness is divided into "I" and "This" which are yet parts of the same figure.

The "This" is at first only by degree and hazily (Dhyamala prayam) presented to the Aham like a picture just forming itself (Unmilitamatra-citrakalpam). For this reason it is said that there is emphasis on the Aham which is indicated in the Diagram by the arrowhead. This is called the "Nimesha" or "closing of the eyes" of Shakti. It is so called because it is the last stage in dissolution before all effects are withdrawn into their first cause. Being the last stage in dissolution it is the first in creation. Then the Idam side becomes clear in the next evolved Ishvara Tattva in which the emphasis is therefore said to be on the "This" which the Aham subjectifies. This is the "Unmesha" or "opening of the eyes" state of Shakti; for this is the state of consciousness when it is first fully equipped to create and does so. The result again of this is the evolved consciousness called Shuddhavidya Tattva in which the emphasis is equal on the "I" and "This". Consciousness is now in the state in which the two halves of experience are ready to be broken up and experienced separately. It is at this state that Maya-Shakti intervenes and does so through its power and the Kancukas which are forms of it.

Maya-Shakti is thus defined as the sense of difference (Bhedabuddhi); that is the power by which things are seen as different from the Self in the dual manifested world. The Kancukas which are evolved from, and are particular forms of, the operation of Maya are limitations of the natural perfections of the Supreme Consciousness. These are Kala which produces division (Pariccheda) in the partless and unlimited; Niyati which affects independence (Svatantrata); Raga which produces interest in, and then attachment to, objects in that which wanted nothing (Purna); Vidya which makes the Purusha a "little knower" in lieu of being all-knower (Sarva-jnata) and Kala which makes Purusha a "little doer," whereas the Supreme was in its Kartrittva or power action of almighty.

The result of Maya and its offshoots which are the Kancukas is the production of the Purusha and Prakriti Tattvas. At this stage the Aham and Idam are completely severed. Each consciousness regards itself as a separate 'I' looking upon the "This" whether its own body or that of others as outside its consciousness.

Each Purusha (and they are numberless) is mutually exclusive the one of the other. Prakriti is the collectivity of all Shaktis in contracted (Sankucadrupa) undifferentiated form. She is Feeling in the form of the undifferentiated mass of Buddhi and the rest and of the three Gunas in equilibrium. The Purusha or Self experiences Her as object. Then on the disturbance of the Gunas in Prakriti the latter evolves the Vikritis of mind and matter. The Purusha at this stage has experience of the multiple world of the twenty-four impure Tattvas.

Thus from the supreme "I" (Parahanta) which is the creative Shiva-Shakti aspect of Parasamvit which changelessly endures as Sacchidananda, Consciousness experiences Itself as object (Sadakhya, Ishvara, Sadvidya Tattvas) and then through Maya and the limitations or contractions which are the Kancukas or Samkocas it loses the knowledge that it is itself its own object. It sees the separate "other"; and the one Consciousness becomes the limited experiencers which are the multiple selves and their objects of the dual universe.

Shakti who in Herself (Svarupa) is Feeling-Consciousness (Cidrupini) becomes more and more gross until physical energy assumes the form and becomes embedded in the "crust" of matter vitalised by Herself as the Life-Principle of all things. Throughout all forms it is the same Shakti who works and appears as Cit-Shakti and Maya-Shakti, the Spirit and Matter aspect of the Power of the Self-Illumining Pure Super-Consciousness or Cit.

Maya-Shakti (The Psycho-Physical Aspect of the Universe)

Spirit, Mind and Matter are ultimately one, the two latter being the twin aspects of the Fundamental Substance or Brahman and Its Power or Shakti. Spirit is the substance of mind-matter, the Reality (in the sense of the lasting changelessness) out of which, by Its Power, all Appearance is fashioned not by the individual mind and senses but by the cosmic mind and senses of which they are but a part. What It creates It perceives. In the last chapter I dealt with the Spirit or Consciousness (Cit) aspect: in this I consider the mind-matter aspect in which Consciousness veils itself in apparent unconsciousness.

These twin principles are called Purusha, Brahman, Shiva on the one hand and Prakriti, Maya, and Maya-Shakti on the other by the Samkhya Mayavada Vedanta and Shaktivada of the Shakta Agama respectively. The latter Shastra, however, alone treats them as aspects of the one Substance in the manner here described and thus most aptly in this respect accommodates itself to the doctrine of Western scientific monism. So, Professor Haeckel points out in conformity with Shakta Advaitavada that Spirit and Matter are not two distinct entities but two forms or aspects of one single Entity or fundamental Substance.

According to him, the One Entity with dual aspect is the sole Reality which presents itself to view as the infinitely varied and wondrous picture of the universe. Whatever be the case transcendentally in what the Buddhist Tantra aptly calls "The Void" (Shunyata. In Tibetan sTongpa-nyid) which is not "nothing" as some have supposed, but That which is like nothing known to us; the ultimate formless (Arupa) Reality as contrasted with appearance (sNang-va-dang) or form (Rupa) of which the Prajnaparamita-hridaya-garbha says only "neti neti" can be affirmed,—in this universe immaterial Spirit is just as unthinkable as spiritless matter.

The two are inseparately combined in every atom which, itself and its forces, possess the elements of vitality, growth and intelligence in all their developments. In the four Atmas which are contemplated in the Citkunda in the Muladhara Cakra, Atma pranarupi represents the vital aspect, Jnanatma the Intelligence aspect, and Antaratma is that spark of the Paramatma which inheres in all bodies, and which when spread (Vyapta) appears as the Bhuta or five forms of sensible matter which go to the making of the gross body. These are all aspects of the one Paramatma *(Jnanarnava Tantra,* Ch. XXI, Vv. 1-9).

The Vedanta recognises four states of experience, Jagrat, Svapna, Sushupti and Turiya. These, as my friend Professor Pramathanatha Mukhyopadhyaya has, in his radical clear-thinking way, pointed out, may be regarded from two stand-points. We may, with Shamkara, from the standpoint of Siddhi alone, regard the last only, that is transcendental or pure experience (Nirvishesha-jnana), as the real Fact or Experience: or we may, with the Shakta Agama, looking at the matter from the standpoint of both Sadhana (that is practical experience) and Siddhi (or transcendental experience), regard not only the supreme experience as alone real, but the whole of experience without any reservation whatever—the whole concrete Fact of Being and Becoming—and call it the Real. This is the view of the Shaiva-Shakta who says that the world is Shiva's Experience and Shiva's Experience can never be unreal.

The question turns upon the definition of "Real". Shamkara's conception of that term is that, That to which it is applied must be absolutely changeless in all the "three times". It is That which absolutely continues through and underlies all the changes of experience; being that which is given in all the four states, Jagrat and the rest. It is That which can never be contradicted (Vadhita) in all the three tenses of time and the four states of Experience. This is the Ether of Consciousness (Cidakasha) and none of Its modes. Our ordinary experience, it is claimed, as well as Supreme non-polar Nirvikalpa Samadhi proves this unchanging aspect of the ultimate Substance, as the changeless principle of all our modes of changing experience, which according to this definition are unreal.

Thus Shamkara's Real = Being = Sat-Cit-Ananda: Unreal = Becoming = Vivartta = Jagat-Prapanca or universe. According to this view, there are three levels or planes of being (Satta), namely transcendental (Paramarthika), empirical (Vyavaharika) and illusory (Pratibhasika). The Real (Satya) is that which is given in all the three planes (Paramarthika Satya): the empirical (Vyavaharika Satya) is that which is given in the second and third planes but not in the first. It is worldly or dual experience, and not undual experience of Samadhi or Videha-Mukti which latter, however, underlies all states of experience, being the Ether of Consciousness Itself.

The last (Pratibhasika Satya) is given or obtains only in the last plane, being only such reality as can be attributed to illusion such as "the rope-snake". A higher plane contradicts a lower: the third is contradicted by the second, the second by the first, and the first by nothing at all. Thus there is a process of gradual elimination from changing to changeless consciousness. Real change or Parinama is said by the Vedanta Paribhasha to exist when the effect or phenomenon and its ground (Upadana or material cause) belong to the same level or plane of existence; as in the case of clay and pot, milk and curd, which both belong to the Vyavaharika plane; milk being the Upadana and curd the effect or change appertaining it (Parinamo hi upadana-sama-sattaka-karya pattih). When, however, the effect's level of existence is different from (Vishama) and therefore cannot be equaled to that of its material cause or Upadana; when, for instance, one belongs to the Vyavaharika experience and the other to the Pratibhasika, there is Nivartta (Vivartto hi upadana-vishama-sattaka-karyapattih).

Thus, in the case of the "rope-snake," the Satta of the rope is Vyavaharika, whilst that of the Rajju-sarpa is only Pratibhasika. For the same reason, the rope, and the whole Jagat-prapanca (universe) for the matter of that, is a Vivartta in relation to the Supreme Experience of pure Cit. On its own plane or level of Satta, every phenomenon may be a Parinama, but in relation to a higher level by which it becomes Vadhita, it is only a Vivartta.

The Shakta Agama differs in its presentment as follows. The Fact or Concrete Experience presents two aspects—what professor Mukhyopadhyaya has aptly called in his work the "Patent Wonder"—the Ether and the Stress—the quiescent background of Cit and the sprouting and evolving Shakti. Agama takes this whole (Shiva-Shakti) embracing all the aspects as its real. If one aspect be taken apart from the others, we are landed in the unreal. Therefore, in the Shakta Agama, all is real; whether the transcendent real of Shamkara (Turiya), or the empirical real waking (Jagrat, dreaming (Svapna) or dreamless sleep (Sushupti).

If it is conceded that Real = Changelessness, then the last three states are not real. But this definition of Reality is not adopted. It is again conceded that the Supreme Substance (Paravastu) is alone real, in the sense of changeless, for the worlds come and go. But the Agama says with the Samkhya, that a thing is not unreal because it changes. The Substance has two aspects, in one of which It is changeless, and in the other of which It changes.

It is the same Substance in both its Prakasha and Vimarsha aspects. Shamkara limits Reality to the Prakasha aspect alone. Agama extends it to both Prakasha and Vimarsha; for these are aspects of the one. As explained later, this divergence of views turns upon the definition of Maya given by Shamkara, and of Maya-Shakti given by the Agama. The Maya of Shamkara is a mysterious Shakti of Ishvara, by which Vivartta is sought to be explained and which has two manifestations, *viz.,* Veiling (Avarana) and moving, changing and projecting (Vikshepa) power. Ishvara is Brahman reflected in Maya; a mystery which is separate, and yet not separate, from Brahman in Its Ishvara aspect. The Shakta Maya-Shakti is an aspect of Shiva or Brahman Itself.

Starting from these premises we must assume a real nexus between the universe and its ultimate cause. The creation is real, and not Maya in Shamkara's sense of Maya, but is the operation of and is Shakti Herself. The cause being thus real, the effect or universe is real though it changes and passes away. Even when it is dissolved, it is merged in Shakti who is real; withdrawn into Her as the Samkhyan tortoise or Prakriti withdraws its limbs (Vikriti) into itself. The universe either *is* as unmanifested Shakti, which is the perfect formless universe of Bliss, or *exists* as manifested Shakti, the limited and imperfect worlds of form.

The assumption of such nexus necessarily involves that what is in the effect is in the cause potentially. Of course, the follower of Shamkara will say that if creation is the becoming patent or actual of what is latent or potential in Shiva, then Shiva is not really Nishkala. A truly Niranjana Brahman cannot admit potential differentiation within Itself (Svagata-bheda.) Again, potentiality is unmeaning in relation to the absolute and infinite Being, for it pertains to relation and finite existence. If it is suggested that Brahman passes from one condition in which Maya lies as a seed in it, to another in which Maya manifests Herself, we are involved in the doctrine of an Absolute in the making. It is illogical to affirm that whilst Brahman in one aspect does not change, It in another aspect, that is as Shakti, does truly change. All such objections have alogical foundation and it is for this reason that Shamkara says that all change (Srishti, Sthiti, Laya) are only apparent, being but a Kalpana or imagination.

But an answer is given to these objections. The Shakta will say that the one Brahman Shiva has two aspects in one of which, as Shakti, It changes and in the other of which, as Shiva, It does not. Reality is constituted of both these aspects. It is true that the doctrine of aspects does not solve the problem. Creation is ultimately inscrutable. It is, however, he urges, better to hold both the reality of the Brahman and the world leaving spiritual experience to synthesise them, than to neglect one at the cost of the other. For this, it is argued, is what Shamkara does. His solution is obtained at the cost of a denial of true reality to the world which all our worldly experience affirms; and this solution is supported by the illogical statement that Maya is not real and is yet not unreal, not partly real and partly unreal.

This also, flies in the face of the logical principle of contradiction. Both theories, therefore, it may be said in different ways, run counter to logic. All theories ultimately do. The matter is admittedly alogical, that is beyond logic, for it is beyond the mind and its logical forms of thinking. Practically, therefore, it is said to be better to base our theory on our experience of the reality of the world, frankly leaving it to spiritual experience to solve a problem for which all logic, owing to the very constitution of the mind, fails. The ultimate proof of authority is Spiritual Experience either recorded in Veda or realised in Samadhi.

As I have already said in my chapter on the spirit-aspect of the One Substance, all occultism, whether of East or West, posits the principle that there is nothing in any one state or plane which is not in some way, actual or potential, in another state or plane. The Western Hermetic maxim, "as above so below," is stated in the Visvasara Tantra in the form, "what is here is there. What is not here is nowhere" *(Yad ihasti tad anyatra yan nehasti na tat kvacit);* and in the northern Shaiva Scripture in the form, "that which appears *without* only so appears *because* it exists *within*", *"Vartamanava-bhasanam bhavanam avabhasanam antahsthitavatam eva ghatate bahiratmana"*.

For these reasons man is rightly called a microcosm (Kshudrabrahmanda; *hominem quasi minorem quendam mundum.* Firm. Maternus Math. III init.) So Caraka says that the course of production, growth, decay and destruction of the universe and of man are the same. But these statements do not mean that what exists on one plane exists in that form or way on another plane. It is obvious that if it did, the planes would be the same and not different. It means that the same thing exists on one plane and on all other levels of being or planes, according either to the form of that plane, if it be what is called an intermediate causal body (Karanavantara-sharira) or ultimately as mere formless potentiality.

According to Shamkara all such argument is itself Maya. And it may be so to those who have realised true consciousness (Citsvarupa) which is beyond all causality. The Tantra Shastra is, however, a practical and Sadhana Shastra. It takes the world to be real and then applies, so far as it may, to the question of its origin, the logic of the mind which forms a part of it. It says that it is true that there is a Supreme or Perfect Experience which is beyond all worlds (Shakti Vishvottirna), but there is also a worldly or (relatively to the Supreme) imperfect (in the sense of limited) and partly sorrowful experience. Because the one exists, it does not follow that the other does not: though mere logic cannot construct an unassailable monism.

It is the one Shiva who is Bliss itself, and who is in the form of the world (Vishvatmaka) which is Happiness-Unhappiness. Shiva is both changeless as Shiva and changeful as Shakti. How the One can be both is a mystery. To say, however, with Shamkara that it is Maya, and in truth Brahman does not change, is not to explain, in an ultimate sense, the problem but to eliminate some other possible cause and to give to what remains a name. Maya by itself does not explain the ultimate. What can? It is only a term which is given to the wondrous power of the Creatrix by which what seems impossible to us becomes possible to Her. This is recognised as it must be, by Shamkara who says that Maya is unexplainable (Anirvacaniya) as of course it is. To "explain" the Creator, one would have to be Creator Himself and then in such case there would be no need of any explanation. Looking, however, at the matter from our own practical standpoint, which is that which concerns us, we are drawn by the fore-going considerations to the conclusion that, what we call "matter," is, in some form, in the cause which according to the doctrine here described, produces it.

But matter as experienced by us is not there; for the Supreme is Spirit only. And yet in some sense it is there, or it would not be here at all. It is there as the Supreme Shakti which is Being-Consciousness-Bliss (Cidrupini, Anandamayi) who contains within Herself the potentiality of all worlds to be projected by Her Shakti. It *is* there as unmanifested Consciousness Power (Cidrupini Shakti). It here *exists* as the mixed conscious-unconsciousness (in the sense of the limited consciousness) of the psychical and material universe. If the ultimate Reality be one, there is thus one Almighty Substance which is both Spirit (Shiva-Shakti Svarupa) and force-mind-matter (Shiva-Shakti-Vishvatmaka). Spirit and Mind-Matter are thus in the end one.

This ultimate Supreme Substance (Paravastu) is Power or Shakti, which is again, of dual aspect as Cit-Shakti which represents the spiritual, and Maya-Shakti which represents the material and mental aspects. The two, however, exist in inseparable connection (Avinabhava-sambandha); as inseparable to use a simile of the Shastra as the winds of heaven from the Ether in which they blow. Shakti, who is in Herself (Svarupa) Consciousness, appears as the Life-force, as subtle Mind, and as gross Matter. See sections in my *World as Power* dealing in detail with Life (Prana-Shakti), Mind (Manasi-Shakti) and Matter (Bhuta-Shakti).

As all is Shakti and as Shakti-svarupa is Being-Consciousness-Bliss, there is, and can be, nothing absolutely unconscious. For Shakti-svarupa is unchanging Being-Consciousness beyond all worlds (Cidrupini Vishvottirna), the unchanging principle of experience in such worlds; and appears as the limited psychical universe and as the apparently unconscious material forms which are the content of man's Experience (Vishvatmika). The whole universe is Shakti under various forms. Therefore it is seen as commingled Spirit-Mind-Matter.

According to Shaiva-Shakta doctrine, Shiva and Shakti are one. Shiva represents the static aspect of the Supreme substance, and Shakti its kinetic aspect: the term being derived from the root "Sak" which denotes capacity of action or power. According to Shamkara, Brahman has two aspects, in one of which as Ishvara, it is associated with Maya and seems to change, and in the other dissociated from Maya (Parabrahman). In the Agama, the one Shiva is both the changeless Parashiva and Parashakti and really changing Shiva-Shakti or universe. As Shiva is one with Himself, He is never associated with anything but Himself. As, however, the Supreme He is undisplayed (Shiva-Shakti Svarupa) and as Shiva-Shakti He is manifest in the form of the universe of mind and matter (Vishvarupa).

Before the manifestation of the universe there was Mahasatta or Grand-being. Then also there was Shiva-Shakti, for there is no time when Shakti is not; though She is sometimes manifest and sometimes not. Power is Power both to Be and to Become. But then Shakti is not manifest and is in its own true nature (Svarupa); that is, Being, Feeling-Consciousness-Bliss (Cinmayi, Anandamayi). As Shiva is consciousness (Cit) and Bliss or Love (Ananda), She is then simply Bliss and Love. Then when moved to create, the Great Power or *Megale Dunamis* of the Gnostics issues from the depths of Being and becomes Mind and Matter whilst remaining what She ever was: the Being (Sat) which is the foundation of manifested life and the Spirit which sustains and enlightens it.

This primal Power (Adya Shakti), as object of worship, is the Great Mother (Magna-Mater) of all natural things (Natura Naturans) and nature itself (Natura Naturata). In herself (Svarupa) She is not a person in man's sense of the term, but She is ever and incessantly *personalising;* assuming the multiple masks (Persona) which are the varied forms of mind-matter. As therefore manifest, She is all Personalities and as the collectivity thereof the Supreme Person (Parahanta). But in Her own ground from which, clad in form, She emerges and personalises, She is beyond all form, and therefore beyond all personality known to us. She works in and as all things; now greatly veiling Her consciousness-bliss in gross matter, now by gradual stages more fully revealing Herself in the forms of the one universal Life which She is.

Let us now first examine Her most gross manifestation, that is, sensible matter (Bhuta), then Her more subtle aspect as the Life-force and Mind, and lastly Her Supreme Shakti aspect as Consciousness. I here deal with the subject in a general way having treated of it in greater detail in the book just now cited *(World as Power).*

The physical human body is composed of certain compounds of which the chief are water, gelatin, fat, phosphate of lime, albumen and fibrin, and, of these, water constitutes some two-thirds of the total weight. These compounds, again, are composed of simpler non-metallic elements of which the chief are oxygen (to the extent of about two-thirds), hydrogen, carbon, nitrogen, calcium and phosphorus. So about two-thirds of the body is water and this is H_2O. Substantially then our gross body is water. But when we get to these simpler elements, have we got to the root of the matter P No. It was formerly thought that matter was composed of certain elements beyond which it was not possible to go, and that these elements and their atoms were indestructible. These notions have been reversed by modern science.

Though the alleged indestructibility of the elements and their atoms is still said by some to present the character of a "practical truth," well-known recent discoveries and experiments go to re-establish the ancient doctrine of a single primordial substance to which these various forms of matter may be reduced, with the resultant of the possible and hitherto derided transmutation of one element into another; since each is but one of the many plural manifestations of the same underlying unity. The so-called elements are varied forms of this one substance which themselves combine to form the various compounds. The variety of our experience is due to permutation and combination of the atoms of the matter into which the primordial energy materialises. We thus find that owing to the variety of atomic combinations of H N O C there are differences in the compounds.

It is curious to note in passing how apparently slight variations in the quantity and distribution of the atoms produce very varying substances. Thus gluten which is a nutrient food, and quinine and strychnine which are in varying degree poisons, are each compounds of C H N O. Strychnine, a powerful poison, is $C_{21}H_{22}N_2O_2$ and quinine is $C_{20}H_{24}N_2O_2$. N and 0 are the same in both and there is a difference of one part only of C and 2 of H. But neither these compounds nor the so-called elements of which they are composed are permanent things. Scientific matter is now found to be only a relatively stable form of cosmic energy. All matter dissociates and passes into the energy of which it is a materialised form and again it issues from it.

Modern Western Science and Philosophy have thus removed many difficulties which were formerly thought to be objections to the ancient Indian doctrine on the subject here dealt with. It has, in the first place dispelled the gross notions which were hitherto generally entertained as to the nature of "matter." According to the notions of quite recent science, "matter" was defined to be that which has mass, weight and inertia. It must be now admitted that the two latter qualities no longer stand the test of examination, since, putting aside our ignorance as to the nature of weight, this quality varies, if we conceive matter to be placed under conditions which admittedly affect it; and the belief in inertia is due to superficial observation, it being now generally conceded that the final elements of matter are in a state of spontaneous and perpetual motion.

In fact, the most general phenomenon of the universe is vibration, to which the human body as all else is subject. Various vibrations affect differently each organ of sensation. When of certain quality and number, they denote to the skin the degree of external temperature; others incite the eye to see different colours; others again enable the ear to hear defined sounds. Moreover "inertia", which is alleged to be a distinguishing quality of "matter," is said to be the possession of electricity, which is considered not to be "material". What, then, is that to which we attribute "mass" P In the first place, it is now admitted that "matter," even with the addition of all possible forces, is insufficient to explain many phenomena, such as those of light; and it has, accordingly, come to be for some an article of scientific *faith* that there is a substance called "Ether": a medium which, filling the universe, transports by its vibrations the radiations of light, heat, electricity, and perhaps action from a distance, such as the attraction exercised between heavenly bodies.

It is said, however, that this Ether is not "matter," but differs profoundly from it, and that it is only our infirmity of knowledge which obliges us, in our attempted descriptions of it, to borrow comparisons from "matter," in its ordinary physical sense, which alone is known by our senses. But if we assume the existence of Ether, we know that "material" bodies immersed in it can change their places therein. In fact, to use an Indian expression, the characteristic property of the vibrations of the Akasha Tattva is to make the space in which the other Tattvas and their derivatives exist. With "Matter" and Ether as their materials, Western purely "scientific" theories have sought to construct the world.

The scientific atom which Du Bois Raymond described as an exceedingly useful fiction—"ausserst nutzliche fiction"—is no longer considered the ultimate indestructible element, but is held to be, in fact, a kind of miniature solar system, formed by a central group or nucleus charged with positive electricity, around which very much smaller elements, called electrons or corpuscles, charged with negative electricity, gravitate in closed orbits. These vibrate in the etheric medium in which they and the positively charged nucleus exist, constituting by their energy, and not by their mass, the unity of the atom.

But what, again, is the constitution of this "nucleus" and the electrons revolving around it? There is no scientific certainty that any part of either is due to the presence of "matter". On the contrary, if a hypothetical corpuscle consisting solely of an electric charge without material mass is made the subject of mathematical analysis, the logical inference is that the electron is free of "matter", and is merely an electric charge moving in the Ether; and though the extent of our knowledge regarding the positive nucleus which constitutes the remainder of the atom is small, an eminent mathematician and physicist has expressed the opinion that, if there is no "matter" in the negative charges, the positive charges must also be free from it.

Thus, in the words of the author upon whose lucid analysis I have drawn, (Houllevigue's *Evolution of Science)* the atom has been *dematerialised,* if one may say so, and with it the molecules and the entire universe. "Matter" (in the scientific sense) *disappears,* and we and all that surround us are physically, according to these views, mere disturbed regions of the ether determined by moving electric charges—a logical if impressive conclusion, because it is by increasing their knowledge of "matter" that physicists have been led to doubt its reality.

But the question, as he points out, does not remain there. For if the speculations of Helmholtz be adopted, there is nothing absurd in imaging that two possible directions of rotation of a vortex formed within, and consisting of, ether correspond to the positive and negative electric charges said to be attached to the final elements of matter. If that be so, then the trinity of matter, ether, and electricity, out of which science has hitherto attempted to construct the world, is reduced to a single element, the ether (which is not scientific "matter") in a state of motion, and which is the basis of the physical universe. The old duality of force and matter disappears, these being held to be differing forms of the same thing. Matter is a relatively stable form of energy into which, on disturbance of its equilibrium, it disappears; for all forms of matter dissociate. The ultimate basis is that energy called in Indian philosophy Prakriti, Maya or Shakti.

Herbert Spencer, the Philosopher of Modern Science, carries the investigation farther, holding that the universe, whether physical or psychical, whether within or without us, is a play of Force, which, in the case of Matter, we experience as object, and that the notion that the ultimate realities are the supposed atoms of matter, to the properties and combinations of which the complex universe is due, is not true. Mind, Life and Matter are each varying aspects of the one cosmic process from the First Cause. Mind as such is as much a "material" organ as the brain and outer sense organs, though they are differing forms of force.

Both mind and matter derive from what Herbert Spencer calls the Primal Energy (Adya Shakti), and Haeckel the fundamental Spirit-Matter Substance. Professor Fitz Edward Hall described the Samkhya philosophy as being "with all its folly and fanaticism little better than a chaotic impertinence". It has doubtless its weaknesses like all other systems. Wherein, however, consists its "fanaticism," I do not know. As for "impertinence," it is neither more nor less so than any other form of Western endeavour to solve the riddle of life. As regards its leading concept, "Prakriti," the Professor said that it was a notion for which the European languages were unable to supply a name; a failure, he added, which was "nowise to their discredit". The implication of this sarcastic statement is that it was not to the discredit of Western languages that they had no name for so foolish a notion. He wrote before the revolution of ideas in science to which I have referred, and with that marked antagonism to things Indian which has been and to some extent still is so common a feature of the more ordinary type of the professional orientalist.

The notion of Prakriti is not absurd. The doctrine of a Primordial Substance was held by some of the greatest minds in the past and has support from the most modern developments of Science. Both now concur to reject what the great Sir William Jones called the "vulgar notion of material substance" (Opera I. 36). Many people were wont, as some still are, to laugh at the idea of Maya. Was not matter solid, permanent and real enough? But according to science what are we (as physical beings) at base P The answer is, infinitely tenuous formless energy which materialises into relatively stable, yet essentially transitory, forms. According to the apt expression of the Shakta Shastra, Shakti, as She creates, becomes Ghanibhuta, that is, massive or thickened; just as milk becomes curd.

The process by which the subtle becomes gradually more and more gross continues until it develops into what has been called the "crust" of solid matter (Parthiva bhuta). This whilst it lasts is tangible enough. But it will not last for ever, and in some radio-active substances dissociates before our eyes. Where does it go, according to Shakta doctrine, but to that Mother-Power from whose womb it came; who exists as all forms, gross and subtle, and is the formless Consciousness Itself. The poet's inspiration led Shakespeare to say, "We are such stuff as dreams are made of."

It is a wonderful saying from a Vedantic standpoint, for centuries before him Advaitavada had said, "Yes, dreams; for the Lord is Himself the Great World-dreamer slumbering in causal sleep as Ishvara, dreaming as Hiranyagarbha the universe experienced by Him as the Virat or totality of all Jivas, on waking." Scientific revision of the notion of "matter" helps the Vedantic standpoint, by dispelling gross and vulgar notions upon the subject; by establishing its impermanence in its form as scientific matter; by positing a subtler physical substance which is not ponderable matter; by destroying the old duality of Matter and Force; and by these and other conclusions leading to the acceptance of one Primal Energy or Shakti which transforms itself into that relatively stable state which is perceived by the senses as gross "matter." As, however, science deals with matter only objectively, that is, from a dualistic standpoint, it does not (whatever hypotheses any particular scientist may maintain) resolve the essential problem which is stated in the world Maya.

That problem is, "How can the apparent duality be a real unity? How can we bridge the gulf between the object and the Self which perceives it? Into whatever tenuous energy the material world is resolved, we are still left in the region of duality of Spirit, Mind and Matter. The position is not advanced beyond that taken by Samkhya. The answer to the problem stated is that Shakti which is the origin of, and is in, all things has the power to veil Itself so that whilst in truth it is only seeing itself as object, it does not, as the created Jiva, perceive this but takes things to be outside and different from the Self. For this reason Maya is called, in the Shastra, Bhedabuddhi or the sense of difference. This is the natural characteristic of man's experience.

Herbert Spencer, the Philosopher of Modern Science, carrying the investigation beyond physical matter, holds, as I have already said, that the universe, whether physical or psychical, whether as mind or matter, is a play of Force; Mind, Life and Matter being each varying aspects of the one cosmic process from the First Cause. This, again, is an Indian notion. For, the affirmation that "scientific matter" is an appearance produced by the play of Cosmic Force, and that mind is itself a product of the same play is what both Samkhya and Mayavada Vedanta hold. Both these systems teach that mind, considered in itself, is, like matter, an unconscious thing, and that both it and matter ultimately issue from the same single Principle which the former calls Prakriti and the latter Maya. Consciousness and Unconsciousness are in the universe inseparate, whatever be the degree of manifestation or veiling of Consciousness.

For the purpose of analysis, Mind in itself—that is, considered hypothetically as dissociated from Consciousness, which, in fact, is never the case, (though Consciousness exists apart from the Mind)—is a force-process like the physical brain.

Consciousness (Cit) is not to be identified with mind (Antahkarana) which is the organ of expression of mind. Consciousness is not a mere manifestation of material mind. Consciousness must not be identified with its *mental modes;* an identification which leads to the difficulties in which western metaphysics has so often found itself. It is the ultimate Reality in which all modes whether subjective or objective exist.

The assertion that mind is in itself unconscious may seem a strange statement to a Western reader who, if he does not identify mind and consciousness, at any rate, regards the latter as an attribute or function of mind. The point, however, is of such fundamental importance for the understanding of Indian doctrine that it may be further developed.

According to the Lokayata School of Indian Materialism, mind was considered to be the result of the chemical combination of the four forms of material substance, earth, water, fire and air, in organic forms. According to the Purva-Mimamsa and the Nyaya-Vaisheshika, the Self or Atma is in itself and that is by nature (Svabhavatah), unconscious (Jada, Acidrupa): for Atma is said to be unconscious (Acetana) in dreamless sleep (Sushupti); and consciousness arises as a produced thing, by association of the Atma with the mind, senses and body. The reader is referred to Pandit Chandra Kanta Tarkalamkara's Bengali Lectures on Hindu Philosophy. At p. 105 he cites Prabhakara Mimamsaka-carya, saying that Vaisheshika-Nyaya supports the view. *Sacetanashcittayogat todyogena vina jadah.* "Atma is conscious by union with knowledge (Jnana) which comes to it by association with mind and body. Without it, it is unconscious." Atma, according to this Darshana, is that in which (Ashraya) Jnana inheres.

Kumarila Bhatta says Atma is partly Prakasha and partly Aprakasha, (luminous and non-luminous) like a fire-fly. But this is denied, as Atma is Niramsha (part-less). Knowledge thus arises from the association of mind (Manas) with Atma, the senses (Indriya) with Manas, and the senses with objects, that, is, worldly (Laukika) knowledge, which is the true—that is, non-illusive—apprehension of objects. Jnana in the spiritual Vedantic sense of Mayavada is Paramatma, or pure

Consciousness realised. The former Jnana, in that it arises without effort on the presentation of the objects is not action (Kriya), and differs from the forms of mental action (Manasi Kriya), such as will (Iccha), contemplation and the like. *Atma manasa samyujyate, mana indriyena, indriyam arthena, tato bhavati jnanam.* Both these theories are refuted by Samkhya and Advaitavada Vedanta (as interpreted by Shamkara, to which unless otherwise stated I refer) which affirm that the very nature of Atma is Consciousness (Cit), and all else, whether mind or matter, is unconscious, though the former appears not to be so. The Jiva mind is not itself conscious, but reflects consciousness, and therefore appears to be conscious. Consciousness as such is eternal and immutable; Mind is a creation and changeable. Consciousness as such is unconditional. In the mind of the Jiva, Consciousness appears to be conditioned by that Maya-Shakti which produces mind, and of which Shakti, mind is a particular manifestation. Mind, however, is not the resultant of the operation of the Bhuta—that is, of gross natural forces or motions—but is, in Samhya and in Shakta monism, an evolution which is logically prior to them.

The mode of exposition in which Consciousness is treated as being in itself something apart from, though associated with, mind, is profound; because, while it recognises the intermingling of Spirit and Matter in the embodied being (Jiva), it yet at the same time clearly distinguishes them. It thus avoids the imputation of change to Spirit (Atma). The latter is ever in Its own true nature immutable. Mind is ever changing, subject to sensations, forming ideas, making resolves, and so forth. Spirit in Itself is neither affected nor acts. Manifold change takes place, through motion and vibration in the unconscious Prakriti and Maya. Mind is one of the results of such motion, as matter is another.

Each of them is a form of specific transformation of the one Principle whence unconsciousness, whether real or apparent, arises. That, however, mind *appears* to be conscious, the Mayavada Vedanta and Samkhya admit. This is called Cidabhasa—that is, the appearance of something as Cit (Consciousness) which is not really Cit. This appearance of

Consciousness is due to the reflection of Cit upon it. A piece of polished steel which lies in the sunshine may appear to be self-luminous, when it is merely reflecting the sun, which is the source of the light it appears to give out. Cit as such is immutable and never evolves. What do evolve are the various forms of natural forces produced by Prakriti or Maya. These two are, however, conceived as being in association in such a way that the result of such association is produced without Cit being really affected at all.

The classical illustration of the mode and effect of such association is given in the Samkhyan aphorism, "Just like the jewel and the flower"—*Kusumavacca manih* (Samkhya-Pravacana-Sutra, II, 35)—that is, when a scarlet hibiscus flower is placed in contiguity to a crystal, the latter appears to be red, though it still in fact retains its pure transparency, as is seen when the flower is removed. On the other hand, the flower as reflected in the crystal takes on a shining, transparent aspect which its opaque surface does not really possess. In the same way Consciousness appears to be conditioned by the force of unconsciousness in the Jiva, but is really not so. "Changeless Cit-Shakti does not move towards anything, yet seems to do so" (Samkhya-pravacana-Sutra). And, on the other hand, Mind as one of such unconscious forces takes on the semblance of Consciousness, though this is borrowed from Cit and is not its own natural quality.

This association of Unconscious Force with Consciousness has a two-fold result, both obscuring and revealing. It obscures, in so far as, and so long as it is in operation, it prevents the realisation of pure Consciousness (Cit). When mind is absorbed pure Consciousness shines forth. In this sense, this Power or Maya is spoken of as a Veil. In another sense, it reveals—that is, it manifests—the world, which does not exist except through the instrumentality of Maya which the world is. Prakriti and Maya produce both Mind and Matter; on the former of which Consciousness is reflected (Cidabhasa). The human mind, then, appears to be conscious, but of its own nature and inherent quality is not so. The objective world of matter is, or appears to be, an unconscious reality. These alternatives are necessary, because, in Samkhya, unconsciousness is a reality; in Vedanta, an appearance. In the Shakta Tantra, apparent unconsciousness is an aspect (Avidya Shakti) of Conscious Shakti. Consciousness is according to Advaita Vedanta, the true existence of both, illumining the one, hidden in the other.

The internal instrument (Antahkarana) or Mind is one only, but is given different names—Buddhi, Ahamkara, Manas—to denote the diversity of its functions. From the second of these issue the senses (Indriya) and their objects, the sensibles (Mahabhuta), or gross matter with the super-sensibles (Tanmatra) as its intermediate cause. All these proceed from Prakriti and Maya.

Therefore, according to these systems, Consciousness is Cit, and Mind or Antahkarana is a transformation of Prakriti and Maya respectively. In itself, Mind is an unconscious specialised organ developed out of the Primordial Energy, Mulaprakriti or Maya. It is thus, not in itself, consciousness but a special manifestation of conscious existence, borrowing its consciousness from the Cit which is reflected on it. Shakta doctrine states the same matter in a different form. Consciousness at rest is Cit-Svarupa. Consciousness in movement is Cit-Shakti associated with Maya-Shakti. The Shiva-Shakti Svarupa is consciousness (Cit, Cidrupini). There is no independent Prakriti as Samkhya holds, nor an unconscious Maya which is not Brahman and yet not separate from Brahman, as Shamkara teaches. What there is, is Maya-Shakti; that is Consciousness (Shakti is in itself such) veiling, as the Mother, Herself to herself as Her creation, the Jiva. There is no need then for Cidabhasa. For mind is consciousness veiling itself in the forms or limitation of apparent unconsciousness.

This is an attractive exposition of the matter because in the universe consciousness and unconsciousness are mingled, and the abolition of unconscious Maya satisfies the desire for unity. In all these cases, however, mind and matter represent either the real or apparent unconscious aspect of things. If man's consciousness is, or appears to be, limited, such limitation must be due to some principle without, or attached to, or inherent in consciousness; which in some sense or other must *ex hypothesi* be really, or apparently different from the consciousness, which it seems to affect or actually affects. In all these systems, mind and matter equally derive from a common *finitising* principle which actually or apparently limits the Infinite Consciousness. In all three, there is, beyond manifestation, Consciousness or Cit, which in manifestation appears as a parallelism of mind and matter; the substratum of which from a monistic standpoint is Cit.

Herbert Spencer, however, as many other Western Philosophers do, differs from the Vedanta in holding that the noumenon of these phenomena is not Consciousness, for the latter is by them considered to be by its very nature conditioned and concrete. This noumenon is therefore declared to be unknown and unknowable. But Force as such is blind, and can only act as it has been predetermined. We discover consciousness in the universe. The cause must, therefore, it is argued, be Consciousness. It is but reasonable to hold that, if the first cause be of the nature of either Consciousness or Matter, and not of both, it must be of the nature of the former, and not of the latter. An unconscious object may wall be conceived to modify Consciousness, but not to produce Consciousness out of its Self. According to Indian Realism, the Paramanus are the material (Upadana) cause (Karana), and Ishvara the instrumental (Nimitta) cause, for He makes them combine. According to Vedanta, Matter is really nothing but a determined modification of knowledge in the Ishvara Consciousness, itself unaffected by such determination. Ishvara is thus both the material and instrumental cause. A thing can only dissolve into its own cause. The agency (Kartritva) of Ishvara is in Mayạvada attributed (Aupadika) only.

The Vedanta, therefore, in its Shakta presentment says, that the Noumenon is knowable and known, for it is the inner Self, which is not an unconscious principle but Being-Consciousness, which, as above explained, is not conditioned or concrete, but is the absolute Self-identity. Nothing can be more intimately known than the Self. The objective side of knowledge is conditioned because of the nature of its organs which, whether mental or material, are conditioned. Sensation, perception, conception, intuition are but different modes in which the one Consciousness manifests itself, the differences being determined by the variety of condition and form of the different organs of knowledge through which consciousness manifests. There is thus a great difference between the Agnostic and the Vedantist. The former, as for instance Herbert Spencer, says that the Absolute cannot be known because nothing can be predicated of it. Whereas the Vedantin when he says, that It cannot be known (in the ordinary sense) means that this is because It is knowledge itself. Our ordinary experience does not know a consciousness of pure being without difference. But, though it cannot be pictured, it may be apprehended. It cannot be thought because it is Pure Knowledge itself. It is that state which is realised only in Samadhi but is apprehended indirectly as the Unity which underlies and sustains all forms of changing finite experience.

What, lastly, is Life? The underlying substance is Being-in-itself. Life is a manifestation of such Being. If by Life we understand life in form, then the ultimate substance is not that; for it is formless. But in a supreme sense it is Life; for it is Eternal Life whence all life in form proceeds. It is not dead Being. If it were It could not produce Life. The Great Mother is Life; both the life of Her children and the Life of their lives. Nor does She produce what is without life or potency of life. What is in the cause is in the effect. Some Western Scientists have spoken of the "Origin of Life," and have sought to find it. It is a futile quest, for Life as such has no origin though life in form has. We cannot discover the beginnings of that which is essentially eternal. The question is vitiated by the false assumption that there is anything dead in the sense that it is wholly devoid of Life or potency of Life. There is no such thing.

The whole world is a living manifestation of the source of all life which is Absolute Being. It is sometimes made a reproach against Hinduism that it knows not a "living God". What is meant I cannot say. For it is certain that it does not worship a "dead God," whatever such may be. Perhaps by "living" is meant "Personal". If so, the charge is again ill-founded. Ishvara and Ishvari are Rulers in whom all personalities and personality itself are. But in their ground they are beyond all manifestation, that is limitation which personality, as we understand it, involves. Man, the animal and the plant alone, it is true, exhibit certain phenomena which are commonly called vital. What exhibits such phenomena, we have commonly called "living".

But it does not follow that what does not exhibit the phenomena which belong to our definition of life is itself altogether "dead". We may have to revise our definition, as in fact we are commencing to do. Until recently it was commonly assumed that matter was of two kinds: inorganic or "dead," and organic or "living". The mineral was "dead," the vegetable, animal and man were endowed with "life". But these living forms are compounded of so-called "dead" matter. How then, is it possible that there is life in the organic kingdom the parts of which are ultimately compounded of "dead" matter? This necessarily started the futile quest for the "origin of life". Life can only come from life: not from death.

The greatest errors arise from the making of false partitions in nature which do not exist. We make these imaginary partitions and then vainly attempt to surmount them. There are no absolute partitions or gulfs. All is continuous, even if we cannot at present establish in each case the connection. That there should be such gulfs is unthinkable to any one who has even in small degree grasped the notion of the unity of things. There is a complete connected chain in the hierarchy of existence, from the lowest forms of apparently inert (but now held to be moving) matter, through the vegetable, animal, human worlds; and then through such Devatas as are superhuman intelligences up to the Brahman. From the latter to a blade of grass (says the Shastra) all are one.

Western scientific notions have, however, in recent years undergone a radical evolution as regards the underlying unity of substance, destructive of the hitherto accepted notions of the discontinuity of matter and its organisation. The division of nature into the animal, vegetable and mineral kingdoms is still regarded as of practical use; but it is now recognised that no such clear line of demarcation exists between them as has hitherto been supposed in the West. Between each of nature's types there are said to be innumerable transitions. The notion of inert, "dead" matter, the result of superficial observation, has given way upon the revelation of the activities at work under this apparent inertia—forces which endow "brute substance" with many of the characteristics of living beings. It is no longer possible to dogmatically affirm where the inorganic kingdom ends and "life" begins. It must be rather asserted that many phenomena, hitherto considered characteristic of "life," belong to "inert matter," composed of molecules and atoms, as "animated matter" is of cells and micellae. It has been found that so-called "inert matter," possesses an extraordinary power of organisation, and is not only capable of apparently imitating the forms of "living" matter, but presents in a certain degree the same functions and properties.

Sentiency is a characteristic of all forms of Existence. Physiologists measure the sensibility of a being by the degree of excitement necessary to produce in it a reaction. Of this it has been said (Le Bon *Evolution of Matter,* 250), "This sensibility of matter, so contrary to what popular observation seems to indicate, is becoming more and more familiar to physicists. This is why such an expression as the "life of matter," utterly meaningless twenty-five years ago has come into common use.

The study of mere matter yields ever-increasing proofs that it has properties which were formerly deemed the exclusive appanage of living beings." Life exists throughout, but manifests in various ways. The arbitrary division which has been drawn between "dead" and "living" matter has no existence in fact, and speculations as to the origin of "life" are vitiated by the assumption that there is anything which exists without it, however much its presence may be veiled from us. Western science would thus appear to be moving to the conclusion that there is no "dead" matter, but that life exists everywhere, not merely in that in which, as in "organic matter," it is to us plainly and clearly expressed, but also in the ultimate "inorganic" atoms of which it is composed—atoms which, in fact, have their organisations as have the beings which they go to build—and that all, to the minutest particle, is vibrating with unending Energy (Tejas). (Author's *World as Power).* Manifested life is

Prana, a form of Kriya Shakti in, and evolved from, the Linga Sharira, itself born of Prakriti. Prana or the vital principle has been well defined *(Hindu Realism,* by J. C. Chatterji) to be, "the special relation of the Atma with a certain form of matter which, by this relation, the Atma *organises* and builds up as a means of having experience." This special relation constitutes the individual Prana in the individual body. Just as in the West, "life" is a term commonly used of organised body only, so also is the term Prana used in the East.

It is the technical name given to the phenomena, called "vital," exhibited by such bodies, the source of which is the Brahman Itself. The individual Prana is limited to the particular body which it vitalises and is a manifestation in all breathing creatures (Prani), of the creative and sustaining activity of the Brahman. All beings exist so long as the Prana is in the body. It is as the Kaushitaki Upanishad says, "the life duration of all". The cosmic all-pervading Prana is the collectivity of all Pranas and is the Brahman as the source of the individual Prana. On the physical plane, Prana manifests as breath through inspiration, "Sa" or Shakti and expiration, "Ha" or Shiva. So the *Niruttara Tantra* (Chapter IV) says: "By Hamkara it goes out and by Sakara it comes in again. A Jiva always recites the Supreme Mantra Hamsa."

Hang-karena bahir yati sah-karena vishet punah
Hangesti paramam mantram jivo japati sarvada.

Breathing is itself the Ajapa Mantra. Prana is thus Shakti as the universally pervading source of life, organising itself as matter into what we call living forms. When the Prana goes, the organism which it holds together disintegrates. Nevertheless each of the atoms which remain has a life of its own, existing as such separately from the life of the organised body of which they formed a part; just as each of the cells of the living body has a life of its own. The gross outer body is heterogeneous (Paricchinna) or made up of distinct or well-defined parts.

But the Pranamaya Self which lies within the Annamaya Self is a homogeneous undivided whole (Sadharana) permeating the whole physical body (Sarvapindavyapin). It is not cut off into distinct regions (Asadharana) as is the Pinda or mircrocosmic physical body. Unlike the latter it has no specialised organs each discharging a specific function. It is a homogeneous unity (Sadharana), present in every part of the body which it ensouls as its inner vital Self. Vayu, as universal vital activity, on entry into each body, manifests itself in ten different ways.

It is the one Prana, though different names are given according to its functions, of which the five chief are Appropriation (Prana), Rejection (Apana), Assimilation (Samana), Distribution (Vyana), and that vital function (Udana) which is connected with self-expression in speech. Prana in its general sense represents the involuntary reflex action of the organism; just as the Indriyas are one aspect of its voluntary activity. Breathing is a manifestation of the Cosmic Rhythm to which the whole universe moves and according to which it appears and disappears. The life of Brahma is the duration of the outgoing breath (Nisvasa) of Kala.

The Samkhya rejecting the Lokayata notion that Vayu is a mere biomechanical force or mechanical motion resulting from such a Vayu, holds, on the principle of the economy of categories, that life is a resultant of the various concurrent activities of other principles or forces in the organism. This, again, the Vedantists deny, holding that it is a separate, independent principle and material form assumed through Maya by the one Consciousness. In either case, it is an unconscious force, since everything which is not the Atma or Purusha, is, according to Mayavada and Samkhya, unconscious, or, in Western parlance, material (Jada).

If we apply Shakta principles, then Prana is a name of the general Shakti displaying itself in the organisation of matter and the vital phenomena which bodies, when organised, exhibit. Manifest Shakti is vitality, which is a limited concrete display in forms of Her own formless Being or Sat. All Shakti is Jnana, Iccha, Kriya, and in its form as Prakriti, the Gunas Sattva, Rajas, Tamas. She desires, impelled by Her nature (Iccha), to build up forms; sees how it should be done (Jnana); and then does it (Kriya). The most Tamasic form of Kriya is the apparently mechanical energy displayed in material bodies. But this is itself the product of Her Activity and not the cause of it. Ultimately then Prana, like everything else, is consciousness which, as Shakti, limits Itself in form which it first creates and sustains; then builds up into other more elaborate forms and again sustains until their life-period is run.

All creation and maintenance is a limiting power, with the appearance of unconsciousness, in so far as, and to the degree that, it confines the boundless Being-Consciousness-Bliss; yet that Power is nothing but Consciousness negating and limiting itself. The Great Mother (Sri Mata) limits Her infinite being in and as the universe and maintains it. In so far as the form and its life is a limited thing, it is apparently unconscious, for consciousness is thereby limited. At each moment there is creation, but we call the first appearance creation (Srishti), and its continuance, through the agency of Prana, maintenance (Sthiti). But both that which is apparently limited and that whose operation has that effect is Being-Consciousness. Prana Vayu is the self-begotten but limited manifestation of the eternal Life. It is called Vayu (Va—to move) because it courses throughout the whole universe. Invisible in itself yet its operations are manifest. For it determines the birth, growth, and decay of all animated organisms and as such receives the homage of all created Being. For it is the Pranarupi Atma, the Prana Shakti.

For those by whom inorganic matter was considered to be "dead" or lifeless, it followed that it could have no Feeling-Consciousness, since the latter was deemed to be an attribute of life. Further, consciousness was denied because it was, and is indeed now, commonly assumed that every conscious experience pre-supposes a subject, conscious of being such, attending to an object. As Professor P. Mukhyopadhyaya *(Approaches to Truth)* has well pointed out, consciousness was identified with intelligence or understanding—that is with directed consciousness; so that where no direction or form is discernible, Western thinkers have been apt to imagine that consciousness as such has also ceased. To their pragmatic eye consciousness is always particular having a particular direction and form.

According, however, to Indian views, there are three states of consciousness: (1) a supramental supreme consciousness dissociated from mind. This is the Paramatma Cit which is the basis of all existence, whether organic or inorganic, and of thought; of which the Shruti says, "know that which does not think by the mind and by which the mind itself is thought." These are then two main manifested states of consciousness: (2) consciousness associated with mind in organic matter working through its vehicles of mind and matter; (3) consciousness associated with and almost entirely veiled by inorganic gross matter (Bhuta) only; such as the muffled consciousness, evidenced by its response to external stimuli, as shown in the experiments with which Sir Jagadish Bose's name is associated.

Where are we to draw the lowest limit of sensation; and if a limit be assigned, why there? As Dr. Ernst Mach has pointed out (*Analysis of Sensations*, 243) the question is natural enough if we start from the commonly current physical conception. It is, of course, not asserted that inorganic matter is conscious to itself in the way that the higher organised life is. The response, however, which it makes to stimuli is evidence that consciousness is there, though it lies heavily veiled in and imprisoned by it. Inorganic matter displays it in the form of that seed or rudiment of sentiency which enlarging into the simple pulses of feeling of the lowest degrees of organised life, at length emerges in the developed self-conscious sensations of human life.

Owing to imperfect scientific knowledge, the first of these aspects was not in antiquity capable of physical proof in the same way or to the same extent, as Modern Science with its delicate instruments have made possible. Starting, however, from the revealed and intuitionally held truth that all was Brahman, the conclusion necessarily followed. All Bhuta is composed of the three Gunas or factors of Prakriti or the psycho-physical potentials. It is the Sattva or Principle of Presentation of Consciousness in gross matter (almost entirely suppressed by Tamas or the Principle of Veiling of Consciousness though it be) which manifests the phenomena of sensibility observed in matter. In short, nature, it has been well said, knows no sharp boundaries or yawning gulfs, though we may ignore the subtle connecting links between things. There is no break in continuity. Being and Consciousness are co-extensive. Consciousness is not limited to those centres in the Ether of consciousness which are called organised bodies. But just as life is differently expressed in the mineral and in man, so is Consciousness which many have been apt to think exists in the developed animal and even in man only.

Consciousness (Cit-Shakti) exists in all the hierarchy of Being, and is, in fact, Being. It is, however, in all bodies veiled by its power or Maya-Shakti which is composed of the three Gunas. In inorganic matter, owing to the predominance of Tamas, Consciousness is so greatly veiled and the life force is so restrained that we get the appearance of insensibility, inertia and mere mechanical energy.

In organised bodies, the action of Tamas is gradually lessened, so that the members of the universal hierarchy become more and more Sattvik as they ascend in the scale of evolution. Consciousness itself does not change. It remains the same throughout. What does change is, its wrappings, unconscious or apparently so, as they may alternatively be called. This wrapping is Maya and Prakriti with their Gunas. The figure of "wrapping" is apt to illustrate the presentment of Samkhya and Mayavada. From the Shakta aspect we may compare the process to one in which it is assumed that in one aspect there is an unchanging light, in another it is either turned up or turned down as the case may be.

In gross matter the light is so turned down that it is not ordinarily perceptible and even delicate scientific experiment may give rise to contending assertions. When the veiling by Tamas is lessened in organic life, and the Jiva is thus less bound in matter, the same Consciousness (for there is no other) which previously manifested as, what seems to us, a mere mechanical reaction, manifests in its freer environment in that sensation which we associate with consciousness as popularly understood. Shakti, who ever negates Herself as Maya-Shakti, more and more reveals Herself as Cit-Shakti. There is thus a progressive *release* of Consciousness from the bonds of matter, until it attains complete freedom or liberation (Moksha) when the Atma is Itself (Atma Svarupi) or Pure Consciousness. At this point, the same Shakti, who had operated as Maya, is Herself Consciousness (Cidrupini).

According to the Hindu books, plants have a sort of dormant Consciousness, and are capable of pleasure and pain. Cakrapani says in the Bhanumati that the Consciousness of plants is a kind of stupefied, darkened, or comatose Consciousness. Udayana also says that plants have a dormant Consciousness which is very dull. The differences between plant and animal life have always been regarded by the Hindus as being one not of kind, but of degree. And this principle may be applied throughout. Life and Consciousness is not a product of evolution.

The latter merely manifests it. Manu speaks of plants as being creatures enveloped by darkness caused by past deeds having, however, an internal Consciousness and a capacity for pleasure and pain. And, in the *Mahabharata,* Bhrigu says to Bharadhvaja that plants possess the various senses, for they are affected by heat, sounds, vision (whereby, for instance, the creeper pursues its path to the light), odours and the water which they taste. I may refer also to such stories as that of the Yamalarjunavriksha of the Srimad Bhagavata mentioned in Professor Brajendra Nath Seal's learned work, *The Positive Sciences of the Ancient Hindus,* and Professor S. N. Das Gupta's scholarly paper on Parinama to which I am indebted for these instances.

Man is said to have passed through all the lower states of Consciousness and is capable of reaching the highest through Yoga. The Jiva attains birth as man after having been, it is said, born 84 lakhs (84,000,000) of times as plants (Vrikshadi), aquatic animals (Jalayoni), insects and the like (Krimi), birds (Pakshi), beasts (Pashvadi), and monkeys (Vanar). He then is born 2 lakhs of times (2,000,000) in the inferior species of humanity, and then gradually attains a better and better birth until he is liberated from all the bonds of matter. The exact number of each kind of birth is in 20, 9, 11, 10, 30 and *4* lakhs, respectively—84 lakhs. As pointed out by Mahamahopadhyaya

Chandrakanta Tarkalankara Lectures on "Hindu Philosophy" (5th year, p. 227, Lecture VII), pre-appearance in monkey form is not a Western theory only.

The Consciousness which manifests in him is not altogether a new creation, but an unfolding of that which has ever existed in the elements of which he is composed, and in the Vegetable and Animal through which prior to his human birth he has passed. In him, however, matter is so re-arranged and organised as to permit of the fullest rnanifestation which has hitherto existed of the underlying Cit. Man's is the birth so "difficult of attainment" (Durlabha). This is an oft-repeated statement of Shastra in order that he should avail himself of the opportunities which Evolution has brought him. If he does not, he falls back, and may do so without limit, into gross matter again, passing intermediately through the Hells of suffering. Western writers in general, describe such a descent as unscientific. How, they ask, can a man's Consciousness reside in an animal or plant'? The correct answer (whatever be popular belief) is that it does not. When man sinks again into an animal he ceases to be a man.

He does not continue to be both man and animal. His consciousness is an animal consciousness and not a human consciousness. It is a, childish view which regards such a case as being the imprisonment of a man in an animal body. If he can go up he can also go down. The soul or subtle body is not a fixed but an evolving thing. Only Spirit (Cit) is eternal and unchanged. In man, the revealing constituent of Prakriti Shakti (Sattvaguna) commences to more fully develop, and his consciousness is fully aware of the objective world and his own Ego, and displays itself in all those functions of it which are called his faculties. We here reach the world of ideas, but these are a superstructure on consciousness and not its foundation or basis. Man's consciousness is still, however, veiled by Maya-Shakti.

With the greater predominance of Sattvaguna in man, consciousness becomes more and more divine, until he is altogether freed of the bonds of Maya, and the Jiva Consciousness expands into the pure Brahman Consciousness.

Thus life and Consciousness exist throughout. All is living. All is Consciousness. In the world of gross matter they seem to disappear, being almost suppressed by the veil of Maya-Shakti's Tamoguna. As however ascent is made, they are less and less veiled, and True Consciousness is at length realised in Samadhi and Moksha. Cit-Shakti and Maya-Shakti exist inseparable throughout the whole universe. There is therefore according to the principles of the Shakta Shastra not a particle of matter which is without life and consciousness variously displaced or concealed though they be. Manifest Maya-Shakti is the universe in which Cit-Shakti *is* the changeless Spirit. Unmanifest Maya-Shakti is Consciousness (Cidrupini).

There are many persons who think that they have disposed of a doctrine when they have given it an opprobrious, or what they think to be an opprobrious, name. And so they dub all this "Animism," which the reader of Census Reports associates with primitive and savage tribes. There are some people who are frightened by names. It is not names but facts which should touch us. Certainly "Animism" is in some respects an incorrect and childlike way of putting the matter.

It is, however, an imperfect presentment of a central truth which has been held by some of the profoundest thinkers in the world, even in an age in which we are apt to think to be superior to all others. Primitive man in his simplicity made the discovery of several such truths. And so it has been well said that the simple savage and the child who regard all existence as akin to their own, living and feeling like himself, have, notwithstanding their errors, more truly felt the pulse of being, than the civilised man of culture. How essentially stupid some of the latter can be needs no proof. For the process of civilisation being one of abstraction, they are less removed from the concrete fact than he is. Hence their errors which seem the more contorted due to the mass of useless verbiage in which they are expressed. And yet, as extremes meet, so having passed through our present condition, we may regain the truths perceived by the simple, not only through formal worship but by that which consists of the pursuit of all knowledge and science, when once the husk of all material thinking is cast aside. For him, who sees the Mother in all things, all scientific research is wonder and worship.

So Gratry said that the *calculus* of Newton and Leibnitz was a supralogical procedure, and that geometric induction is essentially a *process of prayer,* by which he evidently meant an appeal from the finite mind to the Infinite, for light on finite concerns. The seeker looks upon not mere mechanical movements of so-called "dead" matter, but the wondrous play of Her Whose form all matter is. As She thus reveals Herself She induces in him a passionate exaltation and that sense of security which is only gained as approach is made to the Central Heart of things. For, as the Upanishad says, "He only fears who sees duality". Some day may be, when one who unites in himself the scientific ardor of the West and the all-embracing religious feeling of India will create another and a modern Candi, with its multiple salutations to the sovereign World-Mother (Namastasyai namo namah). Such an one, seeing the changing marvels of Her world-play, will exclaim with the Yoginihridaya Tantra, "I salute Her the Samvid Kala who shines in the form of Space, Time and all Objects therein."

Deshakalapadarthatma yad yad vastu yatha yatha,
Tattadrupena ya bhati tam shraye samvidam kalam

This is, however, not mere Nature-worship as it is generally understood in the West, or the worship of Force as Keshub Chunder Sen took the Shakta doctrine to be. All things exist in the Supreme who in Itself infinitely transcends all finite forms. It is the worship of God as the Mother-Creatrix who manifests in the form of all things which are, as it were, but an atom of dust on the Feet of Her who is Infinite Being (Sat), Experience (Cit), Love (Ananda) and Power (Shakti). As Philibert Commerson said: "La vie d'un naturaliste est, je L'ose dire, une adoration presque perpetuelle."

In my paper *Shakti and Maya* contrasted the three different concepts of the Primal Energy as Prakriti, Maya and Shakti of Samkhya, Vedanta and the Agama respectively. I will not, therefore, repeat myself but will only summarise conclusions here. In the first place, there are features common to all three concepts. Hitherto, greater pains have been taken to show the differences between the Darshanas than to co-ordinate them systematically, by regarding their points of agreement or as regard apparent disagreement, their viewpoint. It has been said that Truth cannot be found in such a country as India, in which, there are six systems of philosophy disputing with one another, and where even in one system alone, there is a conflict between Dvaita, Vishishtadvaita and Advaita. One might suppose from such a criticism that all in Europe were of one mind, or that al least the Christian Community was agreed, instead of being split up, as it is, into hundreds of sects. An American humorist observed with truth that there was a good deal of human nature in man everywhere.

Of course there is difference which, as the Radd-ul-Muhtar says, is also the gift of God. This is not to deny that Truth is only one. It is merely to recognise that whilst Truth is one, the nature and capacities of those who seek it, or claim to possess it, vary. To use a common metaphor, the same white light which passes through varicolored glass takes on its various colours. All cannot apprehend the truth to the same extent or in the same way. Hence the sensible Indian doctrine of competency or Adhikara. In the Christian Gospel it is also said, "Throw not your pearls before swine lest they trample upon them and then rend you." What can be given to any man is only what he can receive.

The Six Philosophies represent differing standards according to the manner and to the extent to which the one Truth may be apprehended. Each standard goes a step beyond the last, sharing, however, with it certain notions in common. As regards the present matter, all these systems start with the fact that there is Spirit and Mind, Matter, Consciousness and Unconsciousness, apparent or real. Samkhya, Vedanta and the Shakta Agama called the first Purusha, Brahman, Shiva; and the second Prakriti, Maya, Shakti respectively. All agree that it is from the association together of these two Principles that the universe arises and that such association is the universe. All, again, agree that one Principle, namely, the first, is infinite, formless consciousness, and the second is a *finitising* principle which makes forms. Thirdly, all regard this last as a veiling principle, that is, one which veils consciousness; and hold that it is eternal, all-pervading, existing now as seed (Mula-prakriti, Avyakta) and now as fruit (Vikriti), composed of the Gunas Sattva, Rajas and Tamas (Principles of presentation of Consciousness, Action, and Veiling of Consciousness respectively); unperceivable except through its effects. In all, it is the Natural Principle, the material cause of the material universe.

The word Prakriti has been said to be derived from the root *"Kri,"* and the affix *"Ktin,"* which is added to express Bhava or the abstract idea, and sometimes the Karma or object of the action, corresponding with the Greek affix *Sis. Ktin* inflected in the nominative becomes *tis.* Prakriti, therefore, has been said to correspond with *Phusis* (Nature) of the Greeks. In all three systems, therefore, it is, as the "natural," contrasted with the "spiritual" aspect of things.

The first main point of difference is between Samkhya, on the one hand, and the Advaita Vedanta, whether as interpreted by Shamkara or taught by the Shaiva-Shakta Tantra on the other. Classical Samkhya is a dualistic system, whereas the other two are non-dualistic. The classical Samkhya posits a plurality of Atmans representing the formless consciousness, with one unconscious Prakriti which is formative activity. Prakriti is thus a real independent principle. Vedantic monism does not altogether discard these two principles, but says that they cannot exist as two independent Realities. There is only one Brahman. The two categories of Samkhya, Purusha and Prakriti are reduced to one Reality, the Brahman; otherwise the Vakya, "All this is verily Brahman" (Sarvam khalvidam Brahma), is falsified.

But how is this effected? It is on this point that Mayavada of Shamkara and the Advaita of Shaiva-Shakta Agama differ. Both systems agree that Brahman has two aspects in one of which It is transcendent and in another creative and immanent. According to Shamkara, Brahman is in one aspect Ishvara associated with, and in another one dissociated from Maya which, in his system, occupies the place of the Samkhyan

Prakriti, to which it is (save as to reality and independence) similar. What is Maya P It is not a real independent Principle like the Samkhyan Prakriti. Then is it Brahman or not'? According to Shamkara, it is an unthinkable, alogical, unexplainable (Anirvacantia) mystery.

It is an eternal falsity (Mithyabhuta sanatani), owing what false appearance of reality it possesses to the Brahman, with which in one aspect it is associated. It is not real for there is only one such. It cannot, however, be said to be ur.real for it is the cause of and is empirical experience. It is something which is neither real (Sat) nor unreal (Asat), nor partly real and partly unreal (Sadasat), and which though not forming part of Brahman, and therefore not Brahman, is yet, though not a second reality, inseparably associated and sheltering with (Maya Brahmashrita) Brahman in Its Ishvara aspect. Like the Samkhyan Prakriti, Maya (whatever it be) is in the nature of an unconscious principle. The universe appears by the reflection of consciousness (Purusha, Brahman) on unconsciousness (Prakriti, Maya). In this way the unconscious is made to appear conscious. This is Cidabhasa.

Maya is illusive and so is Shamkara's definition of it. Further, though Maya is not a second reality, but a mysterious something of which neither reality nor unreality can be affirmed, the fact of positing it at all in this form gives to Shamkara's doctrine a tinge of dualism from which the Shakta doctrine is free. For, it is to be noted that notwithstanding that Maya is a falsity, it is not, according to Shamkara, a mere negation or want of something (Abhava), but a positive entity (Bhavarupam ajnanam), that is in the nature of a Power which veils (Acchadaka) consciousness, as Prakriti does in the case of Purusha.

Shamkara's system, on the other hand, has this advantage from a monistic standpoint, that whilst he, like the Shakta, posits the doctrine of aspects saying that in one aspect the Brahman is associated with Maya (Ishvara), and in another it is not (Parabrahman; yet in neither aspect does his Brahman change. Whereas, according to Shakta doctrine, Shiva does, in one aspect, that is as Shakti, change.

Whilst then Shamkara's teaching is consistent with the changelessness of Brahman, he is not so successful in establishing the saying,. "All this is Brahman". The position is reversed as regards Shaiva-Shakta Darshana which puts forth its doctrine of Maya-Shakti with greater simplicity. Shakta doctrine takes the saying, "All this is Brahman" (the realisation of which, as the *Mahanirvana Tantra* states, is the aim and end of Kulacara) in its literal sense. "This" is the universe. Then the universe is Brahman. But Brahman is Consciousness. Then the universe is really That. But in what way P Shamkara says that what we sense with our senses is Maya, which is practically something, but in a real sense nothing; which yet appears to be something because it is associated with the Brahman which alone is Real.

Its appearance of independent reality is thus borrowed and is in this sense said to be "illusory". When, therefore, we say, "All this is Brahman"—according to Shamkara, this means that what is at the back of that which we see is Brahman; the rest or appearance is Maya. Again, according to Shamkara, man is spirit (Atma) vestured in the Mayik falsities of mind and matter. He, accordingly, can then only establish the unity of Ishvara and Jiva by eliminating from the first Maya, and from the second Avidya; when Brahman is left as a common denominator. The Shakta, however, eliminates nothing. For him, in the strictest sense, "All is Brahman." For him, man's Spirit (Atma) is Shiva. His mind and body are Shakti. But Shiva and Shakti are one. Paramatma is Shiva-Shakti in undistinguishable union. Jivatma is Shiva-Shakti in that state in which the Self is distinguished from the not-Self. Man, therefore, according to the Shakta Tantra, is not Spirit seemingly clothed by a non-Brahman falsity, but Spirit covering Itself with its own power or Maya-Shakti. All is Shakti whether as Cit-Shakti or Maya-Shakti. When, therefore, the Shakta Tantric says, "All this is Brahman," he means it literally. "This," here means Brahman as Shakti, as Maya-Shakti, and Cit-Shakti.

Shiva as Parabrahman is Shiva-Shakti in that state when Shakti is not operating and in which She is Herself, that is, pure consciousness (Cidrupini). Shiva as Ishvara is Shiva-Shakti in that state in which Shiva, associated with Maya-Shakti, is the source of movement and change; Shiva-Shakti as Jiva is the state produced by such action which is subject to Maya, from which Ishvara, the Mayin is free.

The creative Shakti is therefore changeless Cit-Shakti and changing Maya-Shakti. Yet the One Shakti must never be conceived as existing apart from, or without the other, for they are only twin aspects of the fundamental Substance (Paravastu). Vimarsha-Shakti (*Kamakalavilasa,* 3rd Edition, 1961, Verses 1-4) as Maya-Shakti produces the forms in which Spirit as Cit-Shakti inheres and which it illuminates (Prakasha). But Maya-Shakti is not unconscious. How can it be; for it is Shakti and one with Cit-Shakti. All Shakti is and must be Consciousness. There is no unconscious Maya which is not Brahman and yet not separate from Brahman. Brahman alone is and exists, whether as Cit or as manifestation of Maya. All is Consciousness, as the so-called "New Thought" of the West also affirms.

But surely, it will be said, there is an unconscious element in things. How is this accounted for if there be no unconscious Maya? It is conscious Shakti veiling Herself and so appearing as limited consciousness. In other words, whilst Shamkara says mind and matter are in themselves unconscious but appear to be conscious through Cidabhasa, the Shakta Agama reverses the position, and says that they are in themselves, that is in their ground, conscious, for they are at base Cit; but they yet appear to be unconscious, or more strictly limited consciousness, by the veiling power of Consciousness Itself as Maya-Shakti. This being so, there is no need for Cidabhasa which assumes, as it were, two things, the Brahman, and unconscious Maya in which the former reflects itself.

Though some of the Shastras do speak of a reflection, Pratibimba is between Shiva and Shakti. Brahman is Maya-Shakti in that aspect in which it negates itself, for it is the function of Shakti to negate (Nishedhavyapararupa shaktih), as it is said by Yoga-Raja or Yoga-Muni (as he is also called) in his commentary on Abhinava Gupta's Paramarthasara. In the Shakta Tantras, it is a common saying of Shiva to Devi,

"There is no difference between Me and Thee." Whilst Shamkara's Ishvara is associated with the unconscious Maya, the Shaiva Shakta's Ishvara is never associated with anything but Himself, that is as Maya-Shakti.

Whether this doctrine be accepted as the final solution of things or not, it is both great and powerful. It is great because the whole world is seen in glory according to the strictest monism as the manifestation of Him and Her. The mind is not distracted and kept from the realisation of unity, by the notion of any unconscious Maya which is not Brahman nor yet separate from It. Next, this doctrine accommodates itself to Western scientific monism, so far as the latter goes, adding to it however a religious and metaphysical basis; infusing it with the spirit of devotion. It is powerful because its standpoint is the 'here' and 'now,' and not the transcendental *Siddhi* standpoint of which most men know nothing and cannot, outside Samadhi, realise.

It assumes the reality of the world which to us is real. It allows the mind to work in its natural channel. It does not ask it to deny what goes against the grain of its constitution to deny. It is, again, powerful because we stand firmly planted on a basis which is real and natural to us. From the practical viewpoint, it does not ask man to eschew and flee from the world in the spirit of asceticism; a course repugnant to a large number of modern minds, not only because mere asceticism often involves what it thinks to be a futile self-denial; but because that mind is waking to the truth that all is one; that if so, to deny the world is in a sense to deny an aspect of That which is both Being and Becoming.

It thinks also that whilst some natures are naturally ascetic, to attempt ascetic treatment in the case of most is to contort the natural being, and to intensify the very evils which asceticism seeks to avoid. Not one man in many thousands has true Vairagya or detachment from the world. Most are thoroughly even glued to it. Again, there are many minds which are puzzled and confused by Mayavada; and which, therefore, falsely interpret it,—may be to their harm. These men, Mayavada, or rather their misunderstanding of it, weakens or destroys. Their grip on themselves and the world is in any case enfeebled. They become intellectual and moral derelicts who are neither on the path of power nor of renunciation, and who have neither the strength to follow worldly life, nor to truly abandon it. It is not necessary, however, to renounce when all is seen to be Her. And, when all is so seen, then the spiritual illumination which transfuses all thoughts and acts makes them noble and pure. It is impossible for a man, who in whatever sense truly sees God in all things, to err. If he does so, it is because his vision is not fully strong and pure; and to this extent scope is afforded to error. But given perfect spiritual eyesight then all "this" is pure. For, as the Greeks profoundly said, "panta kathara tois katharois," "To the pure all things are pure."

The Shakta doctrine is thus one which has not only grandeur but is greatly pragmatic and of excelling worth. It has always been to me a surprise that its value should not have been rightly appreciated. I can only suppose that its neglect is due to the fact that is the doctrine of the Shakta Tantras. That fact has been enough to warrant its rejection, or at least a refusal to examine it. Like all practical doctrines, it is also intensely positive. There are none of those negations which weaken and which annoy those who, as the vital Western mind does, feel themselves to be strong and living in an atmosphere of might and power. For power is a glorious thing. What is wanted is only the sense that all Power is of God and is God, and that Bhava or feeling which interprets all thoughts and acts and their objects in terms of the Divine, and which sees God in and as all things.

Those who truly do so will exercise power not only without wrong, but with that compassion (Karuna) for all beings which is so beautiful a feature of the Buddha of northern and Tantrik Buddhism. For in them Shakti Herself has descended. This is Shaktipata, as it is technically called in the Tantra Shastra; the descent of Shakti which Western theology calls the grace of God. But grace is truly not some exterior thing, though we may pictorially think of it as 'streaming' from above below. Atma neither comes nor goes. To be in grace is that state in which man commences to realise himself as Shiva-Shakti. His power is, to use a Western phrase, "converted". It is turned from the husk of mere outwardness and of limited self-seeking, to that inner Reality which is the great Self which, at base, he (in this doctrine) is.

The principles of Shakta doctrine, which will vary according to race, are a regenerating doctrine, giving strength where there is weakness, and, where strength exists, directing it to right ends. "Shivo' ham," "I am Shiva," "Sha' ham," "I am She (the Devi)," the Tantras say. The Western may call It by some other name. Some call It this and some that, as the Veda says. "I am He," "I am She," "I am It," matters not to the Shakta so long as man identifies himself with the 'Oversoul,' and thus harmonises himself with its Being, with Dharmic actions (as it manifests in the world) and therefore necessarily with Its true ends.

In its complete form the Shakta doctrine is monistic. But to those to whom monism makes no appeal, the Shakta will say that by adopting its spirit, so far as the forms of their belief and worship allow, they will experience a reflection of the joy and strength of those who truly live because they worship Her who is Eternal life—the Mother who is seated on the couch of Shivas (Mahapreta), in the Isle of Gems (Manidvipa), in the "Ocean of Nectar," which is all Being-Consciousness and Bliss.

This is the pearl which those who have churned the ocean of Tantra discover. That pearl is there in an Indian shell. There is a beautiful nacre on the inner shell which is the Mother of Pearl. Outside, the shell is naturally rough and coarse, and bears the accretions of weed and parasite and of things of all kinds which exist, good or bad as we call them, in the ocean of existence (Samsara).

The Scripture leads man to remove these accretions, and to pass within through the crust, gross, though not on that account only, bad; for there is a gross (Sthula) and subtle (Sukshma) aspect of worship. Finally it leads man to seek to see the Mother of Pearl and lastly the Pearl which, enclosed therein, shines with the brilliant yet soft light which is that of the Moon-Cit (Cicchandra) Itself.

Matter and Consciousness

The subject of my lecture today is Consciousness or Cit, and Matter or Unconsciousness, that is, Acit; the unchanging formlessness and the changing forms. According to Shakta Advaitavada, man is Consciousness-Unconsciousness or Cit-Acit; being Cit-Shakti as regards his Antaratma, and the particularised Maya-Shakti as to his material vehicles of mind and body. The reason that I have selected this subject, amongst the many others on which I might have addressed you, is that these two ideas are the key concepts of Indian Philosophy and religion. If they are fully understood both as to their definition and relations, then, all is understood so far as intellect can make such matters intelligible to us; if they are not understood then nothing is properly understood.

Nor are they always understood even by those who profess to know and write on Indian Philosophy. Thus, the work on Vedanta, of an English Orientalist, now in its second edition, describes Cit as the condition of a stone or other inert substance. A more absurd error it is hard to imagine. Those who talk in this way have not learnt the elements of their subject. It is true that you will find in the Shastra, the state of the Yogi described as being like a log (Kashthavat). But this does not mean that his Consciousness is that of a piece of wood; but that he no more perceives the external world than a log of wood does. He does not do so because he has the Samadhi consciousness that is Illumination and true Being itself.

I can to-night only scratch at the surface of a profound subject. To properly expound it would require a series of lectures, and to understand it in its depths, years of thinking thereon. I will look at the matter first from the scientific point of view; secondly, state what those concepts mean in themselves; and thirdly, show how they are related to one another in the Samkhya and the Mayavada and Shaktivada presentments of Vedanta doctrine. The Shaktivada of which I deal to-night may be found in the Tantras. It has been supposed that the Agamas arose at the close of the age of the Upanishads. They are Shastras of the Upasana Kanda dealing with the worship of Saguna Ishvara.

It has been conjectured that they arose partly because of the declining strength of the Vaidika Acara, and partly because of the increasing number of persons within the Hindu fold, who were not competent for the Vaidika Acara, and, for whom some spiritual discipline was necessary. One common feature distinguishes them; namely, their teaching is for all castes and all women. They express the liberal principle that whilst socially differences may exist, the path of religion is open to all, and that spiritual competency and not the external signs of caste determine the position of persons on that path. Ishvara in these Agamas is worshipped in threefold forms as Vishnu, Shiva, Devi. Therefore, the Agamas or Tantras are threefold, Vaishnava, Shaiva and Shakta, such as the Pancaratra Agamas of the first group, the Shaiva Siddhanta (with its 28 Tantras), the Nakulisha Pashupata, and the Kashmirian Trika of the second group; and the alleged division into Kaula, Mishra, Samaya of the third group. I express no opinion on this last division. I merely refer to this matter in order to explain what I mean by the word Agama. The Shaktivada, however, which I contrast with Mayavada today, is taken from the Shakta Agama. By Mayavada I mean Shamkara's exposition of Vedanta.

Now, with reference to the scientific aspect of the subject, I show you that in three main particulars, modern western physics and psychology support Indian philosophy whatever such support may be worth. Indeed, Mr. Lowes Dickinson, in an acute recent analysis of the state of ideas in India, China and Japan observes that the Indian form of religion and philosophy is that which most easily accommodates itself to modern western science. That does not prove it is true, until it is established that the conclusions of western science to which it does conform, are true.

But the fact is of great importance in countering those who have thought that eastern ideas were without rational foundation. It is of equal importance to those two classes who either believe in the ideas of India, or in the particular conclusions of science to which I refer. The three points on this head are firstly, that physicists, by increasing their knowledge of so-called "matter," have been led to doubt its reality, and have dematerialised the atom, and, with it, the entire universe which the various atoms compose. The trinity of matter, ether and electricity out of which science has hitherto attempted to construct the world, has been reduced to a single element—the ether (which is not scientific "matter") in a state of motion.

According to Samkhya, the objective world is composed of Bhutas which derive ultimately from Akasha. I do not say that scientific "ether" is Akasha, which is a concept belonging to a different train of thought. Moreover the sensible is derived from the supersensible Akasha Tanmatra, and is not therefore an ultimate. But it is important to note the agreement in this, that both in East and West, the various forms of gross matter derive from some single substance which is not "matter". Matter is *dematerialised,* and the way is made for the Indian concept of Maya. There is a point at which the mind cannot any longer usefully work outward. Therefore, after the Tanmatra, the mind is turned within to discover their cause in that Egoism which, reaching forth to the world of enjoyment produces sensorial, senses, and objects of sensation.

That the mind and senses are also material has the support of some forms of western philosophy, such as that of Herbert Spencer, for he holds that the Universe, whether physical or psychical, is a play of force which in the case of matter we experience as object. Mind as such is, he says, as much a "material" organ as the brain and outer sense-organs, though they are differing forms of Force. His affirmation that scientific "matter" is an appearance produced by the play of cosmic force, and that mind itself is a product of the same play, is what Samkhya and Vedanta hold. The way again is opened for the concept, Maya. Whilst, however, Spencer and the Agnostic School hold that the Reality behind these phenomena is unknowable, the Vedanta affirms that it is knowable and is Consciousness itself.

This is the Self than which nothing can be more intimately known. Force is blind. We discover consciousness in the Universe. It is reasonable to suppose that if the first cause is of the nature of either Consciousness or Matter, and not of both, it must be of the nature of the former and not of the latter

Unconsciousness or object may be conceived to modify Consciousness, but not to produce Consciousness out of its unconscious Self. According to Indian ideas, Spirit which is the cause of the Universe is pure Consciousness. This is Nishkala Shiva: and, as the Creator, the great Mother or Devi. The existence of pure consciousness in the Indian sense has been decried by some thinkers in the West, where generally to its pragmatic eye, Consciousness is always particular having a particular direction and form.

It assumes this particularity, however, through Maya. We must distinguish between Consciousness as such and modes in consciousness. Consciousness is the unity behind all forms of consciousness, whether sensation, emotion, instinct, will or reason. The claim that Consciousness as such exists can only be verified by spiritual experience. All high mystic experiences, whether in East or West, have been experiences of unity in differing forms and degrees. Even, however, in normal life as well as in abnormal pathological states, we have occasional stretches of experience in which it becomes almost structureless. Secondly, the discovery of the subliminal Consciousness aids Shastric doctrine, in so far as it shows that behind the surface consciousness of which we are ordinarily aware, there is yet another mysterious field in which all its operations grow.

It is the Buddhi which here manifests. Well-established occult powers and phenomena now generally accepted such as telepathy, thought-reading, hypnotism and the like are only explainable on hypotheses which approach more nearly Eastern doctrine than any other theory which has in modern times prevailed in the West. Thirdly, as bearing on this subject, we have now the scientific recognition that from its *materia prima* all forms have evolved; that there is life or its potency in all things: and that there are no breaks in nature. There is the same matter and Consciousness throughout. There is unity of life. There is no such thing as "dead" matter.

The well-known experiments of Dr. Jagadish Bose establish response to stimuli in inorganic matter. This response may be interpreted to indicate the existence of that Sattva Guna which Vedanta and Samkhya affirm to exist in all things organic or inorganic. It is the play of Cit in this Sattva, so muffled in Tamas as not to be recognizable except by delicate scientific experiment, which appears as the so-called "mechanical" response. Consciousness is here veiled and imprisoned by Tamas. Inorganic matter displays it in the form of that seed or rudiment of sentiency which, enlarging into the simple pulses of feeling of the lowest degrees of organised life, at length emerges in the developed self-conscious sensations of human life. Consciousness is throughout the same. What varies is its wrappings. There is, thus, a progressive *release* of Consciousness from gross matter, through plants and animals to man.

This evolution, Indian doctrine has taught in its 84 lakhs of previous births. According to the Hindu books, plants have a dormant consciousness. The *Mahabharata* says that plants can see and thus they reach the light. Such power of vision would have been ridiculed not long ago, but Professor Haberlandt, the well-known botanist, has established that plants possess an organ of vision in the shape of a convex lens on the upper surface of the leaf. The animal consciousness is greater, but seems to display itself almost entirely in the satisfaction of animal's wants. In man, we reach the world of ideas, but these are a superstructure on consciousness, and not its foundation or basis. It is in this modeless basis that the various modes of consciousness with which we are familiar in our waking and dreaming states arise.

The question then arises as to the relation of this principle of Form with Formlessness; the unconscious finite with infinite consciousness. It is noteworthy that in the Thomistic philosophy, Matter, like Prakriti, is the particularising or *finitising* principle. By their definition, however, they are opposed. How then can the two be one?

Samkhya denies that they are one, and says they are two separate independent principles. This, Vedanta in its turn denies for it says that there is in fact only one true Reality, though from the empirical, dualistic standpoint there seem to be two. The question then is asked, Is dualism, pluralism, or monism to be accepted? For the Vedantist the answer of Shruti is that it is the last. But, apart from this, the question is, Does

Shruti record a true experience, and is it the fact that spiritual experience is monistic or dualistic? The answer is, as we can see from history, that all high mystic experiences are experiences of unity in differing forms and degrees.

The question cannot be decided solely by discussion, but by our conclusion as to the conformity of the particular theory held with spiritual experience. But how can we reconcile the unity of pure consciousness with the plurality of unconscious forms which the world of experience gives us? Vedanta gives various intellectual interpretations, though experience alone can solve this question. Shamkara says there is only one Sadvastu, the Brahman.

From a transcendental standpoint, It *is,* and nothing happens. There is, in the state of highest experience (Paramatma), no Ishvara, no creation, no world, no Jiva, no bondage, no liberation. But empirically he must and does admit the world or Maya, which in its seed is the cosmic Samskara, which is the cause of all these notions which from the highest state are rejected. But is it real or unreal? Shamkara says it is neither. It cannot be real, for then there would be two Reals. It is not unreal, for the world is an empirical fact—an experience of its kind, and it proceeds from the Power of Ishvara. In truth, it is unexplainable, and as Sayana says, more wonderful than Cit itself.

But if it is neither Sat nor Asat, then as Maya it is not the Brahman who is Sat. Does it then exist in Pralaya and if so how and where? How can unconsciousness exist in pure consciousness? Shamkara calls it eternal, and says that in Pralaya, Mayasatta is Brahmasatta. At that time, Maya, as the power of the ideating consciousness, and the world, its thought, do not exist: and only the Brahman is. But if so how does the next universe arise on the assumption that there is Pralaya and that there is not with him as Maya the seed of the future universe? A Bija of Maya as Samskara, even though Avyakta (not present to Consciousness), is yet by its terms different from consciousness. To all such questionings, Shamkara would say, they are themselves the product of the Maya of the state in which they are put. This is true, but it is possible to put the matter in a simpler way against which there are not so many objections as may be laid against Mayavada.

It seems to me that Shamkara who combats Samkhya is still much influenced by its notions, and as a result of his doctrine of Maya he has laid himself open to the charge that his doctrine is not Shuddha Advaita. His notion of Maya retains a trace of the Samkhyan notion of separateness, though separateness is in fact denied. In Samkhya, Maya is the real Creatrix under the illumination of Purusha. We find similar notions in Shamkara, who compares Cit to the Ayaskantamani, and denies all liberty of self-determination in the Brahman which, though itself unchanging, is the cause of change. Jnana Kriya is allowed only to Ishvara, a concept which is itself the product of Maya. To some extent the distinctions made are perhaps a matter of words. To some extent particular notions of the Agamas are more practical than those of Shamkara who was a transcendentalist.

The Agama, giving the richest content to the Divine Consciousness, does not deny to it knowledge, but, in its supreme aspect, any dual knowledge; spiritual experience being likened by the Brihadaranyaka Upanishad to the union of man and wife in which duality exists as one and there is neither within nor without. It is this union which is the Divine Lila of Shakti, who is yet all the time one with Her Lord.

The Shakta exposition appears to be both simple and clear. I can only sketch it roughly—having no time for its detail. It is first the purest Advaitavada. What then does it say? It starts with the Shruti, "Sarvam Khalvidam Brahma". Sarvam = world; Brahman= consciousness or Sacchidananda; therefore this world is itself Consciousness.

But we know we are not perfect consciousness. There is an apparent unconsciousness. How then is this explained? The unmanifested Brahman, before all the worlds, is Nirguna Shiva—the Blissful undual consciousness. This is the static aspect of Shiva. This manifests Shakti which is the kinetic aspect of Brahman. Shakti and Shaktiman are one; therefore, Shiva manifests as Shiva-Shakti, who are one and the same. Therefore Shakti is consciousness. But Shakti has two aspects

(Murti), *viz.*, Vidya Shakti or Cit-Shakti, and Avidya Shakti or Maya-Shakti. Both as Shakti (which is the same as Shaktiman) are in themselves conscious. But the difference is that whilst Cit-Shakti is illuminating consciousness, Maya is a Shakti which veils consciousness to itself, and by its wondrous power appears as unconscious. This Maya-Shakti is Consciousness which by its power appears as unconsciousness.

This Maya-Shakti is Triguna Shakti, that is, Shakti composed of the three Gunas. This is Kamakala which is the Trigunatmaka vibhuti. These Gunas are therefore at base nothing but Cit-Shakti. There is no necessity for the Mayavadin's Cidabhasa, that is, the reflection of conscious reality on unconscious unreality, as Mayavada says. All is real except, in the sense that some things endure and are therefore truly real: others pass and in that sense only are not real. All is Brahman. The Antaratma in man is the enduring Cit-Shakti. His apparently unconscious vehicles of mind and body are Brahman as Maya-Shakti, that is, consciousness appearing as unconsciousness by virtue of its inscrutable power. Ishvara is thus the name for Brahman as Shakti which is conjoined Cit-Shakti and Maya-Shakti.

The Mother Devi is Ishvara considered in His feminine aspect (Ishvari) as the Mother and Nourisher of the world. The Jiva or individual self is an Amsha or fragment of that great Shakti: the difference being that whilst Ishvara is Mayavin or the controller of Maya, Jiva is subject to Maya. The World-thinker retains His Supreme undual Consciousness even in creation, but His thought, that is the forms created by His thinking are bound by His Maya that is the forms with which they identify themselves until by the power of the Vidya Shakti in them they are liberated. All is truly Sat—or Brahman. In creation Shiva extends His power, and at Pralaya withdraws it into Himself. In creation, Maya is in itself Consciousness which appears as unconsciousness. Before creation it is as consciousness.

Important practical results follow from the adoption of this view of looking at the world. The latter is the creation of Ishvara. The world is real; being unreal only in the sense that it is a shifting passing thing, whereas Atma as the true Reality endures. Bondage is real, for Bondage is Avidyashakti binding consciousness. Liberation is real for this is the grace of Vidyashakti. Men are each Centres of Power, and if they would achieve success must, according to this Shastra, realise themselves as such, knowing that it is Devata which thinks and acts in, and as, them and that they are the Devata. Their world enjoyment is His, and liberation is His peaceful nature.

The Agamas deal with the development of this Power which is not to be thought of as something without, but as within man's grasp through various forms of Shakti Sadhana. Being in the world and working through the world, the world itself, in the words of the Kularnava Tantra, *becomes the seat of liberation* (Mokshayate Samsara). The Vira or heroic Sadhaka does not shun the world from fear of it. But he holds it in his grasp and wrests from it its secret. Realising it at length as Consciousness the world of matter ceases to be an object of desire. Escaping from the unconscious drifting of a humanity which has not yet realised itself, He is the illumined master of himself, whether developing all his powers, or seeking liberation at his will.

Shakti and Maya

In the Eighth Chapter of the unpublished Sammohana Tantra, it is said that Shamkara manifested on earth in the form of Shamkaracarya, in order to root out Buddhism from India. It compares his disciples and himself to the five Mahapreta (who form the couch on which the Mother of the Worlds rests), and identifies his maths with the Amnayas, namely, the Govardhana in Puri with Purvamnaya (the Sampradaya being Bhogavara), and so on with the rest. Whatever be the claims of Shamkara as destroyer of the great Buddhistic heresy, which owing to its subtlety was the most dangerous antagonist which the Vedanta has ever had, or his claims as expounder of Upanishad from the standpoint of Siddhi, his Mayavada finds no place in the Tantras of the Agamas, for the doctrine and practice is given from the standpoint of Sadhana. This is not to say that the doctrine is explicitly denied.

It is not considered. It is true that in actual fact we often give accommodation to differing theories for which logic can find no living room, but it is obvious that in so far as man is a worshipper he must accept the world-standpoint, if he would not, like Kalidasa, cut from beneath himself the branch of the tree on which he sits. Next, it would be a mistake to overlook the possibility of the so-called "Tantrik" tradition having been fed by ways of thought and practice which were not, in the strict sense of the term, part of the Vaidic cult, or in the line of its descent.

The worship of the Great Mother, the Magna Mater of the Near East, the Adya Shakti of the Shakta Tantras, is in its essentials (as I have elsewhere pointed out) one of the oldest and most widespread religions of the world, and one which in India was possibly, in its origins, independent of the Brahmanic religion as presented to us in the Vaidik Samhitas and Brahmanas. If this be so, it was later on undoubtedly mingled with the Vedanta tradition, so that the Shakta faith of today is a particular presentation of the general Vedantik teaching. This is historical speculation from an outside standpoint. As the Sarvollasa of Sarvanandanatha points out, and as is well-known to all adherents of the Shakta Agamas, Veda in its general sense includes these and other Shastras in what is called the great Shatakoti Samhita.

Whatever be the origins of doctrine (and this should not be altogether overlooked in any proper appreciation of it), I am here concerned with its philosophical aspect, as shown to us today in the teachings and practice of the Shaktas who are followers of the Agama. This teaching occupies in some sense a middle place between the dualism of Samkhya, and Shamkara's ultra-monistic interpretation of Vedanta to which, unless otherwise stated, I refer. Both the Shaiva and Shakta schools accept the threefold aspect of the Supreme known as Prakasha, Vimarsha and Prakasha-Vimarsha called in Tantrik worship, "The Three Feet" (Caranatritaya). Both adopt the Thirty-six Tattvas, Shiva, Shakti, Sadashiva, Ishvara and Shuddhavidya, preceding the Purusha-Prakriti Tattvas with which the Samkhya commences.

For whereas these are the ultimate Tattvas in that Philosophy, the Shaiva and Shakta schools claim to show how Purusha and Prakriti are themselves derived from higher Tattvas. These latter Tattvas are also dealt with from the Shabda side as Shakti, Nada, Bindu and as Kalas which are the Kriya of the various grades of Tattvas which are aspects of Shakti. The Shakta Tantras, such as the Saubhagyaratnakara and other works, speak of ninety-four of such Kalas appropriate to Sadashiva, Ishvara, Rudra, Vishnu, and Brahma, "Sun," "Moon,' and "Fire," (indicated in the form of the Ram Bija with Candrabindu transposed) of which fifty-one are Matrika Kalas, being the subtle aspects of the gross letters of Sanskrit alphabet. This last is the Mimamsaka doctrine of Shabda adapted to the doctrine of Shakti. Common also to both Shakta and Shaiva Sampradayas is the doctrine of the Shadadhva.

I am not however here concerned with these details, but with the general concept of Shakti which is their underlying basis. It is sufficient to say that Shakta doctrine is a form of Advaitavada. In reply to the question what is "silent concealment" (Goptavyam), it is said: Atmaham-bhava-bhavanaya bhavayitavyam ityarthah. Hitherto greater pains have been taken to show the differences between the Darshanas than, by regarding their points of agreement, to co-ordinate them systematically. So far as the subject of the present article is concerned all three systems, Samkhya, Mayavada, Shaktivada, are in general agreement as to the nature of the infinite formless Consciousness, and posit therewith a finitising principle called Prakriti, Maya and Shakti respectively.

The main points on which Samkhya (at any rate in what has been called its classical form) differs from Mayavada Vedanta are in its two doctrines of the plurality of Atmans on the one hand, and the reality and independence of Prakriti on the other. When however we examine these two Samkhya doctrines closely we find them to be mere accommodations to the infirmity of common thought. A Vedantic conclusion is concealed within its dualistic presentment. For if each liberated (Mukta) Purusha is all-pervading (Vibhu), and if there is not the slightest difference between one and another, what is the actual or practical difference between such pluralism and the doctrine of Atma? Again it is difficult for the ordinary mind to conceive that objects cease to exist when consciousness of objects ceases. The mind naturally conceives of their existing for others, although, according to the hypothesis, it has no right to conceive anything at all. But here again what do we find? In liberation Prakriti ceases to exist for the Mukta Purusha. In effect what is this but to say with Vedanta that Maya is not a real independent category (Padartha)?

A critic has taken exception to my statement that the classical Samkhya conceals a Vedantic solution behind its dualistic presentment. I was not then, of course, speaking from historical standpoint. Shiva in the *Kularnava Tantra* says that the Six Philosophies are parts of His body, and he who severs them severs His body. They are each aspects of the Cosmic Mind as appearing in Humanity. The logical process which they manifest is one and continuous. The conclusions of each stage or standard can be shown to yield the material of that which follows. This is a logical necessity if it be assumed that the Vedanta is the truest and highest expression of that of which the lower dualistic and pluralistic stages are the approach.

In Samkhya, the Purusha principle represents the formless consciousness, and Prakriti formative activity. Shamkara, defining Reality as that which exists as the same in all the three times, does not altogether discard these two principles, but says that they cannot exist as two independent Realities. He thus reduces the two categories of Samkhya, the Purusha Consciousness and Prakriti Unconsciousness to one Reality, the Brahman; otherwise the Vakya, "All is Brahman" (Sarvam khalvidam Brahma) is falsified. Brahman, however, in one aspect is dissociated from, and in another associated with Maya, which in his system takes the place of the Samkhyan Prakriti. Rut, whereas, Prakriti is an independent Reality, Maya is something which is neither real (Sat) nor unreal (Asat) nor partly real and partly unreal (Sadasat), and which though not forming part of Brahman, and therefore not Brahman, is yet, though not a second reality, inseparably associated and sheltering with, Brahman (Maya Brahmashrita) in one of its aspects: owing what false appearance of reality it has, to the Brahman with which it is so associated.

It is an Eternal Falsity (Mithyabhuta sanatani), unthinkable, alogical, unexplainable (Anirvacaniya). In other points, the Vedantic Maya and Samkhyan Prakriti agree. Though Maya is not a second reality, but a mysterious something of which neither reality nor unreality can be affirmed, the fact of positing it at all gives to Shamkara's doctrine a tinge of dualism from which Shakta theory is free. According to Samkhya, Prakriti is real although it changes. This question of reality is one of definition. Both Mulaprakriti and Maya are eternal. The world, though a changing thing, has at least empirical reality in either view. Both are unconsciousness. Consciousness is reflected on or in unconsciousness: that is to state one view for, as is known, there is a difference of opinion.

The light of Purusha-Consciousness (Cit) is thrown on the Prakriti-Unconsciousness (Acit) in the form of Buddhi. Vijnanabhikshu speaks of a mutual reflection. The Vedantic Pratibimbavadins say that Atma is reflected in Antahkarana, and the apparent likeness of the latter to Cit which is produced by such reflection is Cidabhasa or Jiva. This question of Cidabhasa is one of the main points of difference between Mayavada and Shaktivada. Notwithstanding that Maya is a falsity, it is not, according to Shamkara, a mere negation or want of something (Abhava), but a positive entity (Bhavarupamajanam): that is, it is in the nature of a power which veils (Acchadaka) consciousness, as Prakriti does in the case of Purusha.

The nature of the great "Unexplained" as it is in Itself, and whether we call it Prakriti or Maya, is unknown. The Yoginihridaya Tantra beautifully says that we speak of the Heart of Yogini who is Knower of Herself (Yogini svavid), because the heart is the place whence all things issue. "What man," it says, "knows the heart of a woman? Only Shiva knows the Heart of Yogini." But from Shruti and its effects it is said to be one, all-pervading, eternal, existing now as seed and now as fruit, unconscious, composed of Gunas (Guna-mayi); unperceivable except through its effects, evolving (Parinami) these effects which are its products: that is the world, which however assumes in each system the character of the alleged cause; that is, in Samkhya the effects are real: in Vedanta, neither real nor unreal.

The forms psychic or physical arise in both cases as conscious-unconscious (Sadasat) effects from the association of Consciousness (Purusha or Ishvara) with Unconsciousness (Prakriti or Maya), *Miyate anena iti Maya.* Maya is that by which forms are measured or limited. This too is the function of Prakriti. Maya as the collective name of eternal ignorance (Ajnana), produces, as the Prapancashakti, these forms, by first veiling (Avaranashakti) Consciousness in ignorance and then projecting these forms (Vikshepashakti) from the store of the cosmic Samskaras. But what is the Tamas Guna of the Samkhyan Prakriti in effect but pure Avidya? Sattva is the tendency to reflect consciousness and therefore to reduce unconsciousness. Rajas is the activity (Kriya) which moves Prakriti or Maya to manifest in its Tamasik and Sattvik aspect.

Avidya means "na vidyate," "is not seen," and therefore is not experienced. Cit in association with Avidya does not see Itself as such. The first experience of the Soul reawakening after dissolution to world experience is, "There is nothing," until the Samskaras arise from out this massive Ignorance. In short, Prakriti and Maya are like the *materia prima* of the Thomistic philosophy, the *finitising* principle; the activity which "measures out" (Miyate), that is limits and *makes forms* in the *formless* (Cit). The devotee Kamalakanta lucidly and concisely calls Maya, the form of the Formless (Shunyasya akara iti Maya).

In one respect, Mayavada is a more consistent presentation of Advaitavada, than the Shakta doctrine to which we now proceed. For whilst Shamkara's system, like all others, posits the doctrine of aspects, saying that in one aspect the Brahman is associated with Maya (Ishvara), and that in another it is not (Parabrahman); yet in neither aspect does his Brahman truly change. In Shakta doctrine, Shiva does in one aspect (Shakti) change. Brahman is changeless and yet changes. But as change is only experienced by Jivatma subject to Maya, there is not perhaps substantial difference between such a statement, and that which affirms changelessness and only seeming change.

In other respects, however, to which I now proceed, Shakta doctrine is a more monistic presentation of Advaitavada. If one were asked its most essential characteristic, the reply should be, the absence of the concept of unconscious Maya as taught by Shamkara. Shruti says, "All is Brahman". Brahman is consciousness: and therefore all is consciousness. There is no second thing called Maya which is not Brahman even though it be "not real", "not unreal"; definition obviously given to avoid the imputation of having posited a second Real. To speak of Brahman, and Maya which is not Brahman is to speak of two categories, however much it may be sought to explain away the second by saying that it is "not real" and "not unreal"; a falsity which is yet eternal and so forth.

Like a certain type of modern Western "New Thought," Shakta doctrine affirms, "all is consciousness," however much unconsciousness appears in it. The Kaulacarya Sadananda says in his commentary on the 4th Mantra of *Isopanishad (Ed.* A. Avalon): "The changeless Brahman, which is consciousness appears in creation as Maya which is Brahman, (Brahmamayi), consciousness (Cidrupini) holding in Herself unbeginning (Anadi) Karmik tendencies (Karmasamskara) in the form of the three Gunas. Hence, She is Gunamayi, despite being Cinmayi. As there is no second principle these Gunas are Cit-Shakti." The Supreme Devi is thus Prakashavimarshasya-rupini, or the union of Prakasha and Vimarsha.

According to Shamkara, man is Spirit (Atma) vestured in the Mayik 'falsities' of mind and matter. He, accordingly, can only establish the unity of Ishvara and Jiva by eliminating from the first Maya, and from the second Avidya, when Brahman is left as common denominator. The Shakta eliminates nothing. Man's spirit or Atma is Shiva, His mind and body are Shakti. Shakti and Shiva are one. The Jivatma is Shiva-Shakti. So is the Paramatma. This latter exists as one: the former as the manifold. Man is then not a Spirit covered by a non-Brahman falsity, but Spirit covering Itself with Its own power or Shakti.

What then is Shakti, and how does it come about that there is some principle of unconsciousness in things, a fact which cannot be denied. Shakti comes from the root *"shak,"* "to be able," "to have power". It may be applied to any form of activity. The power to see is visual Shakti, the power to burn is Shakti of fire, and so forth. These are all forms of activity which are ultimately reducible to the Primordial Shakti (Adya Shakti) whence every other form of Power proceeds. She is called Yogini because of Her connection with all things as their origin.

It is this Original Power which is known in worship as Devi or Mother of Many Names. Those who worship the Mother, worship nothing "illusory" or unconscious, but a Supreme Consciousness, whose body is all forms of consciousness-unconsciousness produced by Her as Shiva's power. Philosophically, the Mother or Daivashakti is the kinetic aspect of the Brahman. All three systems recognise that there is a static and kinetic aspect of things: Purusha, Brahman, Shiva on the one side, Prakriti, Maya, Shakti on the other. This is the time-honoured attempt to reconcile the doctrine of a changeless Spirit, a changing Manifold, and the mysterious unity of the two. For Power (Shakti) and the possessor of the Power (Shaktiman) are one and the same.

In the Tantras, Shiva constantly says to Devi, "There is no difference between Thee and Me." We say that the fire burns, but burning *is* fire. Fire is not one thing and burning another. In the supreme transcendental changeless state, Shiva and Shakti are one, for Shiva is never without Shakti. The connection is called Avinabhavasambandha. Consciousness is never without its Power. Power is active Brahman or Consciousness. But, as there is then no activity, they exist in the supreme state as one Tattva (Ekam tattvam iva); Shiva as Cit, Shakti as Cidrupini. This is the state before the thrill of Nada, the origin of all those currents of force which are the universe. According to Shamkara, the Supreme Experience contains no trace or seed of objectivity whatever.

In terms of speech, it is an abstract consciousness (Jnana). According to the view here expressed, which has been profoundly elaborated by the Kashmir Shaiva School, that which appears "without" only so appears because it, in some form or other, exists "within". So also the Shakta Visvasara Tantra says, "what is here is there, what is not here is nowhere." If therefore we know duality, it must be because the potentiality of it exists in that from which it arises. The Shaivashakta school thus assumes a real derivation of the universe and a causal nexus between Brahman and the world. According to Shamkara, this notion of creation is itself Maya, and there is no need to find a cause for it. So it is held that the supreme experience (Amarsha) is by the Self (Shiva) of Himself as Shakti, who as such is the Ideal or Perfect Universe; not in the sense of a perfected world of form, but that ultimate formless feeling (Bhava) of Bliss (Ananda) or Love which at root the whole world is.

All is Love and by Love all is attained. The Shakta Tantras compare the state immediately prior to creation with that of a grain of gram (Canaka) wherein the two seeds (Shiva and Shakti) are held as one under a single sheath. There is, as it were, a Maithuna in this unity of dual aspect, the thrill of which is Nada, productive of the seed or Bindu from which the universe is born. When the sheath breaks and the seeds are pushed apart, the beginning of a dichotomy is established in the one consciousness, whereby, the "I", and the "This" (Idam or Universe) appear as separate. The specific Shiva aspect is, when viewed through Maya, the Self, and the Shakti aspect the Not-Self. This is to the limited consciousness only.

In truth the two, Shiva and Shakti, are ever one and the same, and never dissociated. Thus each of the Bindus of the Kamakala are Shiva-Shakti appearing as Purusha-Prakriti. At this point, Shakti assumes several forms, of which the two chief are Cit-Shakti or as Cit as Shakti, and Maya-Shakti or Maya as Shakti. Maya is not here a mysterious unconsciousness, a non-Brahman, non-real, non-unreal something. It is a form of Shakti, and Shakti is Shiva who is Consciousness which is real. Therefore Maya Shakti is in itself (Svarupa) Consciousness and Brahman. Being Brahman, It is real.

It is that aspect of conscious power which conceals Itself to Itself. "By veiling the own true form (Svarupa =

Consciousness), its Shaktis always arise", (Svarupavarane casya shaktayah satatotthitah) as the Spandakarika says. This is a common principle in all doctrine relating to Shakti. Indeed, this theory of veiling, though expressed in another form, is common to Samkhya and Vedanta. The difference lies in this that in Samkhya it is a second, independent Principle which veils; in Mayavada Vedanta it is the non-Brahman Maya (called a Shakti of Ishvara) which veils; and in Shakta Advaitavada (for the Shaktas are nondualists) it is Consciousness which, without ceasing to be such, yet veils Itself.

As already stated, the Monistic Shaivas and Shaktas hold certain doctrines in common such as the thirty-six Tattvas, and what are called Shadadhva which also appear as part of the teaching of the other Shaiva Schools. In the thirty-six Tattva scheme, Maya which is defined as "the sense of difference" (Bhedabuddhi), for it is that which makes the Self see things as different from the Self, is technically that Tattva which appears at the close of the pure creation, that is, after Shuddhavidya. This Maya reflects and limits in the Pashu or Jiva, the Iccha, Jnana, Kriya Shaktis of Ishvara. These again are the three Bindus which are "Moon," "Fire," and "Sun". What are Jnana and Kriya (including Iccha its preliminary) on the part of the Pati (Lord) in all beings and things (Bhaveshu) which are His body: it is these two which, with Maya as the third, are the Sattva, Rajas and Tamas Gunas of the Pashu.

This veiling power explains how the undeniable element of unconsciousness which is seen in things exists. How, if all be consciousness, is that principle there "? The answer is given in the luminous definition of Shakti; *"It is the function of Shakti to negate"* (Nishedhavyapararupa Shaktih), that is, to negate consciousness and make it appear to Itself as unconscious (Karika 4 of Yogaraja or Yogamuni's Commentary on Abhinava Gupta's Paramarthasara). In truth the whole world is the Self whether as "I" (Aham) or "This" (Idam). The Self thus becomes its own object. It becomes object or form that it may enjoy dualistic experience. It yet remains, what it was in its unitary blissful experience. This is the Eternal Play in which the Self hides and seeks itself. The formless cannot assume form unless formlessness is negated. Eternity is negated into finality; the all-pervading into the limited; the all-knowing into the "little knower"; the almighty into the "little doer," and so forth. It is only by negating Itself to Itself that the Self becomes its own object in the form of the universe.

It follows from the above that, to the Shakta worshipper, there is no unconscious Maya in Shamkara's sense, and therefore there is no Cidabhasa, in the sense of the reflection of consciousness on unconsciousness, giving the latter the appearance of consciousness which it does not truly possess. For all is Consciousness as Shakti. "Aham Stri," as the Advaitabhavopanisad exclaims. In short, Shamkara says there is one Reality or Consciousness and a not-real not-unreal Unconsciousness. What is really unconscious appears to be conscious by the reflection of the light of Consciousness upon it. Shakta doctrine says consciousness appears to be unconscious, or more truly, to have an element of unconsciousness in it (for nothing even empirically is absolutely unconscious), owing to the veiling play of Consciousness Itself as Shakti.

As with so many other matters, these apparent differences are to some extent a matter of words. It is true that the Vedantists speak of the conscious (Cetana) and unconscious (Acetana), but they, like the Shakta Advaitins, say that the thing in itself is Consciousness. When this is vividly displayed by reason of the reflection (Pratibimbha) of consciousness in Tattva, (such as Buddhi), capable of displaying this reflection, then we can call that in which it is so displayed conscious. Where, though consciousness is all-pervading, Caitanya is not so displayed, there we speak of unconsciousness. Thus, gross matter (Bhuta) does not appear to reflect Cit, and so appears to us unconscious.

Though all things are at base consciousness, some appear as more, and some as less conscious. Shamkara explains this by saying that Caitanya is associated with a non-conscious mystery or Maya which veils consciousness, and Caitanya gives to what is unconscious the appearance of consciousness through reflection. "Reflection" is a form of pictorial thinking. What is meant is that two principles are associated together without the nature (Svarupa) of either being really affected, and yet producing that effect which is Jiva. Shakta doctrine says that all is consciousness, but this same consciousness assumes the appearance of changing degrees of unconsciousness, not through the operation of anything other than itself (Maya), but by the operation of one of its own powers (Mayashakti).

It is not unconscious Maya in Shamkara's sense which veils consciousness, but Consciousness as Shakti veils Itself, and, as so functioning, it is called Mayashakti. It may be asked how can Consciousness become Unconsciousness and cease to be itself '? The answer is that it does not. It never ceases to be Consciousness. It appears to itself, as Jiva, to be unconscious, and even then not wholly: for as recent scientific investigations have shown, even so-called "brute matter" exhibits the elements of that which, when evolved in man, is self-consciousness. If it be asked how consciousness can obscure itself partially or at all, the only answer is Acintya Shakti, which Mayavadins as all other Vedantists admit. Of this, as of all ultimates, we must say with the Western Scholastics, "omnia exeunt in mysterium".

Prakriti is then, according to Samkhya, a real independent category different from Purusha. This both Mayavada and Shaktivada deny. Maya is a not-real, not-unreal Mystery dependent on, and associated with, and inhering in Brahman; but not Brahman or any part of Brahman. Maya-Shakti is a power of, and, in its Svarupa, not different from Shiva: is real, and is an aspect of Brahman itself. Whilst Brahman as Ishvara is associated with Maya, Shiva is never associated with anything but Himself. But the function of all three is the same, namely to make forms in the formless.

It is That, by which the Ishvara or Collective Consciousness pictures the universe for the individual Jiva's experience. Shakti is threefold as Will (Iccha), Knowledge (Jnana), and Action (Kriya). All three are but differing aspects of the one Shakti. Consciousness and its power or action are at base the same. It is true that action is manifested in matter, that is apparent unconsciousness, but its root, as that of all else is consciousness. Jnana is self-proved and experienced (Svatahsiddha), whereas,

Kriya, being inherent in bodies, is perceived by others than by ourselves.

The characteristic of action is the manifestation of all objects. These objects, again, characterised by consciousness-unconsciousness are in the nature of a shining forth (Abhasa) of Consciousness. (Here Abhasa is not used in its sense of Cidabhasa, but as an intensive form of the term Bhasa.) The power of activity and knowledge are only differing aspects of one and the same Consciousness. According to Shamkara, Brahman has no form of self-determination. Kriya is a function of unconscious Maya. When Ishvara is said to be a doer (Karta), this is attributed (Aupadhika) to Him by ignorance only. It follows from the above that there are other material differences between Shakta doctrine and Mayavada, such as the nature of the Supreme Experience, the reality and mode of creation, the reality of the world, and so forth. The world, it is true, is not; as the Mahanirvana Tantra says absolute reality in the sense of unchanging being, for it comes and goes. It is nevertheless real, for it is the experience of Shiva and Shiva's experience is not unreal. Thus again the evolution of the world as Abhasa, whilst resembling the Vivarta of Mayavada, differs from it in holding, as the Samkhya does, that the effect is real and not unreal, as Shamkara contends. To treat of these and other matters would carry me beyond the scope of this essay which only deals, and that in a summary way, with the essential differences and similarities in the concept Prakriti, Maya and Shakti.

I may however conclude with a few general remarks. The doctrine of Shakti is a profound one, and I think likely to be attractive to Western minds when they have grasped it, just as they will appreciate the Tantrik watchword, Kriya or action, its doctrine of progress with and through the world and not against it, which is involved in its liberation-enjoyment (Bhukti-mukti) theory and other matters. The philosophy is, in any case, not, as an American writer, in his ignorance, absurdly called it, "worthless," "religious Feminism run mad," and a "feminisation of Vedanta for suffragette Monists". It is not a "feminization" of anything, but distinctive, original and practical doctrine worthy of a careful study. The Western student will find much in it which is more acceptable to generally prevalent thought in Europe and America—than in the "illusion" doctrine (in itself an unsuitable term), and the ascetic practice of the Vedantins of Shamkara's school. This is not to say that ways of reconciliation may not be found by those who go far enough. It would not be difficult to show ground for holding that ultimately the same intellectual results are attained by viewing the matter from the differing standpoints of Sadhana and Siddhi.

The writer of an interesting article on the same subject in the *Prabuddha Bharata* (August 1916) states that the Samnyasi Totapuri, the Guru of Sri Ramakrishna, maintained that a (Mayavadin) Vedantist could not believe in Shakti, for if causality itself be unreal there is no need to admit any power to cause, and that it is Maya to apply the principle of causation and to say that everything comes from Shakti. The Samnyasi was converted to Shakta doctrine after all. For as the writer well says, it is not merely by intellectual denial, but by *living* beyond the "unreal," that Real is found. He, however, goes on to say, "the Shaktivada of Tantra is not an improvement on the Mayavada of Vedanta, (that is the doctrine of Shamkara) but only its symbolisation through the chromatics of sentiment and concept.".

It is true that it is a form of Vedanta, for all which is truly Indian must be that. It is also a fact that the Agama as a Shastra of worship is full of Symbolism. Intellectually, however, it is an original presentment of Vedanta, and from the practical point of view, it has some points of merit which Mayavada does not possess. Varieties of teaching may be different presentations of one truth leading to a similar end. But one set of "chromatics" may be more fruitful than another for the mass of men. It is in this that the strength of the Shakta doctrine and practice lies. Moreover (whether they be an improvement or not) there are differences between the two. Thus the followers of Shamkara do not, so far as I am aware, accept the thirty-six Tattvas. A question, however, which calls for inquiry is that of the relation of the Shakta and Shaiva (Advaita) Schools Mayavada is a doctrine which, whether true or not, is fitted only for advanced minds of great intellectuality, and for men of ascetic disposition, and of the highest moral development.

This is implied in its theory of competency (Adhikara) for Vedantic teaching. When, as is generally the case, it is not understood, and in some cases when it is understood, but is otherwise not suitable, it is liable to be a weakening doctrine. The Shakta teaching to be found in the Tantras has also its profundities which are to be revealed only to the competent, and contains a practical doctrine for all classes of worshippers (Sadhaka). It has, in this form, for the mass of men, a strengthening pragmatic value which is beyond dispute. Whether, as some may have contended, it is the fruit of a truer spiritual experience I will not here discuss, for this would lead me into a polemic beyond the scope of my present purpose, which is an impartial statement of the respective teachings, on one particular point, given by the three philosophical systems here discussed.

Shakta Sadhana (The Ordinary Ritual)

Sadhana is that, which produces Siddhi or the result sought, be it material or spiritual advancement. It is the means or practice by which the desired end may be attained and consists in the training and exercise of the body and psychic faculties, upon the gradual perfection of which Siddhi follows. The nature or degree of spiritual Siddhi depends upon the progress made towards the realisation of the Atma whose veiling vesture the body is. The means employed are numerous and elaborate, such as worship (Puja) exterior or mental, Shastric learning, austerities (Tapas), Japa or recitation of Mantra, Hymns, meditation, and so forth.

The Sadhana is necessarily of a nature and character appropriate to the end sought. Thus Sadhana for spiritual knowledge (Brahmajnana) which consists of external control (Dama) over the ten senses (Indriya), internal control (Sama) over the mind (Buddhi, Ahamkara, Manas), discrimination between the transitory and eternal, renunciation of both the world and heaven (Svarga), differs from the lower Sadhana of the ordinary householder, and both are obviously of a kind different from that prescribed and followed by the practitioners of malevolent magic (Abhicara). Sadhakas again vary in their physical, mental and moral qualities and are thus divided into four classes, Mridu, Madhya, Adhimatraka, and the highest Adhimatrama who is qualified (Adhikari) for all forms of Yoga.

In a similar way, the Shakta Kaulas are divided into the Prakrita or common Kaula following Viracara with the Pancatattvas described in the following Chapter; the middling (Madhyama) Kaula who (may be) follows the same or other Sadhana but who is of a higher type, and the highest Kaula (Kaulikottama) who, having surpassed all ritualism, meditates upon the Universal Self.

Until a Sadhaka is Siddha, all Sadhana is or should be undertaken with the authority and under the direction of a Guru or Spiritual Teacher and Director. There is in reality but one Guru and that is the Lord (Ishvara) Himself. He is the Supreme Guru as also is Devi His Power one with Himself. But He acts through man and human means.

The ordinary human Guru is but the manifestation on earth of the Adi-natha Mahakala and Mahakali, the Supreme Guru abiding in Kailasa. As the *Yogini Tantra* (Ch. 1) says *Guroh sthanam hi kailasam.* He it is who is in, and speaks with the voice of, the Earthly Guru. So, to turn to an analogy in the West, it is Christ who speaks in the voice of the Pontifex Maximus when declaring faith and morals, and in the voice of the priest who confers upon the penitent absolution for his sins. It is not the man who speaks in either case but God through him. It is the Guru who initiates and helps, and the relationship between him and the disciple (Shishya) continues until the attainment of spiritual Siddhi. It is only from him that Sadhana and Yoga are learnt and not (as it is commonly said) from a thousand Shastras. As the *Shatkarmadipika* says, mere book-knowledge is useless.

Pustake likhitavidya yena sundari jap yate
Siddhir na jayate tasya kalpakoti-shatairapi.

(O Beauteous one! he who does Japa of a Vidya (= Mantra) learnt from a book can never attain Siddhi even if he persists for countless millions of years.)

Manu therefore says, "of him who gives natural birth, and of him who gives knowledge of the Veda, the giver of sacred knowledge is the more venerable father." The Tantra Shastras also are full of the greatness of the Guru. He is not to be thought of as a mere man. There is no difference between Guru, Mantra and Deva. Guru is father, mother and Brahman. Guru, it is said can save from the wrath of Shiva, but in no way, can one be saved from the wrath of the Guru. Attached to this greatness there is, however, responsibility; for the sins of the disciple may recoil upon him.

The Tantra Shastras deal with the high qualities which are demanded of a Guru and the good qualities which are to be looked for in an intending disciple (see for instance *Tantrasara,* Ch. I). Before initiation, the Guru examines and tests the intending disciple for a specified period. The latter's moral qualifications are purity of soul (Shuddhatma), control of the senses (Jitendriya), the following of the Purushartha or aims of all sentient being (Purusharthaparayana).

Amongst others, those who are lewd (Kamuka), adulterous (Para-daratura), addicted to sin, ignorant, slothful and devoid of religion should be rejectsee *Matsyasukta Tantra,* XIII; *Pranatoshini* 108; *Maharudrayamala,* I. XV, II. ii; *Kularnava Tantra,* Ch. XIII). The good Sadhaka who is entitled to the knowledge of all Shastra is he who is pure-minded, self-controlled, ever engaged in doing good to all beings, free from false notions of dualism, attached to the speaking of, taking shelter with and ever living in the consciousness of, the Supreme Brahman *(Gandharva Tantra,* Ch. ii).

All orthodox Hindus of all divisions of worshippers submit themselves to the direction of a Guru. The latter initiates. The Vaidik initiation into the twice-born classes is by the Upanayana. This is for the first three castes only, *viz.,* Brahmana (priesthood and teaching), Kshattriya (warrior) Vaishya (merchant). All are (it is said) by birth Shudra (Janmana jayate Shudrah) and by sacrament (that is, the Upanayana ceremony) twice-born.

By study of the Vedas one is a Vipra. And he who has knowledge of the Brahman is a Brahmana (Brahma jnanati brahmanah). From this well-known verse it will be seen how few there really are, who are entitled to the noble name of Brahmana.

The Tantrik Mantra-initiation is a different ceremony and is for all castes. Initiation (Diksha) is the giving of Mantra by the Guru. The latter should first establish the life of the Guru in his own body; that is the vital power (Pranashakti) of the Supreme Guru in the thousand-petalled lotus (Sahasrara). He then transmits it to the disciple. As an image is the instrument (Yantra) in which Divinity (Devatva) inheres, so also is the body of the Guru. The candidate is prepared for initiation, fasts and lives chastely. Initiation (which follows) gives spiritual knowledge and destroys sin. As one lamp is lit at the flame of another, so the divine Shakti consisting of Mantra is communicated from the Guru's body to that of the Shishya. I need not be always repeating that this is the theory and ideal, which today is generally remote from the fact. The Supreme Guru speaks with the voice of the earthly Guru at the time of giving Mantra. As the *Yogini Tantra* (Ch. I) says:

Mantra-pradana-kale hi manushe Naganandini
Adhishthanam bhavet tatra Mahakalasya Shamkari
Ato na guruta devi manushe natra samshayah.

(At the time the Mantra is communicated, there is in man *(i.e.,* Guru) the Presence of Mahakala. There is no doubt that man is not the Guru.) Guru is the root (Mula) of initiation (Diksha). Diksha is the root of Mantra. Mantra is the root of Devata, and Devata is the root of Siddhi. The *Mundamala Tantra* says that Mantra is born of Guru, and Devata of Mantra, so that the Guru is in the position of Father's Father to the Ishtadevata. Without initiation, Japa (recitation) of the Mantra, Puja, and other ritual acts are useless. The Mantra chosen for the candidate must be suitable (Anukula). Whether a Mantra is Svakula or Akula to the person about to be initiated is ascertained by the Kulakulacakra, the zodiacal circle called Rashicakra and other Cakras which may be found in the Tantrasara. Initiation by a woman is efficacious; that by the mother is eightfold so *(ib.).* For, according to the Tantra Shastra, a woman with the necessary qualifications, may be a Guru and give initiation. The Kulagurus are four in number, each of them being the Guru of the preceding ones. There are also three lines of Gurus.

So long as the Shakti communicated by a Guru to his disciple is not fully developed, the relation of Teacher and Director and Disciple exists. A man is Shishya so long as he is Sadhaka. When, however, Siddhi is attained, Guru and Shishya, as also all other dualisms, and relations, disappear. Besides the preliminary initiation, there are a number of other initiations or consecrations (Abhisheka) which mark greater and greater degrees of advance from Shaktabhisheka when entrance is made on the path of Shakta Sadhana to Purnadikshabhisheka and Mahapurnadikshabhisheka also called Virajagraha-nabhisheka. On the attainment of perfection in the last grade the Sadhaka performs his own funeral rite (Shraddha), makes Purnahuti with his sacred thread and crown lock. The relation of Guru and Shishya now ceases. From this point he ascends by himself until he realises the great saying So'ham "He I am," Sa'ham "She I am". Now he is Jivan-mukta and Paramahamsa.

The word Sadhana comes from the root *Sadh,* to exert or strive, and Sadhana is therefore striving, practice, discipline and worship in order to obtain success or Siddhi, which may be of any of the kinds, worldly or spiritual, desired, but which, on the religious side of the Shastras, means spiritual advancement with its fruit of happiness in this world and in Heaven and at length Liberation (Moksha). He who practices Sadhana is called (if a man) Sadhaka or (if a woman) Sadhika. But men vary in capacity, temperament, knowledge and general advancement, and therefore the means (for Sadhana also means instrument) by which they are to be led to Siddhi must vary. Methods which are suitable for highly advanced men will fail as regards the ignorant and undeveloped for they cannot understand them. What suits the latter has been long outpassed by the former. At least that is the Hindu view.

It is called Adhikara or competency. Thus some few men are competent (Adhikari) to study Vedanta and to follow high mental rituals and Yoga processes. Others are not. Some are grown-up children and must be dealt with as such. As all men, and indeed all beings, are, as to their psychical and physical bodies, made of the primordial substance Prakriti-Shakti (Prakrityatmaka), as Prakriti is Herself the three Gunas, Sattva, Rajas and Tamas, and as all things and beings are composed of these three Gunas in varying proportions, it follows that men are divisible into three general classes, namely, those in which the Sattva, Rajas, and Tamas Gunas, predominate respectively. There are, of course, degrees in each of these three classes.

Amongst Sattvika men, in whom Sattva predominates, some are more and some less Sattvika than others and so on with the rest. These three classes of temperament (Bhava) are known in the *Shakta Tantras* as the Divine (Divyabhava), Heroic (Virabhava) and Animal (Pashubhava) temperaments respectively. Bhava is defined as a property or quality (Dharma) of the Manas or mind *(Pranatoshini,* 570). The Divyabhava is that in which Sattva-guna predominates only, because it is to be noted that none of the Gunas are, or ever can be, absent. Prakriti cannot be partitioned. Prakriti *is* the three Gunas. Sattva is essentially the spiritual Guna, for it is that which manifests Spirit or Pure Consciousness (Cit). A Sattvika man is thus a spiritual man.

His is a calm, pure, equable, refined, wise, spiritual temperament, free of materiality and of passion, or he possesses these qualities imperfectly, and to the degree that he possesses them he is Sattvik. Pashubhava is, on the other hand, the temperament of the man in whom Tamas guna prevails and produces such dark characteristics as ignorance, error, apathy, sloth and so forth. He is called a Pashu or animal because Tamas predominates in the merely animal nature as compared with the disposition of spiritually-minded men. He is also Pashu because he is bound by the bonds (Pasha).

The term pasha comes from the root *Pash* to bind. The Kularnava enumerates eight bonds, namely, pity (Daya, of the type which Taoists call "inferior benevolence" as opposed to the divine compassion or Karuna), ignorance and delusion (Moha), fear (Bhaya), shame (Lajja), disgust (Ghrina), family (Kula), habit and observance (Shila), and caste (Varna). Other larger enumerations are given. The Pashu is the man caught by the world, in ignorance and bondage. Bhaskararaya, on the Sutra "have no converse with a Pashu," says that a Pashu is Bahirmukha or outward looking, seeing the outside only of things and not inner realities. The injunction, he says, only applies to converse as regards things spiritual.

The Shaiva Shastra speaks of three classes of Pashu, namely, Sakala bound by the three Pashas, Anu, Bheda, Karma, that is, limited knowledge, the seeing of the one Self as many by the operation of Maya, and action and its product. These are the three impurities (Mala) called Anavamala, Mayamala, and Karmamala. The Sakala Jiva or Pashu is bound by all three, the Pralayakala by the first and last, and the Vijnanakala by the first only. He who is wholly freed of the remaining impurity of Anu is Shiva Himself. Here however Pashu is used in a different sense, that is, as denoting the creature as contrasted with the Lord (Pati).

In this sense, Pashu is a name for all men. In the Shakta use of the term, though all men are certainly Pashu, as compared with the Lord, yet as between themselves one may be Pashu (in the narrower sense above stated) and the other not. Some men are more Pashu than others. It is a mistake to suppose that the Pashu is necessarily a bad man. He may be and often is a good one. He is certainly better than a bad Vira who is really no Vira at all. He is, however, not, according to this Shastra, an enlightened man in the sense that the Vira or Divya is, and he is generally marked by various degrees of ignorance and material-mindedness.

It is the mark of a bad Pashu to be given over to gross acts of sin. Between these two comes the Hero or Vira of whose temperament (Virabhava) so much is heard in the Shakta Shastras. In him there is prevalent the strongly active Rajas Guna. Rajas is always active either to incite Tamas or Sattva. In the former case the result is a Pashu, in the latter case either a Vira or Divya. Where Sattva approaches perfection of development there is the Divyabhava. Sattva is here firmly established in calm and in high degree.

But, until such time, and whilst man who has largely liberated himself through knowledge of the influence of Tamas, is active to promote Sattva, he is a Vira. Being heroic, he is permitted to meet his enemy Tamas face to face, counter-attacking where the lower developed man flees away. It has been pointed out by Dr. Garbe *(Philosophy of Ancient India,* 481), as before him by Baur, that the analogous Gnostic classification of men as material, psychical, and spiritual also corresponds (as does this) to the three Gunas of the Samkhya Darshana.

Even in its limited Shakta sense, there are degrees of Pashu, one man being more so than another. The Pashas are the creations of Maya Shakti. The Devi therefore is pictured as bearing them. But as She is in Her form as Maya and Avidya Shakti the cause of bondage, so as Vidya Shakti She breaks the bonds (Pashupasa-Vimocini) (see v. 78, *Lalita-sahasranama),* and is thus the Liberatrix of the Pashu from his bondage.

Nitya Tantra says that the Bhava of the Divya is the best, the Vira the next best, and Pashu the lowest. In fact, the state of the last is the starting point in Sadhana, that of the first the goal, and that of the Vira is the stage of one who having ceased to be a Pashu is on the way to the attainment of the goal. From being a Pashu, a man rises in this or some other birth to be a Vira and Divyabhava or Devata-bhava is awakened through Virabhava. The *Picchila Tantra* says (X, see also *Utpatti Tantra,* LXIV) that the difference between the Vira and the Divya lies in the Uddhatamanasa, that is, passionateness or activity by which the former is characterised, and which is due to the great effort of Rajas to procure for the Sadhaka a Sattvik state. Just as there are degrees in the Pashu state, so there are classes of Viras, some being higher than others.

The Divya Sadhaka also is of higher or lower kinds. The lowest is only a degree higher than the best type of Vira. The highest completely realise the Deva-nature wherein Sattva exists in a state of lasting stability. Amongst this class are the Tattvajnani and Yogi. The latter are emancipated from all ritual. The lower Divya class may apparently take part in the ritual of the Vira. The object and end of all Sadhana, whether of Pashu or Vira or Divya, is to develop Sattvaguna. The Tantras give descriptions of each of these three classes. The chief general distinction, which is constantly repeated, between the pure Pashu (for there are also Vibhavapashus) and the Vira, is that the former does not, and the latter does, follow the Pancatattva ritual, in the form prescribed for Viracara.

Other portions of the description are characteristics of the Tamasik character of the Pashu. So *Kubjika Tantra* (VII) after describing this class of man to be the lowest, points out various forms of their ignorance. So it says that he talks ill of other classes of believers. That is, he is sectarian-minded and decries other forms of worship than his own, a characteristic of the Pashu the world over. He distinguishes one Deva from another as if they were really different and not merely the plural manifestations of the One. So, the worshipper of Rama may abuse the worshipper of Krishna, and both decry the worship of Shiva or Devi.

As the Veda says, the One is called by various names. Owing to his ignorance "he is always bathing," that is, he is always thinking about external and ceremonial purity. This, though good in its way, is nothing compared with internal purity of mind. He has ignorant or wrong ideas, or want of faith, concerning (Shakta) Tantra Shastra, Sacrifices, Guru, Images, and Mantra, the last of which he thinks to be mere letters only and not Devata (*Pranatoshini,* 547, *et seq., Picchila,* X). He follows the Vaidik rule relating to Maithuna on the fifth day when the wife is Ritusnata *(Ritu-kalam vina devi ramanam parivrajayet).*

Some of the descriptions of the Pashu seem to refer to the lowest class. Generally, however, one may say that from the standpoint of a Viracari, all those who follow Vedacara, Vaishnavacara and Shaivacara are Pashus. The *Kubjika Tantra* (VII) gives a description of the Divya. Its eulogies would seem to imply that in all matters which it mentions, the Pashu is lacking. But this, as regards some matters, is Stuti (praise) only. Thus he has a strong faith in Veda, Shastra, Deva and Guru, and ever speaks the truth which, as also other good qualities, must be allowed to the Pashu. He avoids all cruelty and other bad action and regards alike both friend and foe. He avoids the company of the irreligious who decry the Devata.

All Devas he regards as beneficial, worshipping all without drawing distinctions. Thus, for instance, whilst an orthodox upcountry Hindu of the Pashu kind who is a worshipper of Rama cannot even bear to hear the name of Krishna, though both Rama and Krishna are each Avatara of the same Vishnu, the Divya would equally reverence both knowing each to be an aspect of the one Great Shakti, Mother of Devas and Men. This is one of the first qualities of the high Shakta worshipper. As a worshipper of Shakti he bows down at the feet of women regarding them as his Guru *(Strinam padatalam drishtva guruvad bhava pet sada).* He offers everything to the supreme Devi regarding the whole universe as pervaded by Stri (Shakti, not "woman") and as Devata. Shiva is (he knows) in all men. The whole universe (Brahmanda) is pervaded by Shiva Shakti.

The description cited also deals with his ritual, saying that he does daily ablutions, Sandhya, wears clean cloth, the Tripundra mark in ashes or red sandal, and ornaments of Rudraksha beads. He does Japa (recitation of Mantras external and mental) and worship (Arcana). He worships the Pitris and Devas and performs all the daily rites. He gives daily charity. He meditates upon his Guru daily, and does worship thrice daily and, as a Bhairava, worships Parameshvari with Divyabhava. He worships Devi at night

(Vaidik worship being by day), and after food (ordinary Vaidik worship being done before taking food). He makes obeisance to the Kaula Shakti (Kulastri) versed in Tantra and Mantra, whoever She be and whether youthful or old. He bows to the Kula-trees (Kulavriksha). He ever strives for the attainment and maintenance of Devatabhava and is himself of the nature of a Devata.

Portions of this description appear to refer to the ritual and not Avadhuta Divya, and to this extent applicable to the high Vira also. The *Mahanirvana* (I. 56) describes the Divya as all but a Deva, ever pure of heart, to whom all opposites are alike

(Dvandvatita) such as pain and pleasure, heat and cold, who is free from attachment to worldly things, the same to all creatures and forgiving. The text I have published, therefore, says that there is no Divya-bhava in the Kaliyuga nor Pashubhava; for the Pashu (or his wife) must, with his own hand, collect leaves, flowers and fruit, and cook his food, which regulations and others are impossible or difficult in the Kali age.

As a follower of Smriti, he should not "see the face of a Shudra at worship, or even think of woman" (referring to the Pancatattva ritual). The Shyamarcana (cited in *Haratattvadidhiti,* 348) speaks to the same effect. On the other hand, there is authority for the proposition that in the Kaliyuga there is only Pashubhava. Thus, the *Pranatoshini* (510-517) cites a passage purporting to come from the *Mahanirvana* which is in direct opposition to the above:

Divpa-vira-mayo bhavah kalau nasti kadacana
Kevalampashu-bhavena mantra-siddhir bhaven nrinam.

(In the Kali age there is no Divya or Virabhava. It is only by the Pashu-bhava that men may attain Mantra-siddhi.)

Dealing with the former passage from the *Mahanirvana,* the Commentator explains it as meaning "that the conditions and characters of the Kaliyuga are not such as to be productive of Pashubhava, or to allow of its Acara (in the sense of the strict Vaidik ritual). No one, he says, can now-a-days fully perform the Vedacara, Vaishnavacara, and Shaiva-cara rites without which the Vaidik and Puranic Yajna and Mantra are fruitless.

No one now goes through the Brahmacarya Ashrama or adopts, after the fiftieth year, Vanaprastha. Those whom the Vaidik rites do not control cannot expect the fruit of their observances. On the contrary, men have taken to drink, associate with the low and are fallen, as are also those who associate with them.

There can, therefore, be no pure Pashu. (That is apparently whilst there may be a natural Pashu disposition the Vaidik rites appropriate to this bhava cannot be carried out.) Under these circumstances, the duties prescribed by the Vedas which are appropriate for the Pashu being incapable of performance, Shiva, for the liberation of men of the Kali age, has proclaimed the Agama. Now there is no other way."

We are, perhaps, therefore, correct in saying that it comes to this: In a bad age, such as the Kali, Divya men are (to say the least) very scarce, though common-sense and experience must, I suppose, allow for exceptions. Whilst the Pashu natural disposition exists, the Vaidik ritual which he should follow cannot be done. It is in fact largely obsolete. The Vaidik Pashu or man who followed the Vaidik rituals in their entirety is non-existent. He must follow the Agamic rituals which, as a fact, the bulk of men do. The Agama must now govern the Pashu, Vira and would-be Divya alike. As I have frequently explained, there are various communities of the followers of Tantra of Agama according to the several divisions of the worshippers of the five Devatas (Pancopasaka). Of the five classes, the most important are Vaishnava, Shaiva and Shakta. I do not, however, hesitate to repeat a statement of a fact of which those who speak of "The Tantra" ignore.

The main elements of Sadhana are common to all such communities following the Agamas; such as Puja (inner and outer), Pratima or other emblems (Linga, Shalagrama), Upacara, Sandhya, Yajna, Vrata, Tapas, Mandala, Yantra, Mantra, Japa, Purashcarana, Nyasa, Bhutasuddhi, Mudra, Dhyana, Samskara and so forth. Even the Vamacara ritual which some wrongly think to be peculiar to the Shaktas, is or was followed (I am told) by members of other Sampradayas including Jainas and Bauddhas. Both, in so far as they follow this ritual, are reckoned amongst Kaulas though, as being non-Vaidik, of a lower class.

A main point to be here remembered, and one which establishes both the historical and practical importance of the Agamas is this: That whilst some Vaidik rites still exist, the bulk of the ritual of today is Agamic, that is, what is popularly called Tantrik. The Puranas are replete with Tantrik rituals.

Notwithstanding a general community of ritual forms, there are some variances which are due to two causes: firstly, to difference in the Devata worship, and secondly, to difference of philosophical basis according as it is Advaita, Vishishtadvaita, or Dvaita. The presentment of fundamental ideas is sometimes in different terms. Thus the Vaishnava Pancaratra Agama describes the creative process in terms of the Vyuhas, and the Shaiva-Shakta Agamas explain it as the Abhasa of the thirty-six Tattvas. I here deal with only one form, namely, Shakta Sadhana in which the Ishtadevata is Shakti in Her many forms.

I will here shortly describe some of the ritual forms above-mentioned, premising that so cursory an account does not do justice to the beauty and profundity of many of them.

There are four different forms of worship corresponding to four different states and dispositions (Bhava) of the Sadhaka himself. The realisation that the Supreme Spirit (Paramatma) and the individual spirit (Jivatma) are one, that everything is Brahman, and that nothing but the Brahman has lasting being is the highest state or Brahma-bhava. Constant meditation with Yoga-processes upon the Devata in the heart is the lower form (Dhyanabhava). Lower still is that Bhava of which Japa (recitations of Mantra) and Hymns of praise (Stava) are the expression; and lowest of all is external worship (Bahyapuja).

Pujabhava is that which arises out of the dualistic notions of worshipper and worshipped, the servant and the Lord, a dualism which necessarily exists in greater or less, degree until Monistic experience (Advaita-bhava) is attained. He who realises the Advaita-tattva knows that all is Brahman. For him there is neither worshipper nor worshipped, neither Yoga, nor Puja nor Dharana, Dhyana, Stava, Japa, Vrata or other ritual or process of Sadhana. For, he is Siddha in its fullest sense, that is, he has attained Siddhi which is the aim of Sadhana. As the *Mahanirvana* says, "for him who has faith in and knowledge of the root, of what use are the branches and leaves'?" Brahmanism thus sagely resolves the Western dispute as to the necessity or advisability of ritual. It affirms it for those who have not attained the end of all ritual. It lessens and refines ritual as spiritual progress is made upwards; it dispenses with it altogether when there is no longer need for it. But, until a man is a real "Knower", some Sadhana is necessary if he would become one. The nature of Sadhana, again, differs according to the temperaments (Bhava) above described, and also with reference to the capacities and spiritual advancement of each in his own Bhava.

What may be suitable for the unlettered peasant may not be so for those more intellectually and spiritually advanced. It is, however, a fine general principle of Tantrik worship that capacity, and not social distinction such as caste, determines competency for any particular worship. This is not so as regards the Vaidik ritual proper. One might have supposed that credit would have been given to the Tantra Shastra for this. But credit is given for nothing. Those who dilate on Vaidik exclusiveness have nothing to say as regards the absence of it in the Agama.

The Shudra is precluded from the performance of Vaidik rites, the reading of the Vedas, and the recital of Vaidik Mantras. His worship is practically limited to that of his Ishtadevata, the Vana-lingapuja with Tantrik and Pauranik mantra and such Vrata as consist in penance and charity. In other cases, the Vrata is performed through a Brahmana. The Tantra Shastra makes no caste distinction as regards worship, in the sense that though it may not challenge the exclusive right of the twice-born to Vaidik rites, it provides other and similar rites for the Shudra.

Thus there is both a Vaidik and Tantrik Gayatri and Sandhya, and there are rites available for worshippers of all castes. All may read the Tantras which contain their form of worship, and carry them out and recite the Tantrik Mantras. All castes, even the lowest Candala may, if otherwise fit, receive the Tantrik initiation and be a member of a Cakra or circle of worship. In the Cakra all the members partake of food and drink together, and are then deemed to be greater than Brahmanas, though upon the break-up of the Cakra the ordinary caste and social relations are re-established. It is necessary to distinguish between social differences and competency (Adhikara) for worship. Adhikara, so fundamental a principle of Brahmanism, means that all are not equally entitled to the same teaching and ritual. They are entitled to that of which they are capable, irrespective (according to the Agama) of such social distinctions as caste. All are competent for Tantrik worship, for, in the words of the Gautamiya which is a *Vaishnava Tantra* (Chap. I) the Tantra Shastra is for all castes and all women.

Sarva-varnadhikarash ca narinam yog ya eva ca.

Though according to Vaidik usage, the wife was co-operator (Sahadharmini) in the household rites, now-a-days, so far as I can gather, they are not accounted much in such matters, though it is said that the wife may, with the consent of her husband, fast, take vows, perform Homa, Vrata and the like. According to the Tantra Shastra, a woman may not only receive Mantra, but may, as Guru, initiate and give it (*Rudrayamala* II, ii, and XV). She is worshipped both as wife of Guru and as Guru herself (*ib.*, I. i. *Matrikabheda Tantra* (c. vii), *Annadakalpa Tantra* cited in *Pranatosini,* p. 68, and as regards the former *Yogini Tantra* chap. i. *Gurupatni Maheshani gurur eva).* The Devi is Herself the Guru of all Shastras and woman, as indeed all females Her embodiments, are in a peculiar sense, Her representatives. For this reason all women are worshipful, and no harm should be ever done them, nor should any female animal be sacrificed.

Puja is the common term for ritual worship, of which there are numerous synonyms in the Sanskrit language such as Arcana, Vandana, Saparyya, Arhana, Namasya, Arca, Bhajana, though some of these stress certain aspects of it. Puja as also Vrata which are Kamya, that is, done to gain a particular end, are preceded by the Sankalpa, that is, a statement of the resolve to worship, as also of the particular object (if any) with which it is done. It runs in the form, "I—of—Gotra and so forth identifying the individual) am about to perform this Puja (or Vrata) with the object—". Thereby the attention and will of the Sadhaka are focused and braced up for the matter in hand. Here, as elsewhere, the ritual which follows is designed both by its complexity and variety (which prevents the tiring of the mind) to keep the attention always fixed, to prevent it from straying and to emphasise both attention and will by continued acts and mental workings. The object of the worship is the Ishtadevata, that is, the particular form of the Deity whom the Sadhaka worships, such as Devi in the case of a Shakta, Shiva in the case of the Shaiva (in eight forms in the case of Ashtamurti-puja as to which *Todala Tantra,* chap. V) and Vishnu as such or in His forms as Rama and Krishna in the case of the Vaishnava Sadhaka.

An object is used in the outer Puja (Bahyapuja) such as an image (Pratima), a picture and emblem such as a jar (Kalasa), Shalagrama (in the case of Vishnu worship), Linga and Yoni or Gauripatta (in the case of the worship) of Shiva (with Devi), or a geometrical design called Yantra. In the case of outer worship the first is the lowest form and the last the highest. It is not all who are capable of worshipping with a Yantra. It is obvious that simpler minds must be satisfied with images which delineate the form of the Devata completely and in material form. The advanced contemplate Devata in the lines and curves of a Yantra.

In external worship, the Sadhaka should first worship inwardly the mental image of the Devata which the outer objects assist to produce, and then by the life-giving (Prana-Pratishtha) ceremony he should infuse the image with life by the communication to it of the light, consciousness, and energy (Tejas) of the Brahman within him to the image without, from which there then bursts the luster of Her whose substance is Consciousness Itself (Caitanyamayi). In every place She exists as Shakti, whether in stone or metal as elsewhere, but in matter is veiled and seemingly inert. Caitanya (Consciousness) is aroused by the worshipper through the Pranapratishtha Mantra. An object exists for a Sadhaka only in so far as his mind perceives it. For and in him its essence as Consciousness is realised.

This is a fitting place to say a word on the subject of the alleged "Idolatry" of the Hindus. We are all aware that a similar charge has been made against Christians of the Catholic Church, and those who are conversant with this controversy will be better equipped both with knowledge and caution against the making of general and indiscriminate charges.

It may be well doubted whether the world contains an idolater in the sense in which that term is used by persons who speak of "the heathen worship of sticks and stones". According to the traveler A. B. Ellis ("The Tshi speaking peoples of the Gold Coast of West Africa"), even "negroes of the Gold Coast are always conscious that their offerings and worship are not paid to the inanimate object itself but to the indwelling God, and every native with whom I have conversed on the subject has laughed at the possibility of its being supposed that he would worship or offer sacrifice to some such object as a stone". Nevertheless a missionary or some traveler might tell him that he did. An absurd attitude on the part of the superior Western is that in which the latter not merely tells the colored races what they should believe, but what notwithstanding denial, they *in fact* believe and *ought* to hold according to the tenets of the latter's religion.

The charge of idolatry is kept up, notwithstanding the explanations given of their beliefs by those against whom it is made. In fact, the conviction that Eastern races are inferior is responsible for this. If we disregard such beliefs, then, anything may be idolatrous. Thus; to those who disbelieve in the "Real Presence," the Catholic worshipper of the Host is an idolater worshipping the material substance, bread. But, to the worshipper who believes that it is the Body of the Lord under the form of bread, such worship can never be idolatrous. Similarly as regards the Hindu worship of images. They are not to be held to worship clay or stone because others disbelieve in the efficacy of the Prana-Pratishtha ceremony. When impartially considered, there is nothing necessarily superstitious or ignorant in this rite.

Nor is this the case with the doctrine of the Real Presence which is interpreted in various ways. Whether either rite has the alleged effect attributed to it is another question. All matter is, according to Shakta doctrine, a manifestation of Shakti, that is, the Mother Herself in material guise. She is present in and as everything which exists. The ordinary man does not so view things. He sees merely gross unconscious matter. If, with such an outlook, he were fool enough to worship what was inferior to himself, he would be an idolater. But the very act of worship implies that the object is superior and conscious. To the truly enlightened Shakta everything is an object of worship, for all is a manifestation of God who is therein worshipped.

But that way of looking at things must be attained. The untutored mind must be aided to see that this is so. This is effected by the Pranapratishtha rite by which "life is established" in the image of gross matter. The Hindu then believes that the Pratima or image is a representation and the dwelling place of Deity. What difference, it may be asked, does this really make? How can a man's belief alter the objective fact? The answer is, it does not. God is not manifested by the image merely because the worshipper believes Him to be there. He is there in fact already. All that the Pranapratishtha rite does is, to enliven the consciousness of the worshipper into a realisation of His presence. And if He be both in fact, and to the belief of the worshipper, present, then the Image is a proper object of worship.

It is the subjective state of the worshipper's mind which determines whether an act is idolatrous or not. The Prana-Pratishtha rite is thus a mode by which the Sadhaka is given a true object of worship and is enabled to affirm a belief in the divine omnipresence with respect to that particular object of his devotion. The ordinary notion that it is mere matter is cast aside, and the divine notion that Divinity is manifested in all that is, is held and affirmed. "Why not then" (some missionary has said) "worship my boot?" There are contemptible people who do so in the European sense of that phrase.

But, nevertheless, there is no reason, according to Shakta teaching, why even his boot should not be worshipped by one who regards it and all else as a manifestation of the One who is in every object which constitutes the Many. Thus this Monistic belief is affirmed in the worship by some Shaktas of that which to the gross and ordinary mind is merely an object of lust. To such minds, this is a revolting and obscene worship. To those for whom such object of worship is obscene, such worship is and must be obscene. But what of the mind which is so purified that it sees the Divine presence in that which, to the mass of men, is an incitement to and object of lust? A man who, without desire, can *truly* so worship must be a very high Sadhaka indeed.

The *Shakta Tantra* affirms the Greek saying that to the pure all things are pure. In this belief and with, as the as the *Jnanarnava Tantra* says, the object of teaching men that this is so, we find the ritual use of substances ordinarily accounted impure. The real objection to the general adoption or even knowledge of such rites lies, from the Monistic standpoint, in the fact that the vast bulk of humanity are either of impure or weak mind, and that the worship of an object which is capable of exciting lust will produce it, not to mention the hypocrites who, under cover of such a worship, would seek to gratify their desires. In thc Paradise Legend, just as amongst some primitive tribes, man and woman go naked.

It was and is after they have fallen that nakedness is observed by minds no longer innocent. Rightly, therefore, from their standpoint, the bulk of men condemn such worship. Because, whatever may be its theoretical justification under conditions which rarely occur, pragmatically and for the bulk of men they are full of danger. Those who go to meet temptation should remember the risk. I have read that it is recorded of Robert d'Arbrissel, the saintly founder of the community of Fonte d'Evrault that he was wont on occasions to sleep with his nuns, to mortify his flesh and as a mode of strengthening his will against its demands. He did not touch them, but his exceptional success in preserving his chastity would be no ground for the ordinary man undertaking so dangerous an experiment.

In short, in order to be completely just, we must, in individual cases, consider intention and good faith. But, practically and for the mass, the counsel and duty to avoid the occasion of sin is, according to Shastrik principles themselves, enjoined. As a matter of fact, such worship has been confined to so limited a class that it would not have been necessary to deal with the subject were it not connected with Shakta worship, the matter in hand. To revert again to the "missionary's boot": whilst all things may be the object of worship, choice is naturally made of those objects which, by reason of their effect on the mind, are more fitted for it.

An image or one of the usual emblems is more likely to raise in the mind of the worshipper the thought of a Devata than a boot, and therefore, even apart from scriptural authority, it would not be chosen. But, it has been again objected, if the Brahman is in and appears equally in all things, how do we find some affirming that one image is more worthy of worship than another. Similarly, in Catholic countries, we find worshippers who prefer certain churches, shrines, places of pilgrimage and representations of Christ, His Mother and the Saints. Such preferences are not statements of absolute worth but of personal inclinations in the worshipper due to his belief in their special efficacy for him. Psychologically all this means that a particular mind finds that it works best in the direction desired by means of particular instruments. The image of Kali provokes in general only disgust in an European mind. But to the race-consciousness which has evolved that image of Deity, it is the cause and object of fervent devotion. In every case, those means must be sought and applied which will produce a practical and good result for the individual consciousness in question. It must be admitted, however, that image worship like everything else is capable of abuse; that is a wrong and (for want of a better term) an idolatrous tendency may manifest. This is due to ignorance.

Thus the aunt of a Catholic schoolboy friend of mine had a statue of St. Anthony of Padua. If the saint did not answer her prayers, she used to give the image a beating, and then shut it up in a cupboard with its "face to the wall" by way of punishment. I could cite numbers of instances of this ignorant state of mind taken from the past and present history of Europe. It is quite erroneous to suppose that such absurdities are confined to India, Africa or other colored countries. Nevertheless, we must, in each case, distinguish between the true scriptural teaching and the acts and notions of which they are an abuse.

The materials used or things done in Puja are called Upacara. The common number of these is sixteen, but there are more and less (*Principles of Tantra,* Part ii). The sixteen which include some of the lesser number and are included in the greater are: (1) Asana (seating of the image), (2) Svagata (welcoming of the Devata), (3) Padya (water for washing the feet), (4) Arghya (offerings which may be general or Samanya and special or Vishesha) made in the vessel, (5), (6) Acamana (water for sipping and cleansing the lips—offered twice), (7) Madhuparka (honey, ghee, milk and curd), (8) Snana (water for bathing), (9) Vasana (cloth for garment), (10) Abharana (jewels), (11) Gandha (Perfume), (12) Pushpa (flowers), (13) Dhupa (incense), (14) Dipa (lights), (15) Naivedya (food), and (16) Vandana or Namaskriya (prayer).

Why should such things be chosen? The Westerner who has heard of lights, flower and incense in Christian worship may yet ask the reason for the rest. The answer is simple. Honour is paid to the Devata in the way honour is paid to friends and those men who are worthy of veneration. So the Sadhaka gives that same honour to the Devata, a course that the least advanced mind can understand. When the guest arrives he is bidden to take a seat, he is welcomed and asked how he has journeyed. Water is given to him to wash his dusty feet and his mouth. Food and other things are given him, and so on. These are done in honour of men, and the Deity is honoured in the same way.

Some particular articles vary with the Puja. Thus, Tulasi leaf is issued in the Vishnu-puja; bael leaf (Bilva) in the Shiva-puja, and to the Devi is offered the scarlet hibiscus (Jaba). The Mantras said and other ritual details may vary according to the Devata worshipped. The seat (Asana) of the worshipper is purified as also the Upacara. Salutation is made to the Shakti of support (Adhara-shakti) the Power sustaining all. Obstructive Spirits are driven away (Bhutapasarpana) and the ten quarters are fenced from their attack by striking the earth three times with the left foot, uttering the weapon-mantra (Astrabija) "Phat," and by snapping the fingers round the head.

Other rituals also enter into the worship besides the offering of Upacara such as Pranayama or Breath control, Bhutasuddhi or purification of the elements of the body, Japa of Mantra, Nyasa (v. *post),* meditation (Dhyana) and obeisance (Pranama).

Besides the outer and material Puja, there is a higher inner (Antarpuja) and mental (Manasapuja). Here there is no offering of material things to an image or emblem, but the ingredients (Upacara) of worship are imagined only. Thus the Sadhaka, in lieu of material flowers offered with the hands, lays at the feet of the Devata the flower of good action. In the secret Rajasik Puja of the Vamacari, the Upacara are the five Tattvas (Pancatattva), wine, meat and so forth described in the next Chapter. Just as flowers and incense and so forth are offered in the general public ritual, so in this special secret ritual, dealt with in the next Chapter, the functions of eating, drinking and sexual union are offered to the Devata.

A marked feature of the Tantra Shastras is the use of the Yantra in worship. This then takes the place of the image or emblem, when the Sadhaka has arrived at the stage when he is qualified to worship with Yantra. Yantra, in its most general sense, means simply instrument or that by which anything is accomplished. In worship, it is that by which the mind is fixed on its object. The Yantra, in lieu of the image or emblem holds the attention, and is both the object of worship, and the means by which it is carried out. It is said to be so called because it subdues (Niyantrana) lust, anger and the other sufferings of Jiva, and the sufferings caused thereby. *(Tantra-tattva.* Sadharana Upasana-tattva.)

The Yantra is a diagram drawn or painted on paper, or other substances, engraved on metal, cut on crystal or stone. The magical treatises mention extraordinary Yantras drawn on leopard's and donkey's skin, human bones and so forth. The Yantras vary in design according to the Devata whose Yantra it is and in whose worship it is used. The difference between a Mandala (which is also a figure, marked generally on the ground) is that whilst a Mandala may be used in the case of any Devata, a Yantra is appropriate to a specific Devata only. As different Mantras are different Devatas, and differing Mantras are used in the worship of each of the Devatas, so variously formed Yantras are peculiar to each Devata and are used in its worship. The Yantras are therefore of various designs, according to the object of worship.

The cover of "Tantrik Texts" shows the great Sri Yantra. In the metal or stone Yantras no figures of Devatas are shown, though these together with the appropriate Mantras commonly appear in Yantras drawn or painted on paper, such as the Devata of worship, Avarana Shaktis and so forth. All Yantras have a common edging called Bhupura, a quadrangular figure with four "doors" which encloses and separates the Yantra from the outside world. A Yantra in my possession shows serpents crawling outside the Bhupura. The *Kaulavaliya Tantra* says that the distinction between Yantra and Devata is that between the body and the self. Mantra is Devata and Yantra is Mantra, in that it is the body of the Devata who is Mantra.

Yantram mantra-ma yam proktam mantratma devataiva hi
Dehatmanor yatha bedo yantradevata yos tatha.

As in the case of the image, certain preliminaries precede the worship of Yantra. The worshipper first meditates upon the Devata and then arouses Him or Her in himself. He then communicates the Divine Presence thus aroused to the Yantra. When the Devata has by the appropriate Mantra been invoked into the Yantra, the vital airs (Prana) of the Devata are infused therein by the Pranapratishtha ceremony, Mantra and Mudra (see for ritual *Mahanirvana,* VI. 63 *et seq.).* The Devata is thereby installed in the Yantra which is no longer mere gross matter veiling the Spirit which has been always there, but instinct with its aroused presence which the Sadhaka first welcomes and then worships.

In Tantrik worship, the body as well as the mind has to do its part, the former being made to follow the latter. This is of course seen in all ritual, where there is bowing, genuflection and so forth. As all else, gesture is here much elaborated. Thus, certain postures (Asana) are assumed in worship and Yoga. There is obeisance (Pranama), sometimes with eight parts of the body (Ashtangapranama), and circumambulation (Pradakshina) of the image. In Nyasa the hands are made to touch various parts of the body and so forth. A notable instance of this practice are the Mudras which are largely used in the Tantrik ritual. Mudra in this sense is ritual manual gesture.

The term Mudra has three meanings. In worship (Upasana,) it means these gestures. In Yoga it means postures in which not only the hands but the whole body takes part. And, in the secret worship with the Pancatattva, Mudra means various kinds of parched cereals which are taken with the wine and other ingredients (Upacara) of that particular worship. The term Mudra is derived from the root "to please" (Mud). The Tantraraja says that in its Upasana form, Mudra is so called because it gives pleasure to the Devatas. These Mudras are very numerous. It has been said that there are 108 of which 55 are in common use (Shabdakalpadruma *Sub Voce,* Mudra and see *Nirvana Tantra,* Chap. XI). Possibly there are more. 108 is favorite number.

The Mudra of Upasana is the outward bodily expression of inner resolve which it at the same time intensifies. We all know how in speaking we emphasise and illustrate our thought by gesture. So in welcoming (Avahana) the Devata, an appropriate gesture is made. When veiling anything, the hands assume that position (Avagunthana Mudra). Thus again in making offering (Arghya) a gesture is made which represents a fish (Matsya Mudra) by placing the right hand on the back of the left and extending the two thumbs finlike on each side of the hands. This is done as the expression of the wish and intention that the vessel which contains water may be regarded as an ocean with fish and all other aquatic animals.

The Sadhaka says to the Devata of his worship, "this is but a small offering of water in fact, but so far as my desire to honour you is concerned, regard it as if I were offering you an ocean." The Yoni in the form of an inverted triangle represents the Devi. By the Yoni Mudra the fingers form a triangle as a manifestation of the inner desire that the Devi should come and place Herself before the worshipper, for the Yoni is Her Pitha or Yantra. Some of the Mudra of Hathayoga which are in the nature both of a health-giving gymnastic and special positions required in Yoga-practice are described in A. Avalon's *The Serpent Power*. The *Gheranda Samhita,* a Tantrik Yoga work says (III. 4. 8. 10) that knowledge of the Yoga Mudras grants all Siddhi, and that their performance produces physical benefits, such as stability, firmness, and cure of disease.

Bhutasuddhi, an important Tantrik rite, means purification of the five "elements" of which the body is composed, and not "removal of evil demons," as Professor Monier-William's Dictionary has it. Though one of the meanings of Bhuta is Ghost or Spirit, it is never safe to give such literal translations without knowledge, or absurd mistakes are likely to be made. The *Mantramahodadhi* (Taranga I) speaks of it as a rite which is preliminary to the worship of a Deva.

Devarca yog yata-praptyai bhuta-shuddhim samacaret.

(For the attainment of competency to worship, the elements of which the body is composed, should be purified). The material human body is a compound of the five Bhutas of "earth," "water," "fire," "air", and "ether". These terms have not their usual English meaning but denote the five forms in which Prakriti the Divine Power as *materia prima* manifests Herself.

These have each a centre of operation in the five Cakras or Padmas (Centres or Lotuses) which exist in the spinal column of the human body. In the lowest of these centres (Muladhara), the Great Devi kundalini, a form of the Saguna Brahman, resides. She is ordinarily sleeping there. In kundalini-yoga, She is aroused and brought up through the five centres, absorbing, as She passes through each, the Bhuta of that centre, the subtle Tanmatra from which it derives and the connected organ of sense (Indriya). Having absorbed all these, She is led to the sixth or mind centre (Ajna) between the eyebrows where the last Bhuta or ether is absorbed in mind, and the latter in the Subtle Prakriti. The last in the form of Kundali Shakti then unites with Shiva in the upper brain called the thousand-petalled lotus (Sahasrara).

In Yoga this involution actually takes places with the result that ecstasy (Samadhi) is attained. But very few are successful Yogis. Therefore, Bhutasuddhi in the case of the ordinary worshipper is an imaginary process only. The Sadhaka imagines Kundali, that She is roused, that one element is absorbed into the other and so on, until all is absorbed in Brahman. The Yoga process will be found described in *The Serpent Power,* and Ch. V. 93 *et seq.* of the *Mahanirvana* gives an account of the ritual process.

The Sadhaka having dissolved all in Brahman, a process which instills into his mind the unity of all, then thinks of the "black man of sin" in his body. The body is then purified. By breathing and Mantra it is first dried and then burnt with all its sinful inclinations. It is then mentally bathed with the nectar of the water-mantra from head to feet. The Sadhaka then thinks that in lieu of his old sinful body a new Deva body has come into being. He who with faith and sincerity believes that he is regenerated is in fact so. To each who truly believes that his body is a Deva body it becomes a Deva body. The Deva body thus brought into being is strengthened by the Earth-mantra and divine gaze (Divyadrishti). Saying, with Bijas, the Mantra "He I am" (So'ham) the Sadhaka by Jiva-nyasa infuses his body with the life of the Devi, the Mother of all.

Nyasa is a very important and powerful Tantrik rite. The word comes from the root, "to place," and means the placing of the tips of the fingers and palm of the right hand on various parts of the body, accompanied by Mantra. There are four general divisions of Nyasa, *viz.,* inner (Antar), outer (Bahir), according to the creative (Srishti) and dissolving (Samhara) order (Krama). Nyasa is of many kinds such as Jiva-nyasa, Matrika or Lipi-nyasa, Rishi-nyasa, Shadamganyasa on the body (Hridayadi-shadamga-nyasa) and with the hands (Amgushthadi-shadamga-nyasa), Pitha-nyasa and so on. The *Kularnava* (IV. 20) mentions six kinds. Each of these might come under one or the other of the four general heads.

Before indicating the principle of this rite, let us briefly see what it is. After the Sadhaka has by Bhuta-shuddhi dissolved the sinful body and made a new Deva body, he, by Jiva-nyasa infuses into it the life of the Devi. Placing his hand on his heart he says, "He I am" thereby identifying himself with Shiva-Shakti. He then emphasises it by going over the parts of the body in detail with the Mantra Am and the rest thus.' saying the Mantra and what he is doing, and touching the body on the particular part with his fingers, he recites: "Am (and the rest) the vital force (Prana) of the blessed Kalika (in this instance) are here. Am (and the rest) the life of the Blessed Kalika is here; Am (and the rest) all the senses of the Blessed Kalika are here; Am (and the rest) may the speech, mind, sight, hearing, sense of smell of the Blessed Kalika coming here ever abide here in peace and happiness. Svaha". By this, the body is thought to become like that of Devata (Devatamaya). Matrika are the fifty letters of the Sanskrit alphabet, for as from a mother comes birth, so from the Brahman who, as the creator of "sound" is called "Shabdabrahman", the universe proceeds.

The Mantra-bodies of the Devata are composed of the Matrika or letters. The Sadhaka first sets the letters mentally (Antar-matrika-nyasa) in their several places in the six inner centres (Cakra), and then externally by physical action (Bahya-matrika-nyasa). The letters of the alphabet form the different parts of the body of the Devata which is thus built up in the Sadhaka himself. He places his hand on different parts of his body, uttering distinctly at the same time the appropriate Matrika for that part. The mental disposition in the Cakra is that given in *Serpent Power* by A. Avalon, each letter being repeated thus, Om Ham Namah (obeisance), Om Ksham Namah and so on with the rest. The external disposition is as follows: The vowels are placed on the forehead, face, right and left eye, right and left ear, right and left nostril, right and left cheek, upper and lower lip, upper and lower teeth, head and hollow of the mouth.

The consonants, 'Ka' to 'Va' are placed on the base of the right arm and the elbow, wrist base and tips of fingers, left arm, and right and left leg, right and left side, back navel, belly, heart, right and left shoulder, and space between the shoulders (Kakuda). Then, from the heart to the right palm, Sa; from the heart to the left palm, Sa (second); from the heart to the right foot, Sa; from the heart to the left foot, Ha; and lastly from the heart to the belly and the heart to the mouth, Ksha. This Matrikanyasa is of several kinds.

One form of Rishi-nyasa is as follows: "In the head, salutation to Brahma and the Brahmarishis; in the mouth, salutation to Gayatri and other forms of Verse; in the heart, salutation to the primordial Devata Kali; in the hidden part (Guhya), salutation to the Bija Krim; in the two feet, salutation to Hrim; in all the body, salutation to Shrim and Kalika. In Shadamganyasa on the body, certain letters are placed with the salutation Namah, and with the Mantras Svaha, Vashat, Vaushat, Hrim, Phat on the heart, head, crown-lock (Shikha), eyes, the front and back of the palm.

In Karanyasa, the Mantras are assigned to the thumbs, index fingers, middle fingers, fourth fingers, little fingers, and the front and back of the palm. From the above examples the meaning of Nyasa is seen. By associating the Divine with every part of the body and with the whole of it, the mind and body are sought to be made divine to the consciousness of the Sadhaka. They are that already, but the mind is made to so regard them. "What if it does?" the English reader may ask. How can the regarding a thing as divine make it so? In one sense it does not, for mind and body are as Shakti divine, whether this be known or not. But this must be known to the Sadhaka or they are not divine *for him.* His mind is trained to look upon them as divine manifestations of the One Supreme Essence which at base he and they are. According to Hindu views, primary importance is attached to mental states, for as the Divine Thought made the World, man makes his character therein by what he thinks. If he is always thinking of material things and has desires therefor, he becomes himself material and is given over to lust and other passions. If, on the contrary, he has always his mind on God, and associates everything with the thought of Him, his mind becomes pure and divine. As the Upanishad says, "What a man thinks that he becomes."

Thought is everything, molding our bodily features, moral and intellectual character and disposition, leading to and appearing in our actions. Much superficial criticism is levelled at this or other ritual, its variety, complexity, its lengthy character and so forth. If it is performed mechanically and without attention, doubtless it is mere waste of time. But if it is done with will, attention, faith and devotion, it must necessarily achieve the result intended. The reiteration of the same idea under varying forms brings home with emphasis to the consciousness of the Sadhaka the doctrine his Scripture teaches him, *viz.*, that his essence is Spirit and his mind and body are its manifestation. All is divine. All is Consciousness.

The object of this and all the other ritual is to make that statement a real experience for the Sadhaka. For the attainment of that state in which the Sadhaka feels that the nature (Bhava) of the Devata has come upon him, Nyasa is a great auxiliary. It is as it were the wearing of Divine jewels in different parts of the body.

The Bijas of the Devatas (which are Devatas) are the jewels which the Sadhaka places on the different parts of his body. By the particular Nyasa he places his Abhishtadevata in such parts, and by Vyapaka-Nyasa he spreads its presence throughout himself. He becomes thus permeated by the Divine and its manifestations, thus merging or mingling himself in or with the Divine Self or Lord.

Nyasa, Asana and other ritual are necessary, for the production of the desired state of mind and its purification (Cittashuddhi). The whole aim and end of ritual is Citta-shuddhi. Transformation of thought is transformation of being, for particular existence is a projection of thought, and thought is a projection from the Consciousness which is the Root of all.

This is the essential principle and rational basis of this, as of all, Tantrik Sadhana. Nyasa also has certain physical effects, for these are dependent on the state of mind. The pure restful state of meditation is reflected in the body of the worshipper. The actions of Nyasa are said to stimulate the nerve centres and to effect the proper distribution of the Shaktis of the human frame according to their dispositions and relations, preventing discord and distraction during worship, which itself holds steady the state thus induced.

Mantra is Devata and by Sadhana therewith the sought-for (Sadhya) Devata is attained, that is, becomes present to the consciousness of the Sadhaka or Mantrin. Though the purpose of Worship (Puja), Reading (Patha), Hymn (Stava), Sacrifice (Homa), Meditation (Dhyana), and that of the Diksha-mantra obtained on initiation are the same, yet the latter is said to be far more powerful, and this for the reason that in the first, the Sadhaka's Sadhana-shakti only operates whilst in the case of Mantra that Sadhana-shakti works in conjunction with Mantra-shakti which has the revelation and force of fire, than which nothing is more powerful. The special Mantra which is received at initiation (Diksha) is the Bija or Seed-Mantra sown in the field of the Sadhaka's heart, and the Tantrik Sandhya, Nyasa, Puja, and the like are the stem and branches upon which hymns of praise (Stuti) and prayer and homage (Vandana) are the leaves and flower, and the Kavaca consisting of Mantra, the fruit.

The utterance of a Mantra without knowledge of its meaning or of the Mantra-sadhana is a mere movement of the lips and nothing more. The Mantra sleeps. This is not infrequently the case in the present degeneracy of Hindu religion. For example, a Brahman lady confided to me her Diksha-mantra and asked me for its meaning, as she understood that I had a Bija-kosha or Lexicon which gave the meaning of the letters. Her Guru had not told her of its meaning, and inquiries elsewhere amongst Brahmanas were fruitless. She had been repeating the Mantra for years, and time had brought the wisdom that it could not do her much good to repeat what was without meaning to her. Japa is the utterance of Mantra as described later. Mantra-sadhana is elaborate. There are various processes preliminary to and involved in its right utterance which again consists of Mantra.

There are the sacraments or purifications (Samskara) of the Mantra (*Tantrasara,* p. 90). There are "birth" and "death" defilements of a Mantra *(ib.,* 75, *et seq.,)* which have to be cleansed. This and, of course, much else mean that the mind of the Mantrin has to be prepared and cleansed for the realisation of the Devata. There are a number of defects (Dosha) which have to be avoided or cured. There is purification of the mouth which utters the Mantra (Mukha-shodhana) (see as to this and the following *Sharada Tilaka* (Chap. x), purification of the tongue (Jihva-shodhana) and of the Mantra (Ashauca-bhanga). Mantra processes called Kulluka, Nirvana, Setu (see *Sharada Tilaka, loc cit,* Tantrasara, and Purashcaranabodhini, p. 48) which vary with the Devata of worship, awakening of Mantra (Nidrabhanga) its vitalising through consciousness (Mantracaitanya), pondering on the meaning of the Mantra and of the Matrikas constituting the body of the Devata (Mantrartha bhavana). There are Dipani, Yonimudra with meditation on the Yoni-rupa-bhagavati with the Yonibija (Eng) and so forth.

In ascertaining what Mantra may be given to any particular individual, certain Cakra calculations are made, according to which Mantras are divided into those which are friendly, serving, supporting or destroying (Siddha, Sadhya, Susiddha, Ari). All this ritual has as its object the establishment of that pure state of mind and feeling which are necessary for success (Mantra-siddhi). At length the Mantrin through his Cit-shakti awakening and vitalising the Mantra which in truth is one with his own consciousness (in that form) pierces through all its centres and contemplates the Spotless One *(Kubjika Tantra* V). The Shakti of the Mantra is called the Vacika Shakti or the means by which the Vacya Shakti or ultimate object is attained. The Mantra lives by the energy of the former. The Saguna-Shakti in the form of the Mantra is awakened by Sadhana and worshipped and She it is who opens the portals whereby the Vacya-Shakti is reached. Thus the Mother in the Saguna form is the Presiding Deity (Adhishthatri Devata) of the Gayatri Mantra.

As the Nirguna (formless) One, She is its Vacya Shakti. Both are in truth one and the same. But the Sadhaka, by the laws of his nature and its three Gunas, must first meditate on the gross (Sthula) form before he can realise the subtle (Sukshma) form which is his liberator. So for from being merely superstition, the Mantra-sadhana is, in large part, based on profound notions of the nature of Consciousness and the psychology of its workings. The Sadhaka's mind and disposition are purified, the Devata is put before him in Mantra form and by his own power of devotion (Sadhana Shakti) and that latent in the Mantra itself (Mantra-shakti) and expressed in his mind on realisation therein, such mind is first identified with the gross, and then with the subtle form which is his own transformed consciousness and its powers. Japa is defined as *Vidhanena mantroccaranam,* that is (for default of other more suitable words), the utterance or recitation of Mantra according to certain rules. Japa may however be of a nature which is not defined by the word, recitation. It is of three kinds *(Jnanarnava Tantra,* XX) namely, Vacika Japa, Upamshu Japa, Manasa Japa. The first is the lowest and the last the highest form. Vacika is verbal Japa in which the Mantra is distinctly and audibly recited (Spashta-vaca). Upamshu Japa is less gross and therefore superior to this. Here the Mantra is not uttered (Avyakta) but there is a movement of the lips and tongue (Sphuradvaktra) but no articulate sound is heard.

In the highest form or mental utterance (Manasa-japa) there is neither articulate sound nor movement. Japa takes place in the mind only by meditation on the letters (Chintanakshararupavan). Certain conditions are prescribed as those under which Japa should be done, relating to physical cleanliness, the dressing of the hair, garments worn, the seated posture (Asana), the avoidance of certain states of mind and actions, and the nature of the recitation. Japa is done a specified number of times, in lakhs by great Sadhakas. If the mind is really centred and not distracted throughout these long and repeated exercises the result must be successful. Repetition is in all things the usual process by which a certain thing is fixed in the mind.

It is not considered foolish for one who has to learn a lesson to repeat it himself over and over again until it is got by heart. The same principle applies to Sadhana. If the "Hail Mary" is said again and again in the Catholic rosary, and if the Mantra is similarly said in the Indian Japa, neither proceeding is foolish, provided that both be done with attention and devotion. The injunction against "vain repetition" was not against repetition but that of a vain character. Counting is done either with a Mala or rosary (Mala-japa) or with the thumb of the right hand upon the joints of the fingers of that hand according to a method varying according to the Mantra (Kara-japa).

Purashcarana is a form of Sadhana in which, with other ritual, Japa of Mantra, done a large number of times, forms the chief part. A short account of the rite is given in the *Purashcarana-bodhini* by Harakumara Tagore (1895). (See also *Tantrasara* 71 and the *Purashcaryarnava* of the King of Nepal.) The ritual deals with preparation for the Sadhana as regards chastity, food, worship, measurements of the Mandapa or Pandal and of the altar, the time and place of performance and other matters. The Sadhaka must lead a chaste life (Brahmacarya) during the period prescribed. He must eat the pure food called Havishyannam or boiled milk (Kshtra), fruits, Indian vegetables, and avoid all other food which has the effect of stimulating the passions. He must bathe, do Japa of the Savitri Mantra, entertain Brahmanas and so forth.

Pancagavya is eaten, that is, the five products of the cow, namely, milk, curd, ghee, urine, and dung, the two last (except in the case of the rigorously pious) in smaller quantity. Before the Puja there is worship of Ganesha and Kshetrapala and the Sun, Moon, and Devas are invoked. Then follows the Samkalpa. The Ghata or Kalasa (jar) is placed in which the Devata is invoked. A Mandala or figure of a particular design is marked on the ground and on it the jar is placed. Then the five or nine gems are placed in the jar which is painted red and covered with leaves. The ritual then prescribes for the tying of the crown lock (Shikha), the posture (Asana) of the Sadhaka, Japa, Nyasa, and the Mantra ritual. There is meditation as directed, Mantra-chaitanya and Japa of the Mantra the number of times for which vow has been made.

The daily life of the religious Hindu was in former times replete with worship. I refer those who are interested in the matter to the little work, *The Daily Practices of the Hindus* by Srisha Candra Vasu, the Sandhyavandana of all Vedic Shakhas by B. V. Kameshvara Aiyar, the Kriyakandavaridhi and Purohita-darpanam. The positions and Mudras are illustrated in Mrs. S. C. Belons' *Sandhya or daily prayer of the Brahmin* published in 1831. It is not here possible to do more than indicate the general outlines of the rites followed.

As the Sadhaka awakes he makes salutation to the Guru of all and recites the appropriate Mantras and confessing his inherent frailty ("I know Dharma and yet would not do it. I know Adharma and yet would not renounce it,")—the Hindu form of the common experience "Video meliora," he prays that he may do right and offers all the actions of the day to God. Upon touching the ground on leaving his bed he salutes the Earth, the manifestation of the All-Good. He then bathes to the accompaniment of Mantra and makes oblation to the Devas, Rishis or Seers and the Pitris who issued from Sandhya, Brahma the Pitamaha of humanity, and then does rite.

This is the Vaidik form which differs according to Veda and Shakha for the twice-born and there is a Tantriki Sandhya for others. It is performed thrice a day at morn, at noon, and evening. The Sandhya consists generally speaking, of Acamana (sipping of water), Marjjana-snana (sprinkling of the whole body), Pranayama (Breath-control), Aghamarshana (expulsion of sin), prayer to the Sun and then (the canon of the Sandhya) Japa of the Gayatri-mantra. Rishi-nyasa and Shadamga-nyasa (v. *ante),* and meditation of the Devi Gayatri, in the morning as Brahmani (Shakti of Creation), at midday as Vaisnavi (Shakti of maintenance), and in evening as Rudrani (Shakti which "destroys" in the sense of withdrawing creation). The Sandhya with the Aupasana fire-rite and Pancayajna are the three main daily rites, the last being offerings to the Devas, to the Pitris, to animals and birds (after the Vaishvadeva rite), to men (as by entertainment of guests) and the study of Vaidik texts. By these five Yajnas, the worshipper daily places himself in right relations with all being, affirming such relation between Devas, Pitris, Spirits, men, the organic creation and himself.

The word "Yajna" comes from the root *Yaj* (to worship) and is commonly translated "sacrifice," though it includes other rituals than what an English reader might understand by that term. Thus, Manu speaks of four kinds of Yajna as Deva, Bhauta (where ingredients are used), Niryaja and Pitryajna. Sometimes the term is used in connection with any kind of ceremonial rite, and so one hears of Japa-yajna (recitation of Mantra), Dhyana-yajna (meditation) and so on. The Pancatattva ritual with wine and the rest is accounted a Yajna. Yajnas are also classified according to the dispositions and intentions of the worshipper into Sattvika, Rajasika and Tamasika Yajna.

A common form of Yajna is the Devayajna Homa rite in which offerings of ghee are made (in the Kunda or fire-pit) to the Deva of Fire who is the carrier of oblations to the Devas. Homa is an ancient Vaidik rite incorporated with others in the General Tantrik ritual. It is of several kinds, and is performed either daily, or on special occasions, such as the sacred thread ceremony, marriage and so forth. Besides the daily (Nitya) ceremonies such as Sandhya there are occasional rites (Naimittika) and the purificatory sacraments (Samskara) performed only once.

The ordinary ten Samskaras are Vaidik rites done to aid and purify the individual in the important events of his life, namely, the Garbhadhana sanctifying conception prior to the actual placing of the seed in the womb, the Pumsavana and Simantonnayaṇa or actual conception and during pregnancy. It has been suggested that the first Samskara is performed with reference to the impulse to development from the "fertilisation of the ovum to the critical period: the second with reference to the same impulse from the last period to that of the viability stage of the fetus," and the third refers to the period in which there is viability to the full term (see Appendix on Samskaras. *Pranavavada,* I. 194). Then follows the Samskara on birth (Jata-karma), the naming ceremony (Nama-karana), the taking of the child outdoors for the first time to see the sun (Nishkramana), the child's first eating of rice (Annaprasana), his tonsure (Cudakarana), and the investiture in the case of the twice-born with the sacred thread (Upanayana) when the child is reborn into spiritual life. This initiation must be distinguished from the Tantrik initiation (Mantra-diksha) when the Bija-mantra is given by the Guru. Lastly there is marriage (Udvaha). These Samskaras, which are all described in the ninth Chapter of the *Mahanirvana Tantra,* are performed at certain stages in the human body with a view to effect results beneficial to the human organism through the superphysical and subjective methods of ancient East science.

Vrata is a part of Naimittika—occasional ritual or Karma. Commonly translated as vows, they are voluntary devotions performed at specified times in honour of particular Devatas (such as Krishna's birthday), or at any time (such as the Savitrivrata). Each Vrata has its peculiarities, but there are certain features common to all, such as chastity, fasting, bathing, taking of pure food only and no flesh or fish. The great Vrata for a Shakta is the Durga-puja in honour of the Devi as Durga.

The fasting which is done in these or other cases is called Tapas, a term which includes all forms of ascetic austerity and zealous Sadhana such as the sitting between five fires (Pancagni-tapah) and the like. Tapas has however a still wider meaning and is then of three kinds, namely, bodily (Shariraka), by speech (Vacika) and by mind (Manasa), a common division both of Indian and Buddhist Tantra. The first includes external worship, reverence, support of the Guru, Brahmanas and the wise (Prajna), bodily cleanliness, continence, simplicity of life and avoidance of hurt to any being (Ahimsa).

The second form includes truth, good, gentle and affectionate speech and study of the Vedas. The third or mental Tapas includes self-restraint, purity of disposition, tranquillity and silence. Each of these classes has three sub-divisions, for Tapas may be Sattvika, Rajasika, or Tamasika according as it is done with faith, and without regard to its fruit, or for its fruit; or is done through pride and to gain honour or respect or power; or lastly which is done ignorantly or with a view to injure and destroy others such as Abhicara or the Sadhana of the Tantrik Shatkarma (other than Shanti), that is, fascination or Vashikarana, paralysing or Stambhana, creating enmity or Vidveshana, driving away or Uccatana, and killing or Marana when performed for a malevolent purpose. Karma ritual is called Kamya when it is done to gain some particular end such as health, prosperity and the like.

The highest worship is called Nishkama-karma, that is, it is done not to secure any material benefit but for worship's sake only. Though it is not part of ordinary ritual, this is the only place where I can conveniently mention a peculiar Sadhana, prevalent, so far as I am aware, mainly if not wholly amongst Tantrikas of a Shakta type which is called Nilasadhana or Black Sadhana. This is of very limited application being practiced by some Vira Sadhakas in the cremation ground. There are terrifying things in these rituals and therefore only the fearless practice them.

The Vira trains himself to be indifferent and above all fear. A leading rite is that called Shava Sadhana which is done with the means of a human corpse. I have explained elsewhere (*Serpent Power*) why a corpse is chosen. The corpse is laid with its face to the ground. The Sadhaka sits on the back of the body of the dead man on which he draws a Yantra and then worships. If the rite is successful it is said that the head of the corpse turns round and asks the Sadhaka what is the boon he craves, be it liberation or some material benefit. It is believed that the Devi speaks through the mouth of the corpse which is thus the material medium by which She manifests Her presence. In another rite, the corpse is used as a seat (Shavasana). There are sittings also (Asana) on skulls (Mundasana) and the funeral pyre (Citasana). However repellent or suspect these rites may appear to be to a Western, it is nevertheless the fact that they have been and are practiced by genuine Sadhakas of fame such as in the past the famed Maharaja of Nattore and others. The interior cremation ground is within the body that being the place where the passions are burnt away in the fire of knowledge.

The Adya Shakti or Supreme Power of the Shaktas is, in the words of the Trishati, concisely described as Ekananda-cidakritih. Eka = Mukya, Ananda = Sukham, Cit = Caitanyam or Prakasha = Jnanam; and Akritih = Svaruipa. She is thus Sacchidananda-brahmarupa,. Therefore, the worship of Her is direct worship of the Highest. This worship is based on Advaitavada. Therefore, for all Advaitins, its Sadhana is the highest. The Shakta Tantra is thus a Sadhana Shastra of Advaitavada. This will explain why it is dear to, and so highly considered by Advaitins.

It is claimed to be the one and only stepping stone which leads directly to Kaivalya or Nirvanamukti; other forms of worship procuring for their followers (from the Saura to the Shaiva) various ascending forms of Gaunamukti. Others of course may claim this priority. Every sect considers itself to be the best and is in fact the best for those who, with intelligence, adopt it. Were it not so its members would presumably not.

belong to it but would choose some other. No true Shakta, however, will wrangle with others over this. He will be content with his faith of which the *Nigamakalpataru* says, that as among castes the Brahmanas are foremost, so amongst Sadhakas are the Shaktas. For, as *Niruttara Tantra* says, there is no Nirvana without knowledge of Shakti *(Shaktijnanam vina devi nirvanam naiva jayate).* Amongst the Shaktas, the foremost are said to be the worshippers of the Kali Mantra.

The Adimahavidya is Kalika. Other forms are Murttibheda of Brahmarupini Kalika. Kalikula is followed by Jnanis of Divya and Vira Bhavas; and Shrikula by Karmin Sadhakas. According to Niruttara, Kalikula includes Kali, Tara, Raktakali, Bhuvana, Mardini, Triputa, Tvarita, Pratyamgiravidya, Durga, and Shrikula includes Sundari, Bhairavi, Bala, Bagala, Kamala, Dhumavati, Matamgi, Svapnavatividya, Madhumati Mahavidya. Of these forms Kalika is the highest or Adyamurti as being Shuddhasattvagunapradhana, Nirvikara, Nirgunabrahma-svarupaprakashika, and, as the *Kamadhenu Tantra* says, directly Kaivalyadayini. Tara is Sattvagunatmika, Tattvavidyadayini, for by Tattvajnana one attains Kaivalya. Shodashi, Bhuvaneshvari, Cinnamasta are Rajahpradhana Sattvagunatmika, the givers of Gaunamukti and Svarga. Dhumavati, Kamala, Bagala, Matangi are Tamahpradhana whose action is invoked in the magical Shatkarma.

The most essential point to remember as giving the key to all which follows is that Shaktadharma is Monism (Advaitavada). *Gandharva Tantra* says, "Having as enjoined saluted the Guru and thought "So'ham,' the wise Sadhaka, the performer of the rite should meditate upon the unity of Jiva and Brahman."

Gurun natva vidhanena so'ham iti purodhasah

Aikyam sambhavayet dhiman jivasya brahmano'pica.

Kali Tantra says: "Having thus meditated, the Sadhaka should worship Devi with the notion, 'So'ham'."

Evam dhyatva tato devim so'ham atmanam arcayet.

Kubjika Tantra says: "A Sadhaka should meditate upon himself as one and the same with Her" (*Taya sahitamatmanam ekibhutam vicintayet).* The same teaching is to be found throughout the Shastra: *Nila Tantra* directing the Sadhaka to think of himself as one with Tarini; *Gandharva Tantra* telling him to meditate on the self as one with Tirupura not different from Paramatma; and Kalikulasarvasva as one with Kalika and so forth. For as the *Kularnava Tantra* says: "The body is the temple of God. Jiva is Sadashiva. Let him give up his ignorance as the offering which is thrown away (Nirmalya) and worship with the thought and feeling, 'I am He'."

Deho devalayah proktah jivo devah Sadashivah

Tyajed ajnananirmalyam so'ham bhavena pujayet.

This Advaitavada is naturally expressed in the ritual.

The Samhita and Brahmanas of the four Vedas are (as contrasted with the Upanishads) Traigunyavishaya. There is therefore much in the Vaidik Karmakanda which is contrary to Brahmajnana. The same remarks apply to the ordinary Pashu ritual of the day. There are differences of touchable and untouchable, food, caste, and sex. How can a man directly qualify for Brahmajnana who even in worship is always harping on distinctions of caste and sex and the like? He who distinguishes does not know. Of such distinctions the higher Tantrik worship of the Shakta type knows nothing.

As the *Yogini Tantra* says, the Shastra is for all castes and for women as well as men. Tantra Shastra is Upasana Kanda and in this Shakta Upasana the Karma and Jnana Kanda are mingled (Mishra). That is, Karma is the ritual expression of the teaching of Jnana Kanda and is calculated to lead to it. There is nothing in it which contradicts Brahmajnana. This fact, therefore, renders it more conducive to the attainment of such spiritual experience. Such higher ritual serves to reveal Jnana in the mind of the Pashu.

So it is rightly said that a Kula-jnani even if he be a Candala is better than a Brahmana. It is on these old Tantrik principles that the Indian religion of today can alone, if at all, maintain itself. They have no concern, however, with social life and what is called "social reform". For all secular purposes the Tantras recognise caste, but in spiritual matters spiritual qualifications alone prevail. There are many such sound and high principles in the Tantra Shastra for which it would receive credit, if it could only obtain a fair and unprejudiced consideration. But there are none so blind as those who will not see. And so we find that the "pure and high" ritual of the Veda is set in contrast with theca supposed "low and impure" notions of the Tantra. On the contrary, a Tantrik Pandit once said to me: "The Vaidik Karmakanda is as useful for ordinary men as is a washerman for dirty clothes. It helps to remove their impurities. But the Tantra Shastra is like a glorious tree which gives jeweled fruit."

Sadhana, as I have said, is defined as that which leads to Siddhi. Sadhana comes from the root "Sadh"—to exert, to strive. For what'? That depends on the Sadhana and its object. Sadhana is any means to any end and not necessarily religious worship, ritual and discipline. He who does Hatha-yoga, for physical health and strength, who accomplishes a magical Prayoga, who practices to gain an "eightfold memory" and so forth are each doing Sadhana to gain a particular result (Siddhi), namely, health and strength, a definite magical result, increased power of recollection and so forth. A Siddhi again is any power gained as the result of practice.

Thus, the Siddhi of Vetala Agni Sadhana is control over the fire-element. But the Sadhana which is of most account and that of which I here speak, is religious worship and discipline to attain true spiritual experience. What is thus sought and gained may be either Heaven (Svarga), secondary liberation (Gaunamukti) or full Nirvana. It is the latter which in the highest sense is Siddhi, and striving for that end is the chief and highest form of Sadhana. The latter term includes not merely ritual worship in the sense of adoration or prayer, but every form of spiritual discipline such as sacraments (Samskara), austerities (Tapas), the reading of Scripture (Svadhyaya), meditation (Dhyana) and so forth. Yoga is a still higher form of Sadhana; for the term Yoga means strictly not the result but the means whereby Siddhi in the form of Samadhi may be had.

Ordinarily, however, Sadhana is used to express all spiritual disciplines based on the notion of worshipper and worshipped;

referring thus to Upasana, not Yoga. The latter passes beyond these and all other dualisms to Monistic experience (Samadhi). The first leads up to the second by purifying the mind (Cittashuddhi), character and disposition (Bhava) so as to render it capable of Jnana or Laya Yoga; or becomes itself Parabhakti which, as the *Devibhagavata* says, is not different from Jnana. The great Siddhi is thus Moksha; and Moksha is Para-matma, that is, the Svarupa of Atma.

But the Sadhaka is Jivatma, that is, Atma associated with Avidya of which Moksha or Paramatma is free. Avidya manifests as mind and body, the subtle and gross vehicles of Spirit. Man is thus therefore Spirit (Atmasvarupa), which is Saccidananda, Mind (Antahkarana) and body (Sthula-sharira). The two latter are forms of Shakti, that is, projections of the Creative Consciousness through and as its Maya. The essential operation of Maya and of the Kancukas is to seemingly *contract* consciousness. As the *Yoginihridaya Tantra* says, the going forth (Prashara) of Consciousness (Samvit) is in fact a contraction (Sankoca as Matri, Mana, Meya or known, knowing, being known). Consciousness is thus finilised into a limited self which and other selves regard one another as mutually exclusive.

The Self becomes its own object as the many forms of the universe. It conceives itself as separate from them. Oblivious in separateness of its essential nature it regards all other persons and things as different from itself. It acts for the benefit of its limited self. It is in fact selfish in the primary sense of the term; and this selfishness is the root of all its desires, of all its sins. The more mere worldly desires are fostered, the greater is the bondage of man to the mental and material planes. Excessively selfish desires display themselves as the sins of lust, greed, anger, envy and so forth. These bind more firmly than regulated desire and moreover lead to Hell (Naraka).

The most general and ultimate object of Sadhana is therefore to cast off from the Self this veil of Avidya and to attain that Perfect experience which is Atmasvarupa or Moksha. But to know Brahman is to *be* Brahman. *Brahma veda brahmaiva bhavati* as Shruti says. In essence man is Brahman. But owing to Avidya it is necessary to do something in order that this ever existent fact may be realised. That action (Kriya) is the work of Sadhana in its endeavour to clear away the veiling of Avidya which is ignorance.

In the sense that Avidya is being removed man may be said by Sadhana to become Brahman: that is, he realises himself as what he truly is and was. Sadhana, therefore, by the grace of Devi or "descent of Shakti" (Shaktipata) "converts" (to use an English term) the Sadhaka, that is, turns him away from separatist worldly enjoyment to seek his own true self as the pure Spiritual Experience. This transformation is the work and aim of Sadhana. But this experience is not to be had in its completest sense at once and at a bound.

It is, as Patanjali says, very rare. Indeed those who truly desire it are very few. Brahman is mindless (Amanah); for mind is a fetter on true consciousness. This mindlessness (Niralambapuri) is sought through the means of Yoga. But no would-be Yogi can attain this state unless his mind is already pure, that is, not only free from gross sin, but already possessing some freedom from the bondage of worldly desires, cultivated and trained, and desirous of liberation (Mumukshu). The aim, therefore, of preliminary Sadhana is to secure that purification of mind (Cittashuddhi) which is alone the basis on which Yoga works. The first object then is to restrain the natural appetites, to control the senses, and all that excessive selfishness beyond the bounds of Dharma which is sin (Papa). Dharma prescribes these bounds because unrestricted selfish enjoyment leads man downward from the path of his true evolution.

Man is, as regards part of his nature, an animal, and has, according to the Shastra, passed through all animal forms in his 84 lakhs of previous births. But he has also a higher nature and if he conforms to the path laid out for him will progress by degrees to the state of that Spirit whose limited form he now is. If he strays from that path he falls back, and continued descent may bring him again to the state of apparently unconscious matter through many intervening Hells in this and other worlds. For this reason, the Shastra repeats that he is a "self-killer" who, having with difficulty attained to manhood, neglects the opportunities of further progress which they give him *(Kularnava Tantra* I). Therefore, he must avoid sin which leads to a fall.

How can the impure realise the Pure? How can the mere seeker of sensual enjoyment desire formless liberating Bliss? How can he recognise his unity with all if he is bound in selfishness which is the root of all sin? How can he realise the Brahman who thinks himself to be the separate enjoyer of worldly objects and is bound by all sensualities? In various forms this is the teaching of all religions. It would be hardly necessary to elaborate what is so plain were it not apparently supposed that the Tantra Shastra is a strange exception to these universally recognised principles. "I thought," said a recent English correspondent of mine, "that the Tantra was a wholly bad lot belonging to the left hand path." This is not so: common though the notion be.

The Shastra teaches that the Sadhaka must slay his "Six Enemies" which are the six cardinal sins and all others allied with them. Whether all the *means* enjoined are good, expedient, and fitting for the purpose is a different matter. This is a distinction which none of its critics ever makes; but which accuracy and justice require they should make if they condemn the method. It is one thing to say that a particular method prescribed for a good end is bad, dangerous, or having regard to the present position of the generality of men, unadvisable; and a totally different thing to say that the *end* which is sought is itself bad. The Tantra, like all Shastras, seeks the Paramartha and nothing else. Whether all the forms of search are good (and against the bulk of them no moral objection can be raised) is another question. Let it be for argument supposed that one or other of the means prescribed is not good but evil. Is it accurate or just to condemn not only the particular Shastra in which they occur (as the discipline of a particular class of Sadhakas only), but also the whole of the Agamas of all classes of worshippers under the misleading designation "The Tantra"?

I am here speaking from the point of view of one who is not a Hindu. Those, however, who are Hindus must logically either deny that the Tantra Shastra is the Word of Shiva or accept all which that Word says. For if a Tantra prescribes what is wrong this vitiates the authority, in all matters, of the Tantra in which wrong is ordained. It may be that other matters dealt with should be accepted, but this is so not because of any authority in the particular Tantra, but because they have the countenance elsewhere of a true authoritative scripture. From this logical position no escape is possible.

Let us for the moment turn to the celebrated Hymn to Kali (of, as those who read it might call, the extremist, that is Vira Shakta worship) entitled the Karpuradi Stotra *(Tantrik Texts,* Vol. IX), which like most (probably all) of its kind has both a material (Sthula) and a subtle (Sukshma) meaning. In the 19th verse it is said that the Devi delights to receive in sacrifice flesh, with bones and hair, of goat, buffalo, cat, sheep, camel and of man. In its literal sense this passage may be taken as an instance of the man-sacrifice of which we find traces throughout the world (and in some of the Tantras) in past stages of man's evolution. Human sacrifices permitted by other Semites were forbidden by the Mosaic Code, although there is an obvious allusion to such a custom in the account of the contemplated sacrifice of Isaac by Abraham (Gen. xxii).

The Israelites, however, offered bloody sacrifices the savor of which God (Yahweh) is represented as enjoying, they being necessary in His honour and to avert His wrath (Gen. viii. 21; Lev. i. 9. 13, 17; Judges vi. 17, xii. 15; Gen. viii. 20-21; 1 Sam xxvi. 19). Nothing is more common in all religions (and Christianity as by some understood provides many examples) than to materially understand spiritual truths. For such is the understanding of material of Sthuladarshin (grossly seeing) men. But, even in the past, those who were spiritual referred all sacrifice to the self; an inner sacrifice which all must make who would attain to that Spirit which we may call Kali, God, Allah, or what we will.

But what is the Svarupa-vyakhya or true meaning of this apparently revolting verse? The meaning is that inner or mental worship (Antaryaga) is done to Her who is black (Asita) because She is the boundless (Sita = Baddha) Consciousness (Cidrupa) whose true nature is eternal liberation (Nityamukta-Svabhava). And just as in outer worship material offerings (Upacara) are made, so the Sadhaka sacrifices to Her his lust (the Goat-Kama), his anger (the Buffalo-Krodha), his greed (the Cat-Lobha), his stupidity of illusion (the Sheep-Moha), his envy (the Camel-Matsaryya) and his pride and infatuation with worldly things (the Man-Mada). All will readily recognise in these animals and man the qualities (Guna) here attributed to them. It is to such as so sacrifice to whom is given Siddhi in the form of the five kinds of Mukti.

Competency for Tantra (Tantrashastradhikara) is described in the second Chapter of the *Gandharva Tantra* as follows: The aspirant must be intelligent (Daksha), with senses controlled (Jitendriya), abstaining from injury to all beings (Sarva himsa-vinirmukta), ever doing good to all (Sarvapranihite rata), pure (Shuci), a believer in Veda (Astika), a non-dualist (Dvaitahina), whose faith and refuge is in Brahman (Brahmanishtha, Brahmavadi, Brahma, Brahma-parayana). "Such an one," it adds, "is competent for this Scripture *otherwise he is no Sadhaka" (So'smin shastre'dhikari tad anyatra na sadhakah).* It will be allowed by all that these are strange qualifications for a follower of "a bad scripture of the left hand path." Those who are on such a path are not supposed to be seekers of the Brahman, nor solicitous for the good of all being. Rather the reverse.

The *Kularnava Tantra* (which I may observe deals with the ill-famed Pancatattva ritual) gives in the thirteenth Chapter a long list of qualifications necessary in the case of a Tantrik disciple (Shishya). Amongst these, it rejects the slave of food and sexual pleasure (Jihvopasthapara); the lustful (Kamuka), shameless (Nirlajja), the greedy and voracious eater, the sinner in general who does not follow Dharma and Acara, who is ignorant, who has no desire for spiritual knowledge, who is a hypocrite, with Brahman on his lips but not in his heart, and who is without devotion (Bhakti). Such qualifications are inconsistent with its alleged intention to encourage sensuality unless we assume that all such talk in all the Shastras throughout all time is mere hypocrisy.

It is not however sufficient for the Sadhaka to turn from sin and the occasions of it. It is necessary to present the mind with a pure object and to busy it in pure actions. This not only excludes other objects and actions but trains the mind in such a way towards goodness and illumination that it at length no longer desires wrongful enjoyment; or lawful Pashu enjoyment or even enjoyment infused with a spiritual Bhava, and thus finally attains desirelessness (Nishkama-bhava). The mind dominated *by* matter, then regulated *in* matter, consciously releases itself to first work *through* matter, then *against* matter; then rising *above* matter it, at length, enters the Supreme State in which all the antithesis of Matter and Spirit have gone.

What then are the means by which spiritual Siddhi is attained? Some are possibly common to all religions; some are certainly common to more than one religion, such as objective ritual worship (Bahyapuja), inner or mental worship (Manasa-Puja or Antarpuja) of the Ishtadevata, prayer (Prarthana), sacraments (Samskara), self-discipline for the control of the will and natural appetites (Tapas), meditation (Dhyana) and so forth. There is, for instance, as I have elsewhere pointed out, a remarkable similarity between the Tantrik ritual of the Agamas and Christian ritual in its Catholic form.

It has been suggested that Catholicism is really a legacy of the ancient civilization, an adaptation of the old religions (allied in many respects with Shakta worship) of the Mediterranean races; deriving much of its strength from its non-Christian elements. I will not observe on this except to say that you do not dispose of the merits of any ritual by showing (if it be the fact) that it is extremely old and non-Christian. Christianity is one of the great religions, but even its adherents, unless ignorant, will not claim for it the monopoly of all that is good.

To deal in detail with Tantrik Sadhana would take more than a volume. I have shortly summarised some important rituals. I will now shortly indicate some of the general psychological principles on which it is based and which if understood, will give the key to an understanding of the extraordinary complexity and variety of the actual ritual details.

I will also illustrate the application of these principles in some of the more common forms of worship.

It is recognised in the first place that mind and body mutually react upon one another. There must therefore be a physical Sadhana as the groundwork of the mental Sadhana to follow. India has for ages recognised what is now becoming generally admitted, namely, that not only health but clarity of mind, character, disposition, and morals are affected by the nourishment, exercise, and general treatment of the body. Thus, from the moral aspect, one of the arguments against the use of meat and strong drink is the encouragement they give to animal passions. Why then it may be asked do these form a part of some forms of Shakta Sadhana'? I answer this later. It is however a Hindu trait to insist on purity of food and person. Tantrik Hathayoga deals in full with the question of bodily cleanliness, food, sexual continence, and physical exercise. But there are injunctions, though less strict, for the ordinary householder to whom wine and other intoxicating drinks and the eating of beef (thought by some to be a material foundation of the British Empire, but now recognised by several medical authorities to be the source of physical ills) and some other foods, as also all gluttony, as regards permitted food, are forbidden. Periodical fasts are enjoined; as also, during certain religious exercises, the eating of the pure food called Havishyannam made of fruit, vegetable and rice.

The sexual life has also its regulations. In short, it is said, let the body be well treated and kept pure in order to keep the mind sane and pure and a good and not rebellious instrument for mental Sadhana. In the Tantras will be found instances of several necessary bodily perfections in the Sadhaka. Thus he should not be deformed, with defective limbs, wanting in, or having excess of any limb, weak of limb, crippled, blind, deaf, dirty, diseased, with unnatural movements, paralysed, slothful in action *(Kularnava,* XIII).

Let us now pass to the mind. For the understanding of Hindu ritual it is necessary to understand both Hindu philosophy and Hindu psychology. This point, so far as I am aware, has never been observed Certainly Indian ritual has never been dealt with on this basis. It has generally been considered sufficient to class it as "Mummery" and then to pass on to something supposed to be more worthy of consideration. It is necessary to remember that (outside successful Yoga) the mind (at any rate in its normal state) is never for one moment unoccupied. At every moment of time worldly objects are seeking to influence it.

Only those actually do so, to which the mind, in its faculty as Manas, gives attention. In one of the *Tantrik Texts* (Satcakranirupana), the Manas is aptly spoken of as a doorkeeper who lets some enter and keeps others outside. For this reason it is called Samkalpavikalpatmaka: that is, it selects (Samkalpa) some things which the senses (Indriyas) present to it and rejects (Vikalpa) others. If the Manas attends to the sensation demanding entrance, it is admitted and passed on to the Buddhi and not otherwise. So the *Brihadaranyaka Upanishad* says, "My Manas was elsewhere and therefore I did not hear." This is a secret for the endurance of pain which not only the martyrs and the witches knew, but some others who have suffered lesser pains. When the sensation is passed on to the Buddhi, as also when the latter acts upon the material of remembered precepts, there is formed in the Buddhi a Vritti.

The latter is a modification of the Mind into the form of the perceived object. Unless a man is a Siddhayogi, it is not possible to avoid the formation of mental Vrittis. The object, there fore, of Sadhana is firstly to take the attention away from undesirable objects and then to place a desirable object in their stead. For the mind must feed on something. The object is the Ishtadevata. When a Sadhaka fully, sincerely and deeply contemplates and worships his Ishtadevata, his mind is formed into a Vritti in the form of the Devata. As the latter is all purity, the mind, which contemplates it, is during and to the depth of such contemplation pure. By prolonged and repeated worship the mind becomes naturally pure and of itself tends to reject all impure notions.

What to others is a source of impurity is pure. To the pure, as the Hellenes said, all things are pure. Things are not impure. It is the impure mind which makes them so. He learns to see that everything and all acts are manifestations of the Divine. He who realises Consciousness in all objects no longer has desire therefor. In this way a good disposition or Bhava, as it is called, is attained which ripens into that which is divine or Devatabhava. This is the principle on which all Sadhana, as well as what is called specifically Mantrayoga, is based. It is profoundly said in the *Kularnva Tantra* that a man must rise by means of the same things which are the cause of his fall.

If you fall on the ground you must raise yourself by it. The mind is thus controlled by means of its own object (Vishaya); that is, the world of name and form (Namarupa). The unregulated mind is distracted by Namarupa. But the same Namarupa may be used as the first means of escape therefrom. A particular form of Namarupa productive of pure Bhava is therefore given as the object of meditation. This is called Sthula or Saguna Dhyana of the five Devatas. Material media are used as the first steps whereby the Formless One is, through Yoga, attained, such as Images (Pratima), emblems (Linga, Shalagrama), pictures (Citra), mural markings (Bhittirekha), Jar (Ghata), Mandalas and Yantras. To these worship (Puja) is done with other rites such as Japa, Nyasa and so forth, and gestures (Mudra). Siddhi in this, is the Samadhi called Mahabhava.

The second principle to be noted is that the object or mind's content, as also the service (Seva) of it, may be either gross (Sthula) or subtle (Sukshma). This distinction pervades all the rituals and rightly so. Men are not all at the same degree of intellectual and spiritual advancement. For the simple-minded there are simple material and mental images. Progressively considered, the objects used to fix in the mind the thought of the Devata are images in human or semihuman form, similar pictures, non-human forms or emblems (such as Linga and Gauripatta, Shalagrama, the Jar or Ghata, Mandalas) and lastly Yantras.

The image is not merely used for instruction *(ut pictura pro scriptura haberetur),* or to incite in the mind a mental picture, but after the Prana-Pratishtha rite is itself worshipped. So also amongst Christians, where however this rite is unknown, "eikones acheiropoietoi" (what are called in Sanskrit Svayambu emblems) and wonder-working images have been directly venerated. Superficial persons doubtless think themselves profound when they ask how the Devata can be invoked (Avahana). To them also the dismissal (Visarjana) savors of childish impudence and absurdity. How (I have read) can God be told to come and go P A Christian who sings the Hymn, "Veni creator Spiritus," is indeed ignorant if he fancies that at his request the Holy Ghost comes to him flying through the skies. As Shamkara says, Spirit (Atma) never comes and never goes. That which in fact moves is the mind of the Sadhaka in which, if pure, Spirit manifests Itself.

That Spirit is in all places, and when the Sadhaka's mind fully realises its presence in the Image, the latter as the manifestation of that Spirit is a fitting object of worship. Some knowledge of Vedanta is needful for the understanding and performance of image worship. Yantra worship is however higher and is fitter for those who have reached a more advanced stage in Sadhana. The term, as I have said, literally means an instrument; that by which anything is accomplished. In Upasana it is that instrument by which the mind is fixed upon the Devata of worship.

It is, as drawn, a diagram consisting of lines, angles and curves, varying with the Devata worshipped as also, to some extent, according as it is a Puja or Dharana Yantra, the whole being included in a common Bhupura. A Yantra is three-dimensional, though it is very generally represented by a drawing on the flat. The Yantra and each part of it as representing certain Shaktis, has a significance which is known to the instructed Sadhaka. On the great Sri Yantra with its Baindava and other Cakras there is an entire literature. It is neglected now-a-days. Those who have fully understood it are masters in *Tantra Shastras.* The subject is shortly dealt with in the Introduction to the *Tantraraja Tantra* (Vol. VIII, *Tantrik Texts).* Not only is the object of worship subtle or gross, but so also is the ritual with which it is worshipped. For the simple Indian, worship avails itself of the ordinary incidents of daily life understood by even the most ignorant.

And so we see the tending of the idol, waking it, bathing it, giving it food, putting it to sleep and so forth. In ordinary worship there is the offer of flowers, light, incense and the like Upacara. In the subtle inner or mental worship (Antarpuja) these are but symbols. Thus the Jnaneshvara Samhita cited in the Mantrayogarahasyanirnaya speaks of the offering of "flowers of feeling" (Bhavapushpa) to the Divinity—namely, the virtue of selflessness (Anahamkara), desirelessness (Araga), guilelessness (Adambha), freedom from malice and envy (Advesha, Amatsaryya), and infatuation and delusion (Amada and Amoha) and control over the feelings and mind (Akshobhaka, Amanaka). He who can truly make such offerings to Devi is a high Sadhaka indeed. The Shastra makes wonderful provision for all types.

It recognises that there must be a definite object to which the mind must turn; chooses that object with a view to the capacities of the Sadhaka; and similarly regulates the ensuing worship. Much ignorant talk takes place as to the supposed worship of the Formless. Worship implies an object of worship and every object has some form. But that form and the ritual vary to meet the needs of differing capacities and temperaments; commencing with the more or less anthropomorphic image (Doll or Puttali, as those who dislike such worship call it) with its material service reproducing the ways of daily life, passing through pictures, emblems, Yantras, and mental worship to adoration of the Point of Light (Jyotirbindu) in which at length, consciousness being merged, all worship ceases.

The Shaktirahasya summarises the stages of progress in a short verse, thus: "By images, ceremonies, mind, identification, and knowing the Self, a mortal attains Liberation (Kaivalya)".

In the same way, meditation is either gross (Sthula) or subtle (Sukshma). The forms of the Mother of the Universe are threefold. There is first the Supreme (Para) form of which the *Vishnuyamala* says "None know". There is next Her subtle form which consists of Mantra. But as the mind cannot settle itself upon that which is formless, She appears also in physical form as celebrated in the Devi-stotras of the Puranas and Tantras.

The third principle to be noticed is the part which the body is made to take in the ritual. Necessarily there is action in any case to carry out the ritual, but this is so prescribed as to emphasise the mental operation (Manasikriya), and in addition certain symbolic gestures (Mudra) are prescribed. The body is made to take its part in the ritual, the mental processes being thus emphasised and intensified. This is based on a well-known natural tendency. When we speak with conviction and intensity of feeling, we naturally adopt appropriate movements of the body and gestures of the hands. We thus speak with the whole body.

Take for example Nyasa which like Yantra is peculiar to the Tantras. The object of the Sadhaka is to identify himself with the Devata he contemplates and thus to attain Devatabhava for which it is, in its many forms, a most powerful means. Regarding the body of the Devata as composed of Bija Mantras, he not merely imagines that his own body is so composed but he actually places (Nyasa means placing) these Bijas with the tip of his fingers on the various parts of his own body. The Abhishta Devata is thus in imagination (expressed by outward acts) placed in each of the parts and members of the Sadhaka's body, and then with the motion of his arms he, by Vyapaka Nyasa, as it were, spreads the presence of the Devata all over his body. He thus feels himself permeated in every part by the presence of the Devata and identified with the Divine Self in that its form. How, it may be asked, can the Devata be spread as it were butter on bread? These are crude questionings and because critics of the ritual do not get beyond this crude state of mind, this ritual is not understood. Devata is not spread. God is everywhere and He is not to be placed by man's fingers anywhere. What is done is to produce in man's mind the notion that he is so spread. Again with certain ritual acts Mudra is made. This Mudra expresses by the hands the thought of the worshipper of which it is sometimes a kind of manual shorthand.

A further important point for consideration is that the mental Vritti is not only strengthened by the accompanying physical action, but by a prolonged repetition of either or both. There may be a literal repetition of either or both, of which a prominent example is Japa of Mantra with which I have dealt in the Chapters on Shakti as Mantra and on the Varnamala; or the object of contemplation may be severed into parts, as where meditation is done not simply on the Devata as a whole, but on each of the parts of His body and then on the whole; or a particular result, such as the dissolution of the Tattvas in Bhutasuddhi, may be analysed into the component parts of a process commencing with the first movement and ending with the last. Repetition of a word and idea fixes it in the mind, and if the same essential thought can be presented in varied forms, the effect is more powerful and at the same time less calculated to tire. "Vain repetition" is itself in the mouths of many a vain criticism when not a platitude.

If it is in fact vain, it is vain. But it need not be so. In the current gross way of looking at things it is asked, "Will the Deity yield (like a modern politician) to repeated clamor?" The answer is the Devata is not so affected. What is in fact affected is, the mind of the Sadhaka himself, which, being thus purified by insistent effort, becomes a fit medium for the manifestation of a divine consciousness (Devatabhava). In short fact Indian ritual cannot be understood unless the Vedantik *principles* of which they are a particular practical *application* are understood. Even when in devotion, complete understanding and feeling are not attained, the intention to gain both will achieve success by quickening worshipper's interest and strengthening the forces of the will.

A word now as to Symbolism, which exists in all religions in varying degrees. The Tantra Shastra is extraordinarily full of it in all its kinds—form, colour, language, number, action. The subject is a highly interesting but very lengthy one. I can only make two remarks with regard to it here. Red is a favourite colour in the *Shakta Tantras.* As pointed out in the *Bhavanopanisad* (Sutra 28) an Upanishad of the Kadimata and Bhaskararaya's commentary thereon, Redness denotes Raga and Vimarsha Shakti. (See Introduction to *Tantraraja Tantra* Vol. VIII, *Tantrik Texts,* and Vol. XI, *Tantrik Texts.)*

There is a good deal of what is called erotic symbolism in some of the *Tantras.* This is apt to shock many English people who are by no means all so moral in fact as some might think this sensitivity suggests. "The Hindus are very natural as regards sexual matters." An English clergyman remarks (E. F. Elwin *India and the Indians,* p. 70) "A leading Indian Christian said to me 'there is no reserve among us in the sense that you English people have it. There is nothing which our children do not know."

It should be added, says this author, "that the knowledge of evil (why I may ask is it always evil?) does not as a matter of course produce evil". The mind of the ancients was a natural one and they called a spade a spade and not an horticultural instrument, and were not shocked thereby. For instance, coupled *Yab-Yum* figures were not thought impure. Another point has been observed upon by the Italian author Guido Gozzano, namely, that the European has lost the power of "worshipping through the flesh" which existed in antique pagan times. (Verso la cuna del Mondo). Fear of erotic symbols is rather indicative in the generality of cases of a tendency to weakness and want of self-control.

The great Edward Carpenter speaks of the "impure hush" in these matters. A person whose mind is naturally bent towards sensual thoughts but who desires to control them has no doubt a fear, which one readily understands, of anything which may provoke such thoughts. But such a man is, in this respect, lower than him who looks upon natural things in a natural way without fear of injury to himself; and greatly lower than him to whom all is a manifestation of the One Consciousness, and who realises this in those things which are the cause of all to the imperfectly self-governed Pashu. Nothing is in itself impure. It is the mind which makes it so.

It is however absolutely right that persons who feel that they have not sufficient self-control should, until they gain it, avoid what they think may do them injury. Apart from symbolism there are statements in some Shastras or so-called Shastras which are, in the ordinary modern sense, obscene. Some years ago a man wrote to me that he had come across in the Tantras "obscenities the very reading of which was demoralising". The very fact that these portions of the Scripture had such an effect on him is a sufficient reason that he and others similarly situated should not read them. The *Tantra Shastra* recognises this principle by certain injunctions into which I cannot enter here. The *Kularnava* expressly says that the Chapter on the Wine ritual is not to be read *(Na pathed asavollasam);* that is, by the unqualified.

Again it is not necessary to admit either that every Text which calls Itself a Tantra is a genuine one or if so that it was the product of a high class Sadhaka. What is authoritative is that which is generally admitted to be so. Even if the Scripture be one of general acceptance, there is another matter to be remembered. As pointed out in *Karpuradistotra (Hymn to Kali,* where instances are given), an apparently "obscene" statement may disguise something which is not so. Why it may be asked? An intending disciple may be questioned as to such passages. If he is a gross-minded or stupid man his answers will show it. Those who are not fit for the reception of the doctrine may be kept off on hearing or reading such statements which may be of such a character that anyone but a fool would know that they were not to be taken literally. It may be that the passages which my correspondent read were of this character.

As regards erotic symbolism, however, (for to this I now limit myself) it is not peculiar to the Tantras. It is as old as the hills and may be found in other Scriptures. It is a matter of embarrassment to the class I have mentioned that the Bible is not free from it. Milton, after referring to Solomon's wedded leisures says, "In the Song of Songs which is generally believed, even in the jolliest expressions, to figure the spousals of the Church with Christ, sings of a thousand raptures between those two lovely ones far on the hither side of carnal enjoyment." If we would picture the cosmic processes we must take the materials therefore from our own life.

It is not always necessary to go to the erotic life. But man has generally done so for reasons I need not discuss here; and his selections must sometimes be admitted to be very apt. It has however been said that "throughout Shakta symbolism and pseudo-philosophising, there lies at the basis of the whole system, the conception of sexual relationship as the ultimate explanation of the universe." Reading these words as they stand, they are nonsense. What is true is that some *Shakta Tantras* convey philosophic and scientific truths by the media of erotic imagery; which is another matter. But so also does *Upanishad.* The charge of pseudo-philosophy is ill-founded, unless the Advaita-vedanta is such. The *Shakta Tantra* simply presents the Vedantik teachings in a symbolical ritualistic form for the worshipper to whom it also prescribes the means whereby they may be realised in fact. Those who think otherwise have not mastered the alphabet of the subject.

I will conclude with a reply to a possible objection to what I have above written. It may be said that some of the rituals to which I have alluded are not merely the property of the Tantra Shastras and that they are not entitled to any credit for them. It is a fact that some (many have become extinct) Vaidik rituals such as the ten Samskaras, Sandhya, Homa and so forth are imbedded in and have been adopted by the Agamas. These and other rituals are to be found also in the Puranas.

In any case, the Agama is what it is whether its elements are original or derived. If the rites adopted are creditable then praise must be given for the adoption of that which is good. If they are not, blame equally attaches to the original as to the copy. What however the Agamas have adopted has been shaped so as to be suitable for all, that is, for others than those for whom the original rituals were intended. Further many of the rituals here described seem to have been introduced by and to be peculiar to the Agamas. Possibly some of these may have been developed from other forms or seeds of form in the *Vaidik ritual.*

The whole subject of Indian ritual and its origins is still awaiting inquiry. Personally I am disposed to favour the view that the Agamas have made a contribution which is both original and considerable. To me also the contribution seems to have greater conformity with Vedantik doctrine, which is applied by the ritual in a psychological manner which is profound. On an "historical" view of the matter this seems necessarily to be so. For, according to that view, the early Vaidik ritual either antedated or was contemporaneous with the promulgation of the Vedantik doctrine to be found in the Upanishads, for the general acceptance of which considerable time was necessary.

It could not therefore (if at all) embody that doctrine in the same way or to the same degree as a Ritual developed at a time when that doctrine had been widely disseminated, generally accepted and at least to a greater degree systematised. Ritual is only a practical expression of doctrine, and the Agamas, according to a generally accepted view, did not come into being earlier than a date later than the first and chief Upanishads, and perhaps at the close of what is generally called the Aupanishadic age. No "historical" argument, however, is yet entirely trustworthy, as the material upon which it is to be based has not been sufficiently explored.

For myself I am content to deal with present-day facts. According to the Indian view, all Shastras are various parts of one whole and that Part which as a present-day fact contains the bulk of the ritual, now or recently in practice, consists of the Tantras of the various schools of Agama. As an Indian author and follower of the Shaivagama has said—the Temple ritual throughout India is governed by the Agamas. And this must be so, if it be the fact as alleged, that Temples, Images, and other matters were unknown to the original Vaidik Aryas.

If the Agamas have adopted some of the ritual of the latter, those in their turn in course of time took to themselves the practices of those outside the body of men for whom the Vaidik Karma-kanda was originally designed. Vedanta in its various forms has now for centuries constituted the religious notions of India, and the Agamas in their differing schools are its practical expression in worship and ritual affording the means whereby Vedantik doctrine is realised.

6

Spiritual Evolution

Spiritual evolution is the philosophical, theological, esoteric or spiritual idea that nature and human beings and/or human culture evolve along a predetermined cosmological pattern or ascent, or in accordance with certain pre-determined potentials. This predeterminism of evolution concept is also complemented by the idea of a creative impulse in human beings, known as epigenesis. Within this broad definition, theories of spiritual evolution are very diverse. They may be cosmological (describing existence at large), personal (describing the development of the individual), or both. They can be holistic (holding that higher realities emerge from and are not reducible to the lower), idealist (holding that reality is primarily mental or spiritual) or nondual (holding that there is no ultimate distinction between mental and physical reality). All of them can be considered to be teleological to a greater or lesser degree.

Philosophers, scientists, and educators that have proposed theories of spiritual evolution include Nader Angha, Schelling, Hegel, Max Theon, Henri Bergson, Sri Aurobindo, Jean Gebser, Pierre Teilhard de Chardin, Arthur M. Young, Edward Haskell, E. F. Schumacher, Erich Jantsch, Clare W. Graves, Aristotle, Alfred North Whitehead, Terrence McKenna, P.R. Sarkar, and Ken Wilber. These theorists tend (for the most part) to be non-materialistic or non-reductionistic.

Precursors to the Idea

The Cyclic Cosmos: Mircea Eliade has suggested that in many pre-modern cultures one finds the concept of the Fall and a "nostalgia for paradise". However for those cultures that have a cyclic cosmology, the concept of a progressive deterioration of the universe (as in the Hesiodic, Hindu, and Lurianic cosmologies of a degradation from a Golden Age to an Iron Age or Kali Yuga) might be balanced by a corresponding ascent to more spiritual stages and a return to paradisical conditions. This is what one finds in Buddhist and especially Jaina cosmologies.

Emanation: Many premodern cosmologies and esoteric systems of thought are based on an emanationist view of reality. If the Cyclic view is temporal, then emanation is a non-temporal precursor to the theory of spiritual evolution.

According to this paradigm, Creation proceeds as an outpouring or even a transformation in the original Absolute or Godhead. The Supreme Light or Consciousness descends through a series of stages, gradations, worlds or hypostases, becoming progressively more material and embodied, before finally turning around to return to the One, retracing its steps through spiritual knowledge, contemplation and ascent.

A supreme example of this form of thinking is the Neoplatonism of Plotinus and his successors. Other examples and interpretations might be found in Kashmir Shaivism and Tantra in general, Gnosticism, Sufism, and Kabbalah. The Hindu idea of the Chakras might also considered here as the "microcosmic" counterpart of macrocosmic involution and evolution (the Yogi raises the Kundalini or life force through and thus transcends each chakra in turn, until he reaches the crown chakra and liberation (Avalon).

Samkhya: An early example of the doctrine of spiritual evolution is found in Samkhya, a teaching that goes back more than two and a half thousand years (although it's present form dates to around the 4th or 5th century c.e.). Unlike classic Hinduism, the traditional Samkhyan philosophy is atheistic and dualistic. Pure spirit (called *purusha*) comes into proximity with *prakriti* (psychophysical nature), disturbing its equilibrium. As a result the original root-prakriti (*mulaprakriti*) undergoes a series of progressive transformations or unfoldings, in the form of successive essences called *tattvas*. The most subtle tattwas emerge first, then progressively grosser ones, each in a particular order, and finally the elements and the organs of sense. The goal of evolution however is, paradoxically, the release of prurusha and the return to the unmanifest condition. Hence everything is tending towards a goal of spiritual quiescence (Larson 1979).

The Great Chain of Being: The concept of the Great Chain of Being developed by Plato and Aristotle whose ideas were taken up and synthesised by Plotinus. Plotinus in turn heavily influenced Augustine's theology, and from there Aquinas and the Scholastics. The Great Chain of Being was an important theme in Renaissance and Elizabethan thought, had an under-acknowledged influence on the shaping of the ideas of the Enlightenment and played a large part in the worldview of 18th century Europe.

And while essentially a static worldview, by the 18th and early 19th century it had been "temporalised" by the concept of the soul ascending or progressing spiritually through the successive rungs or stages, and thus growing or evolving closer to God. (Lovejoy 1936) It also had at this time an impact on theories of biological evolution.

E. F. Schumacher, author of *Small is Beautiful*, has recently proposed a sort of simplified Great Chain of Being, based on the idea of four "kingdoms" (mineral, vegetable, animal, human) (Schumacher, 1977). Schumacher rejects modernist and scientific themes, his approach recalling the universalist orientation of writers like Huston Smith (Smith 1976), and quite likely contributing to (unless the latter developed his ideas completely independently) Ken Wilber's "holonomic" hierarchy or "Great Nest of Being" (Wilber 2000).

German Idealism

Occult Concepts of Spiritual Evolution: Theories of Spiritual Evolution are important in many Occult and Esoteric teachings, which emphasise the progression and development of the individual either after death (Spiritualism) or through successive reincarnations (Theosophy, Hermeticism).

Spiritualism: In the 19th century Anglo-American Spiritualist ideas emphasise the progression of the soul after death to higher states of existence, in contrast to the French and Brazilian Spiritualism of Allan Kardec, which admits reincarnation. The Anglo-American position recalls (and is presumably inspired by) 18th century concepts regarding the temporalisation of The Great Chain of Being. Spiritual evolution, rather than being a physical (or physico-spiritual) process is based on the idea of realms or stages through which the soul or spirit passes in a non-temporal, qualitative way. This is still an important part of some spiritualist ideas today, and is similar to some mainline (as opposed to fundamentalist) Protestant Christian beliefs, according to which after death the person goes to "a better place" or "heaven" (in English Spiritualism, Summerland).

Theosophical Conceptions: Theosophy presents a more sophisticated and complex cosmology than Spiritualism, although coming out of the same general milieu. H. P. Blavatsky developed a highly original cosmology, according to which the human race (both collectively and through the succession of individual reincarnation and spiritual evolution) passes through a number of Root Races, beginning with the huge ethereal and mindless Polarian or First Root Race, through the Lemurian (3rd), Atlantean (4th) and our present "Aryan" 5th Race. This will give rise to a future, Post-Aryan 6th Root Race of highly spiritual and enlightened beings, and an even more sublime 7th Root Race, before ascending to totally superhuman and cosmic states of existence.

Blavatsky's ideas were further developed by her successors, such as C.W. Leadbeater, Rudolph Steiner, and Alice Bailey, each of whom went into huge and often tedious detail in constructing baroque cycles of rounds, races, and sub-races. Although including elements of the science of her day as well as both eastern and western esoteric thought, Blavatsky rejected the Darwinian idea that man evolved from apes, and most subsequent esotericists followed this lead. Darwinism, with its explanation of evolution through material factors like natural selection and random mutation, does not sit well with many spiritual evolutionists, for whom evolution is initiated or guided by metaphysical principles or is tending towards a final spiritual or divine state.

Despite this, Theosophists and Anthroposophists have tried to incorporate the facts of geology and paleontology into their cosmology and spiritual evolution (in Anthroposophy Hermann Poppelbaum is a particularly creative thinker in this regard). Some have attempted to equate Lemuria with Gondwanaland, for example. Today all these ideas have little influence outside their specialised followings, but for a time Theosophical concepts were immensely influential.

Theurgy: Theurgy has a clear relationship to neo-Platonism and Kabbalah and contains the concept of spiritual evolution and ultimately unification with God or the Godhead at its core. Theurgy is considered by many to be another term for high magic and is known to have influenced the members of the Hermetic Order of the Golden Dawn many of whom considered the order to be Theurgic in nature. Aleister Crowley also considered his Thelemic system of magical philosophy to be a Theurgic tradition as it emphasised the Great Work, which is essentially another form of spiritual evolution. The Great Work is believed to result in communication with one's personal angel or higher self.

Evolution Towards Godhead

A Common Vision: Although contemporaries, Sri Aurobindo and Pierre Teilhard de Chardin did not meet, or even seem to have been aware of each other's work. Nevertheless there are amasing similarities between the two in their respective evolutionary philosophies. (*e.g.* Bruteau 1974, Sethna 1973). Both describe a progression from inanimate matter through life and mind to a future state of Divine consciousness, not as an otherworldly realisation but a consummation and Divinisation of the collective consciousness on Earth. Teilhard de Chardin refers to this as the Omega Point, and Sri Aurobindo as the Supermind (Teilhard de Chardin 1955, Sri Aurobindo 1977). Neither Teilhard nor Sri Aurobindo have a problem with Darwinism the way that the Theosophists, or even someone like Ken Wilber (Wilber 2000 p.20), do. For them this material process is merely part of a larger picture.

Teilhard de Chardin: Teilhard, who was a Jesuit Paleontologist who played an important role in the discovery of Peking Man, presented a teleological view of planetary and cosmic evolution, according to which the formation of atoms, molecules and inanimate matter is followed by the development of the biosphere and organic evolution, then the appearance of man and the noosphere as the total envelope of human thought. According to Teilhard evolution does not cease here but continues on to its culmination and unification in the Omega Point, which he identifies with Christ.

Sri Aurobindo: Sri Aurobindo-who incorporates western as well as Indian thought-refers to individual as well as collective spiritual evolution. As described in his great opus *The Life Divine*, and more poetically in *Savitri*, an aspect of the original Divine consciounsess or *Superconscient* descends into the inertia and total non-consciousness of Matter (the Inconscient) to become the physical universe. From there, Life (which, like all the higher levels, remains veiled or hidden, but still present) emerges, and then Mind.

Man as a mental being passes both collectively (*e.g.* social evolution) and individually (through spiritual effort) through the levels of "tamasic", rajasic" and "sattvic" (these are the gunas of Samkhyan philosophy). Future evolution requires dedicated spiritual effort, by which the faculties of Body, Life and Mind are transformed through the action of the Divine Soul ("Psychicisation") and the transcendent Spirit ("Spiritualisation"), leading to the realisation of progressive levels of Spiritual Mind and culminating in the individual *and* collective realisation of the Supermind. This last, is a unitary Divine consciousness that constitutes an utterly new state of perfected existence, which will bring about the transformation of matter itself.

But perhaps it was Swami Vivekananda who did more than any other Hindu thinker to synthesise Darwinian evolutionary ideas with Hinduism...

Surat Shabda Yoga: Surat Shabda Yoga esoteric cosmology depicts the whole of creation (the macrocosm) as being emanated and arranged in a spiritually differentiated hierarchy, often referred to as eggs, regions, or planes. Typically, eight spiritual levels are described above the physical plane, although names and subdivisions within these levels will vary to some extent by mission and Master. (One version of the creation from a Surat Shabda Yoga perspective is depicted at the Sant Ajaib Singh Ji Memorial Site in "The Grand Scheme of All Creation".)

The constitution of the individual (the microcosm) is an exact replica of the macrocosm. Consequently, the microcosm consists of a number of bodies, each one suited to interact with its corresponding plane or region in the macrocosm. These bodies developed over the yugas through involution (emanating from higher planes to lower planes) and evolution (returning from lower planes to higher planes), including by karma and reincarnation in various states of consciousness (Holtje 1995).

Dynamic Evolution through Successive Kingdoms: Arthur M. Young and Edward Haskell have each independently incorporated the findings of science into a larger theory of spiritual evolution, and extended the traditional human, animal, vegetable, and mineral categories with kingdoms representing photons, atoms and molecules. (Haskell 1972, Young 1976). Arthur M. Young goes further in considering the human state as a subset of a larger kingdom of "Dominion", of which the sixth stage is represented for example by Christ and Buddha, and the seventh (final) stage an even higher level of Enlightenment or God-realisation. (Young 1976, diagram pp.86-7). Moreover, both Haskell and Young present profound accounts of evolution through these kingdoms in terms of cybernetic principles.

A more "mainstream" scientific presentation of this same idea is provided by Erich Jantsch in his consummate account of how self-organising systems evolve and develop as a series of "symmetry breaks" through the sequence of matter, life, and mind (Jantsch 1980). Although abiding strictly by the understanding of science, Jantsch arranges the various elements of cosmic, planetary, biological, psychological, and human evolution in a single overall framework of emergent evolution that may or may not be considered teleological (Jantsch 1980 p.224).

Energy Driven Evolution: The book *Tuning the Diamonds: Electromagnetism and Spiritual Evolution* written by Susan Joy Rennison claims that evolution on Earth is driven by cosmic energy originating from deep space.

New Age Ideas: New Age thought is strongly syncretic and based on a superficial but creative interpretation of previous spiritual and esoteric traditions, especially Eastern thought, Theosophy, and popular (mis)interpretations of science. A common theme is the evolution or the transcendence of the human or collective planetary consciousness in a higher state or higher "vibratory" (a metaphor taken from G. I. Gurdjieff) level. Among the better thinkings of the "New Age", David Spangler's communications speak of a "New Heaven and a new Earth", while Christopher Hills refers (perhaps influenced by Sri Aurobindo) to the divinisation of man (Hills 1977, p.30).

Jonathan Livingston Seagull narrated the idea of evolution in a fascinating fashion. James Redfield in his novel *The Celestine Prophecy* suggested that through experiencing a series of personal spiritual insights, humanity is becoming aware of the connection between our evolution and the Divine. More recently in his book *God and the Evolving Universe: The Next Step in Personal Evolution* (2002) co-written with Michael Murphy, he claims that humanity is on the verge of undergoing a change in consciousness.

Integral Theory and Spiral Dynamics: An interpretation of social and psychological development that could also be considered a theory of spiritual evolution is Spiral Dynamics, based on the work of Clare W. Graves.

More recently the concept of spiritual evolution has been given a sort of respectability it has not had since the early 19th century through the work of Ken Wilber, in whose writings both the cosmological and the personal dimensions are described. In this "Integral Philosophy", reality is said to consist of several realms or stages, including more than one of the following: the physical, the vital, the psychic, (after the Greek *psyche*, "soul"), the causal (referring to "that which causes, or gives rise to, the manifest world"), and the ultimate (or non-dual), through which the individual progressively evolves. Although this schema is derived in large part from Tibetan Buddhism, Wilber argues (and uses many tables of diagrams to show) that these same levels of being are common to all wisdom teachings.

Described simplistically, Wilber sees humans developing through several stages, including magic, mythic, pluralistic, and holistic mentalities. But he also sees cultures as developing through these stages. And, much like Hegel, he sees this development of individuals and cultures *as* the evolution of existence itself. Wilber has also teamed up with Don Beck to integrate Spiral Dynamics into his own Integral philosophy, and vice versa.

Bibliography

Anand, B.S. : *Baba Farid*, Sahitya Akademi, New Delhi, 1975.

Anwarul Haq, M. : *The Faith Movement of Mawlana Muhammad Ilyas*, George Allen & Unwin Ltd., London, 1972.

Banerji, S. K. : *Shaikh Salim Chishti, the Shaikh-ul-Islam of Fathpur Sikri*, The Indian Press, Ltd., Allahabad, 1945.

Begg, W.D. : *The Big Five of India in Sufism*, W. E. Begg, Ajmer, 1972.

Bhajjan, Samuel Victor : *The Chishti Sufis of India*, Hartford Seminary, M.A. Thesis, 1959.

Chaudhry, Hafeezur Rehman : *The Shrine and Lunger of Golra Sharif*, Oxford University Press, Karachi, 1990.

Currie, P. M. : *The Shrine and Cult of Mu'in al-Din Chishti of Ajmer*, Oxford University Press, Delhi, 1989.

Desai, Ziyaud-Din A. : *Malfuz Literature: As a Source of Political, Social, and Cultural History of Gujarat and Rajasthan*, Patna, 1991.

Digby, Simon : *In According to Tradition: Hagiographical Writing in India*, Harrasowitz Verlag, Wiesbaden, 1994.

Digby, Simon : *In Delhi Through the Ages: Essays in Urban History, Culture and Society*, Oxford University Press, Delhi, 1986.

Digby, Simon : *In Socio-cultural Impact of Islam on India*, University of the Panjab, Chandigarh, 1976.

Eaton, Richard M. : *In Moral Conduct and Authority: the Place of Adab in South Asian Islam*, University of California Press, Berkeley, 1984.

Eaton, Richard M. : *Sufis of Bijapur 1300-1700: Social Roles of Sufis in Medieval India*, Princeton University Press, 1978.

Eaton, Richard M. : *The Rise of Islam and the Bengal Frontier*, University of California Press, Berkeley, 1993.

Elahi, M. : *Couplets of Baba Farid*, Majlis Shah Hussain, Lahore, 1967.

Ernst, Carl W. : *In The Religions of South Asia*, Princeton University Press, Princeton, 1995.

Faruqi, Nisar Ahmed : *In Contemporary Relevance of Sufism*, Indian Council for Cultural Relations, New Delhi, 1993.

Gilmartin, David : *In Pakistan: The Social Sciences' Perspective*, Oxford University Press, Karachi, 1990.

Habib, Mohammad : *Hazrat Amir Khusrau of Delhi*, Islamic Book Service, Lahore, 1979.

Habib, Mohammad : *Politics and Society During the Early Medieval Period, Collected Works of Professor Mohammad Habib*, People's Publishing House, New Delhi, 1974.

Haq, Muhammad Enamul : *A History of Sufi-ism in Bengal*, Asiatic Society of Bangladesh, Dacca, 1975.

Islam, Riazul : *A Comparative Study of the Treatment of Futuh in the Principal Chishti Records,* Asiatic Society of Bangladesh, Dacca, 1975.

Jackson, Paul : *In Islam in India: Studies and Commentaries*, Vikas Publishing House Pvt Ltd, Delhi, 1985.

Jeffery, Patricia : *In Ritual & Religion among Muslims of the Sub-continent*, Vanguard, Lahore, 1985.

Köszegi, Michael : *In Islam in North America: A Sourcebook*, Garland Publishing, Inc., New York, 1992.

Latif, S. A. : *In Bias in Indian Historiography*, D. K. Publications, Delhi, 1980.

Lawrence, Bruce B. : *The Chishtiya of Sultanate India: A Case Study of Biographical Complexities in South Asian Islam*, Scholars Press, Chico, 1981.

Maududi, Abul A'la : *A Short History of the Revivalist Movement in Islam*, Islamic Publications Limited, Lahore, 1963.

Metcalfe, Barbara : *Islamic Revival in British India: Deoband, 1860-1900*, Princeton University Press, Princeton, 1982.

Moinuddin, Abu Abdullah Ghulam : *The Book of Sufi Healing*, Inner Traditions International, New York, 1985.

Nabi, Mohammad Noor : *Development of Muslim Religious Thought in India from 1200 A.D. to 1450 A.D.*, Aligarh Muslim University Press, Aligarh, 1962.

Nizam Ad-Din Awliya. *Morals for the Heart*. Recorded by Amir Hasan Sijzi. Trans. Bruce B. Lawrence. Classics of Western Spirituality, 74. New York: Paulist Press, 1992.

Nizami, K. A. : *Historical Significance of the Malfuz Literature of Medieval India, In On History and Historians of Medieval India,* Munshiram Manoharlal Publishers Pvt. Ltd., New Delhi, 1982.

Nizami, K. A. : *The Life and Times of Shaikh Farid-u'd-Din Ganj-i-Shakar*, Idarah-i Adabiyat-i Delli, Delhi, 1955.

Nizami, K. A. : *The Life and Times of Shaikh Nizam-u'd-Din Auliya*, Idarah-i Adabiyat-i Delli, Delhi, 1991.

Pinto, Desiderio : *Piri-Muridi Relationship: A Study of the Nizamuddin Durgah*, Manohar, 1995.

Qadri, Syed Abdul Shakoor : *Diwan-i Masud Bakk*, Nagpur University, Dissertation, 1972.

Qamar Jahan Begam : *Princess Jahan Ara Begam, Her Life and Works,* S. M. Hamid 'Ali, Karachi, 1991.

Rashid, S. Khalid : *Wakf Administration in India: A Socio-Legal Study*, Vikas Publishing House Pvt Ltd, New Delhi, 1978.

Rasool, Ghulam : *Chishti Nizami Sufi Order of Bengal till mid 15th Century and its Socio-religious Contribution*, Idarah-i Adabiyat-Delli, Delhi, 1990.

Rawlinson, Andrew : *The Book of Enlightened Masters: Western Teachers in Eastern Traditions*, Open Court, Chicago, 1997.

Rizvi, Saiyd Athar Abbas : *A History of Sufism in India*, Munshiram Manoharlal Publishers Pvt. Ltd., Delhi, 1978.

Saeed, Mian Muhammad : *The Sharqi Sultanate of Jaunpur: A Political & Cultural History*, University of Karachi, Karachi, 1972.

Sanyal, Usha : *Devotional Islam and Politics in British India: Ahmad Riza Khan Barelwi and his Movement, 1870-1920*, Oxford University Press, New York, 1996.

Schimmel, Annemarie : *Islam in the Indian Subcontinent*, E. J. Brill, Leiden, 1980.

Schimmel, Annemarie : *Islamic Literatures of India*, Harrassowitz, Wiesbaden, 1973.

Talib, Gurbachan Singh : *Baba Sheikh Farid: His Life and Teaching*, Punjabi University, Patiala, 1973.

Troll, Christian W. : *In Islam in India: Studies and Commentaries*, Vikas Publishing House Pvt Ltd, Delhi, 1985.

Valiuddin, Mir : *Contemplative Disciplines in Sufism*, East-West Publications, London, 1980.

Wahid Bakhsh Sial Rabbani : *Islamic Sufism: The Science of Flight in God, with God, by God and Union and Communion with God, Also showing the Tremendous Sufi Influence on Christian and Hindu Mystics and Mysticism*, Sufi Foundation, Lahore, 1984.

Zaki, Mohammad : *In Bias in Indian Historiography*, D. K. Publications, Delhi, 1980.

Zilli, I. A. : *Successors of Shaikh Nasiruddin Mahmud and the Disintegration of the Central Chishti Organization*, *Proceedings of the Indian History Congress*, D. K. Publications, Delhi, 1983.

Index

❑❑❑